SMALL FIRMS IN SINGAPORE

SMALL FIRMS IN SINGAPORE

CHEW SOON BENG

Published for
Centre for Advanced Studies,
Faculty of Arts and Social Sciences,
National University of Singapore

SINGAPORE
OXFORD UNIVERSITY PRESS
OXFORD NEW YORK
1988

Oxford University Press

Oxford   New York   Toronto
Delhi   Bombay   Calcutta   Madras   Karachi
Petaling Jaya   Singapore   Hong Kong   Tokyo
Nairobi   Dar es Salaam   Cape Town
Melbourne   Auckland
and associated companies in
Berlin   Ibadan

Oxford is a trade mark of Oxford University Press

© Oxford University Press Pte. Ltd. 1988

Published in the United States by
Oxford University Press, Inc., New York

ISBN 0 19 588883 9

Library of Congress Cataloging-in-Publication Data

Chew, Soon Beng, 1948–
Small firms in Singapore.

"Published for the Centre for Advanced Studies,
Faculty of Arts and Social Sciences, National
University of Singapore."
Bibliography: p.
Includes index.
1. Small business—Singapore. 2. Singapore—
Manufactures. I. Title.
HD2346.S54C46 1988   338.6'42'095957   87–28331
ISBN 0-19-588883-9 (pbk.)

British Library Cataloguing in Publication Data

Chew, Soon Beng
Small firms in Singapore.
1. Small business—Singapore
I. Title
338.6'42'095957   HD2346.S55

ISBN 0-19-588883-9

Printed in Malaysia by Peter Chong Printers Sdn. Bhd.
Published by Oxford University Press Pte. Ltd.,
Unit 221, Ubi Avenue 4, Singapore 1440

To Rosalind

ACKNOWLEDGEMENTS

My research interest in small firms started when I worked with Professor Lim Chong Yah in 1985. Indeed, it was Professor Lim who encouraged me to pursue an indepth study of small firms which culminated in the present book. I am very grateful to Professor Lim for his intellectual stimulation as well as moral support of the study.

Most studies on small firms examine the characteristics of such firms without taking into account why they exist in the first place. This book attempts to present a new approach to a systematic assessment of the contribution and characteristics of small firms using Singapore as the principal case study.

I am indebted to the Institute of Developing Economies of Japan for funding the field surveys, and to the Asia Foundation and the Centre for Advanced Studies (NUS), for financial support of the study. Thanks are also due to Ruby Toh for her excellent research assistance and Lela Hassan for typing the earlier drafts of the study.

At the personal level, I would like to express my gratitude to my parents, who supported me through my education. Next, I owe much to my wife, Rosalind. This book would never have been completed without her understanding, affection and inspiration. My son, Tze-Shern and twin daughters, Tian-En and Tian-Ning, also provided inspiration and incentive towards the completion of the book.

CONTENTS

TABLES

FIGURES

NOTES

In the literature, the term 'small industries' is used interchangeably with 'small firms'. In this book, 'small firms' refers strictly to firms with fewer than 100 workers. Small firms are further subdivided into three categories: tiny establishments (firms with 5–9 workers), small establishments (firms with 10–49 workers), and medium establishments (firms with 50–99 workers).

In the cross-country analysis, Singapore, Taiwan, Thailand, and Japan carry the same definition of small firms, i.e. firms with fewer than 100 workers. In discussions on Singapore, there is no reference to 'medium firms'. Instead, the term 'large firms', used interchangeably with 'large establishments', refers to firms with 100 workers or more.

For Taiwan, 'medium firms' refers to firms with 100–499 workers, and 'large firms' to those with 500 workers or more. For Thailand, 'medium firms' are those with 100–199 workers, while 'large firms' are those with 200 workers or more. For Japan, 'medium firms' are firms with 100–299 workers, while 'large firms' are those with 300 workers or more.

Currency
All figures are in Singapore dollars unless otherwise stated.

ABBREVIATIONS

CPF	Central Provident Fund
DBS	Development Bank of Singapore
EDB	Economic Development Board
GDP	Gross Domestic Product
GNP	Gross National Product
HDB	Housing and Development Board
LAC	long-run average-cost curve
LIS	Light Industries Service
MDAS	Market Development Assistance Scheme
MNC	multinational corporation
NIC	Newly Industrializing Country
NPB	National Productivity Board
NWC	National Wages Council
OECD	Organization of Economic Cooperation and Development
PAP	People's Action Party
SDF	Skills Development Fund
SEB	Small Enterprise Bureau
SES	Stock Exchange of Singapore
SIFS	Small Industries Finance Scheme
SISIR	Singapore Institute of Standards and Industrial Research
SME	small and medium establishments
TDB	Trade Development Board
URA	Urban Renewal Authority

I

AN OVERVIEW

Introduction

THERE is an extensive literature on the performance of small firms in many countries.[1] Despite the fact that both the scope and pace of industrial development are dominated by large firms, small firms have also played an important role in the industrialization process in both developed and developing countries.

In the United States, for example, firms employing fewer than 100 workers accounted for 52 per cent of the total number of manufacturing establishments in 1972.[2] In Japan, small firms in 1979 accounted for 80 per cent of the total number of establishments in non-primary industries and 33 per cent of the total work-force.[3] In Sweden, small firms accounted for one-third of the total work-force.[4] In Thailand, small firms were responsible for 24 per cent of the total employment.[5]

Indeed, some researchers claim that small firms are indispensable to industrialization. Rothwell and Zegveld argue that small firms in the US are seen as the cornerstone of a free market economy, and small firms, by vigorously competing in the market-place, inject a certain dynamism into the economy and act as a countervailing force against overweening monopoly power.[6] Small firms in Japan basically play the major role of supporting the principal industries.[7] They furnish parts and sub-assemblies to large firms at competitive prices. In return, large firms, by relying on subcontracting small firms, can avoid committing themselves to excessive capital investment. It has been estimated in 1979 that at least 60 per cent of all small firms in Japan were subcontracting firms.[8] The Swedish small firms bring employment to the countryside and promote technical development and also play the role of exporters and subcontractors.

Staley and Morse have carefully examined the contributions of small firms in various countries and conclude that, 'in a given country, once a critical minimum level of modern industry is established, the role of small firms does not decline with time but holds an equal position in the farther development and expansion of the manufacturing economy'.[9] It may be argued that small firms in newly industrializing countries (NICs)—South Korea, Taiwan, Hong Kong, and Singapore—follow a rather different pattern. The development strategy of the NICs is to allow multinational corporations (MNCs) to operate in their countries so that the NICs gain access to technology, capital, and world markets. But the impact of the MNCs on the development and potential of small firms varies from country to country. In Singapore, many local firms are small subcontracting firms to the MNCs.

The purpose of this book is to analyse the contribution of small firms in the industrial development of Singapore and more importantly to assess the role which small firms can play in the manufacturing sector in the future.

Historical Perspective

Singapore was a traditional fishermen's town. In 1819 it was chosen by Stamford Raffles of the East India Company as a British maritime base for its trade in the Malay Archipelago and the Far East. By the nineteenth century, Singapore had already become an important commercial and trading centre in South-East Asia. Several factors contributed to her rapid development:

1. She lies at the southern tip of the Malay Peninsula and is at the international waterway between east and west Asia;

2. She has an excellent deep-water harbour and sheltered anchorage; and

3. Her British administrators allowed free trade.

As an island, trade naturally became the cornerstone of Singapore's economic development. Indeed, with the rapid rise in economic activity in South-East Asia in general, and the growth of the tin and rubber industries in the Malay Peninsula in particular, Singapore by 1918 had become the major rubber export centre of the world, functioning as a grading, packing and processing base for the re-export of not only rubber but other primary products from South-East Asia to the world.

By the end of World War I, Singapore had become a major entrepôt in South-East Asia, importing manufactured goods from the world for re-export in the region and re-exporting raw materials produced in the area to the world. As a growing port, the rising demand for service and maintenance needs and consumer goods, coupled with the rising building and construction activity, stimulated other manufacturing activities; but trade continued to dominate the economy.

The manufacturing sector, nevertheless, continued to grow.[10] By 1947, it accounted for 16.5 per cent of the labour force. By 1959, it was regarded as the third major source of employment.[11] The manufacturing activities, however, involved mainly the processing of imported raw materials and the manufacturing of simple consumer goods. Three broad categories of industrial activities were classified:[12]

1. Industrial activities involving the processing of rubber, coconut and vegetable oils, timber, tin, and other tropical products;

2. Industrial activities involving the production of beverages, clay products, and furniture; and

3. Ancillary and service activities such as engineering, printing and publishing, motor vehicles, and ship building and repairing.

Most industrial establishments were small prior to 1960. According to the Census of Industrial Production in 1959, firms which employed 10–39 workers accounted for 71 per cent of the total number of establishments with 10 or more workers. However, small firms did not contribute proportionately to employment, output, and value-added. They accounted for less than one-third of total employment, about one-quarter of total output, and only one-fifth of value-added.[13] Small firms were generally found in food manufacturing, printing and publishing, and engineering industries, and they were household units or backyard repair and service units using little capital equipment.

Thus, in the pre-1960 period, Singapore relied heavily on trade and commerce for her economic activities, while the manufacturing sector was regarded as a secondary sector in terms of employment, output and value-added. The manufacturing sector was of low value-added, was very labour intensive and only catered to local and regional markets.

The Rationale for Industrialization

Singapore obtained self-government from Britain in 1959, and the People's Action Party (PAP) was elected to power. The newly elected government immediately embarked on a deliberate strategy for industrialization. The rationale for industrialization lay in the following factors:[14]

1. There was massive unemployment. Moreover, the rapid population growth in the post-war period and the consequent number of youths entering the labour market aggravated the already serious unemployment problem. The normal expansion of traditional trade and commerce was unable to solve the unemployment problem.

2. A dynamic manufacturing sector was regarded as the way by which Singapore could develop into a prosperous country.

3. There was a need to diversify the economy because entrepôt trade was unreliable owing to: (i) the instability of world demand for primary products, and (ii) the desire of neighbouring countries to have direct trade and also to develop their industrial infrastructure and industries.

Singapore's industrialization programme was officially launched in 1960. The PAP government was quick to provide the necessary fiscal incentives to stimulate industrial growth. Tax incentives included tax holidays for pioneer industries, tax concessions for capital spending by established firms, and accelerated depreciation allowances. The Economic Development Board (EDB) was set up in 1961 as the government agency to promote industrial development.

Besides extending fiscal incentives, one of the great achievements of the PAP government was to eliminate the industrial and labour unrest which plagued Singapore in the pre-1960 period. Consequently, to enforce industrial stability and to control labour costs, a series of legislative measures, such as the Industrial Relations Ordinance of 1960, the Industrial Relations Amendment Act of 1966, and the Employment Act of 1968, were imposed.

The Economic Development of Singapore since 1959

Since attaining self-government, Singapore has made remarkable prog-
ress in economic development and has earned for herself the title of an
Asian Newly Industrializing Country. This section briefly looks at
Singapore's economic development since 1959.

Economic development includes both economic growth and social
development. Indicators of economic development are numerous. We
will examine a few important and common indicators:

Growth in Real Gross Domestic Product (GDP)

Singapore, as Table 1.1 shows, achieved a double-digit growth rate
during 1966–73. Against unfavourable international economic conditions in the 1970s and early 1980s, Singapore still managed to attain
4–10 per cent growth rates for the period 1974–85, except in 1985
when the growth rate was –1.8 per cent.

With respect to the growth rate in real per capita income, in the 1960s
it was 6.7 per cent per annum and went up to 7.4 per cent in the 1970s.
Lim Chong Yah has compared Singapore's real GDP growth rate with
those of other countries.[15] He found that Singapore's real growth rate
of 8.8 per cent in the 1960s exceeded the 4.4 per cent for developing
countries in the UN First Development Decade (see Table 1.2).
Similarly, Singapore's 8.5 per cent per annum performance in the 1970s
also exceeded the 4.6 per cent for developing countries in the same
period. On the basis of a global comparison, Singapore's performance
both in the 1960s and 1970s was among the highest in the world.

Unemployment and Population

An important aspect of rapid economic development is the reduction in
unemployment rate. Table 1.1 shows that the unemployment rate in
Singapore has declined steadily. In actual fact, the unemployment rate
does not give us a complete picture of the labour market. Since 1971,
there has been a significant inflow of foreign workers into Singapore.
Indeed, Singapore has reached a point where she has to worry about the
negative externality of the presence of a large number of foreign
workers.

One of the reasons why she has to rely on foreign workers is the
steady decline in her population growth rate (see Table 1.1). Both the
sharp decline in the fertility rate and the stringent immigration policy
are responsible for the low population growth rate. The decline in the
fertility rate is attributed to the effectiveness of the government family
planning programme as well as various social and economic factors
favouring low reproductive performance.

Inflation

Inflation in Singapore has been rather low. As indicated in Table 1.1,
inflation in Singapore was around 1–5 per cent in the 1960s and 1970s

except for 1973 and 1974 when oil prices escalated. But inflation rates in 1980 and 1981 were much higher than in the earlier period. However, due to the 1985 economic recession, the inflation rate fell to 0.5 per cent in 1985.

Wages

Table 1.3 shows that wages in all sectors have increased substantially. The annual average growth rate of wages in various sectors for 1972–83 ranged from 9.2 per cent in construction to 20.4 per cent in quarrying. It should be noted that the growth rate of wages was very much greater than the inflation rate, indicating that real wages increased significantly during these years.

Housing

One of the great achievements of the Singapore government is the provision of good government housing at affordable prices. Since 1982, 75 per cent of the population have been housed in government-built flats. More importantly, 66 per cent of the people who lived in government-built flats were home-owners.

Income Distribution

Economic development cannot be successful until it has achieved the twin objectives of economic growth and income distribution. There are various indicators of income distribution. According to Lim Chong Yah,[16] the most useful and meaningful way to examine income distribution is to observe favourable changes in all the above variables, namely, GDP growth, unemployment, population growth, wages, and housing. On the basis of the performance of the above six variables, Singapore's income distribution has been equitable, which implies that the sharing of the fruits of economic growth has been achieved.

1. See, for example, E. Staley and R. Morse, *Modern Small Industry for Developing Countries*, New York, McGraw-Hill Book Company, 1965.

2. A. D. Star, 'Estimates of the Number of Quasi and Small Businesses 1948 to 1972', *American Journal of Small Business*, Vol. IV, No. 2, October 1979.

3. Japan, Ministry of International Trade and Industry, 'Small and Medium Enterprises', *White Papers of Japan 1979–80*, Tokyo, Institute of National Affairs, 1979, p. 128.

4. Helge Herzog, 'Small and Medium-sized Firms in Sweden and Government Policy', *American Journal of Small Business*, Vol. VII, No. 2, December 1982.

5. Busaba Kunasirin, *The Role of Small- and Medium-Scale Industries in the Economic Development of Japan and Thailand: A Comparative Analysis*, Tokyo, Institute of Developing Economies, Visiting Research Fellow Monograph Series No. 109, March 1984, p. 13.

6. R. Rothwell and W. Zegveld, *Innovation and the Small and Medium-Sized Firm*, Hingham, Massachusetts, Kluwer Nijhoff Publishing, 1981, p. 244.

7. See note 3 above.

8. Tetsuo Minato, 'The Japanese System of Subcontracting', *Sumitomo Corporation News*, Vol. 48, January 1985.

9. See note 1 above.

10. For a detailed discussion on how Singapore developed from entrepôt trade to manufacturing, see H. Hughes and You Poh Seng, *Foreign Investment and Industrialization in Singapore*, Canberra, Australian National University Press, 1969, and Lee Soo Ann, *Industrialization in Singapore*, Camberwell, Victoria, Longman, 1973.

11. See Lee Soo Ann, *Industrialization*, Chapter 6.

12. Ibid., and also Lim Chong Yah and You Poh Seng, *The Singapore Economy*, Singapore, Eastern Universities Press, 1971, Chapter 8, and also Pang Eng Fong and Augustine Tan, 'Employment and Export-led Industrialization: The Experience of Singapore', in Rashid Amjad (ed.), *The Development of Labour-Intensive Industry in ASEAN Countries*, Bangkok, Asian Regional Team for Employment Promotion, 1981.

13. See Chia Siow Yue, Chapter 8, in Lim and You, op. cit., pp. 190–1.

14. Much literature has been written on this. See Lee Soo Ann, *Industrialization*, and also Pang and Tan, op. cit.

15. Lim Chong Yah, 'Economic Development of Singapore since Self-Government in 1959', in K. E. Boulding (ed.), *The Economics of Human Betterment*, London, The Macmillan Press, 1984.

16. Ibid.

TABLE 1.1

GDP, Unemployment, Inflation, and Population Growth, 1966–1985
(Percentage)

Year	Rate of Growth of Gross Domestic Product at 1968 Market Prices	Unemployment Rate	Inflation Rate[a]	Population Growth Rate[b]
1966	11.1	8.9	1.9	2.3
1967	11.8	8.1	3.3	2.0
1968	13.9	7.3	0.7	1.6
1969	13.7	6.7	−0.3	1.5
1970	13.7	6.0	0.4	1.7
1971	12.5	4.8	1.9	1.8
1972	13.4	4.7	2.1	1.9
1973	11.5	4.5	19.6	1.8
1974	6.3	4.0	22.3	1.6
1975	4.1	4.5	2.6	1.4
1976	7.5	4.5	−1.9	1.4
1977	7.9	3.9	3.2	1.3
1978	8.6	3.6	4.8	1.2
1979	9.4	3.4	4.0	1.3
1980	10.3	3.5	8.5	1.2
1981	9.9	2.9	8.2	1.2
1982	6.3	2.6	3.9	1.2
1983	7.9	3.3	1.2	1.1
1984	8.2	2.7	2.6	1.1
1985	−1.8	4.2	0.5	1.1

Source: Singapore, Department of Statistics, *Yearbook of Statistics*, various years.

[a] Consumer Price Index, June 1977–May 1978 = 100.

[b] Data on population growth were taken from *Report on Registration of Births and Deaths*, Singapore, Registrar-General of Births and Death, 1985.

TABLE 1.2

Comparative Economic Performance, 1960–1982

Country	Real GDP Average Annual Growth (%)			
	1960–1970	1970–1980	1981	1982p
Low-income countries	4.4	4.6	n.a.	n.a.
Middle-income countries	5.9	5.6	n.a.	n.a.
Industrial market economies	5.2	3.2	1.5*	−0.5*
ASEAN				
Singapore	8.8	8.5	9.9	6.3
Indonesia	3.9	7.6	7.6	4.5
Malaysia	6.5	7.8	6.9	3.9
Philippines	5.1	6.3	3.7	2.6
Thailand	8.4	7.2	7.6	4.5
Other Asian NICs				
South Korea	8.6	9.5	6.4	6.0
Hong Kong	10.0	9.3	11.0	4.0
Taiwan	8.8	10.1	5.5	4.0

Sources: World Bank, *World Development Report*, 1982, and *Economic Survey of Singapore*, 1982. Figures for Taiwan are obtained from Republic of China, Directorate-General of Budget, Accounting and Statistics, *Statistical Yearbook of China*, 1984.
* Total of Organization for Economic Cooperation and Development (OECD) countries.
p = preliminary.
n.a. = Data not available.

TABLE 1.3

Growth of Average Weekly Earnings by Industry, 1972–1983

Industry	Year ($)		1972–1983 Annual Average Growth Rate (%)
	1972	1983	
Agriculture and fishing	55.4	194.3	12.6
Quarrying	69.1	490.7	20.4
Manufacturing	63.2	191.6	10.6
Utilities	80.5	274.1	11.5
Construction	77.6	200.9	9.2
Trade	68.5	220.7	11.3
Transport and communications	84.7	258.9	10.8
Financial and business services	108.9	299.5	9.4
Other services	86.8	277.2	11.4
All industries	75.6	231.3	10.8

Source: See Table 1.1.

2

THE INDUSTRIALIZATION
PROCESS

WITHIN a short span of twenty-five years, Singapore has emerged as one of the NICs. Only Japan and Brunei have a higher per capita income than Singapore in Asia. However, for Singapore, the struggle with industrialization is by no means over. Indeed, rising trade protectionism in the West has forced Singapore to restructure her economy. Her success in the restructuring of the economy depends upon complete cooperation between the government, the private sector and the labour force.

A Sectoral Analysis

As has been discussed in Chapter 1, Singapore depended heavily upon entrepôt trade for her growth and development in the pre-1960 period. Table 2.1 shows that, in 1963, the trade sector accounted for 36.0 per cent of Singapore's GDP while the manufacturing sector only contributed 13.5 per cent. Two other important sectors were the transport and communications sector and the financial and business services sector, each contributing 13.0 per cent and 11.0 per cent respectively in the same year.

The government is fully aware that the manufacturing sector cannot be developed in isolation. In fact, through a strong manufacturing sector, the transport and communications sector and the financial and business services sector can be simultaneously stimulated, thereby achieving the objective of diversifying the economy. Singapore's industrialization experience confirms that this is true to a large extent.

Singapore's manufacturing sector has been expanding very rapidly. Its contribution to Singapore's GDP increased from 16 per cent in 1967 to 22 per cent in 1980, but fell to 20 per cent in 1983. Both the GDP contributions of the transport and communications industry and the financial and business services industry fell behind that of the manufacturing sector in the 1960s and 1970s, but surpassed it in 1983. Thus, the government has successfully transformed the Singapore economy from a trade-dominated economy into an economy which relies equally on four sectors: trade, manufacturing, transport and communications, and financial and business services.

The sectoral contribution by employment presents a rather different picture. Table 2.2 shows that in 1963, more than 40 per cent of her work-force were engaged in the manufacturing sector. This implies that the manufacturing sector was very labour intensive because it only accounted for 13.5 per cent of Singapore's GDP in the same year. The manufacturing sector continued to be the dominant absorber of the work-force until the 1970s when Singapore had a labour shortage instead of the old unemployment problem.

Due to the labour shortage in the 1970s, all sectors were urged to economize on labour. The manufacturing sector was no exception. The percentage of workers engaged in the manufacturing sector was under 30 per cent in the 1970s and early 1980s. In terms of employment contribution, the three main pillars of the economy were, and still are, manufacturing, trade, and financial and business services.

The above discussion implies that the relative contribution of the manufacturing sector in terms of GDP and employment is not likely to increase. In fact, its employment contribution fell from 29.2 per cent in 1980 to 27.8 per cent in 1983 and its GDP contribution also decreased from 22 per cent in 1980 to 20 per cent in 1983. This suggests that the manufacturing sector should be selective and invest in the right types of industries. It should move away from low value-added and labour-intensive industries to high value-added and capital-intensive industries. It is hoped that small firms can help to restructure the manufacturing sector along these lines.

Industrial Development

Singapore's industrialization process since 1960 has been tremendous, aided greatly by a manufacturing sector that has been dynamic enough to cope with the problems faced by the economy. The process may be divided into four phases corresponding to changes in government policies.

The Import-substitution Phase, 1960–1966

The industrialization programme started off with an emphasis on import substitution so as to create jobs for the expanding labour force and to provide manufacturers with the opportunity for exploiting the then anticipated pan-Malaya (Malaya and Singapore) common market. Incentives were given to local and foreign investors to encourage them to set up 'pioneer industries' which were generally protected by tariffs and quotas from competing imports.

The import-substitution strategy was abandoned upon two unanticipated crises: Singapore's separation from the Federation of Malaysia in August 1965 and the British announcement of the phased withdrawal of her troops from Singapore by the mid-1960s.

The Employment-creating Export-orientation Phase, 1967–1969

The announcement of the British military withdrawal by the mid-1960s spelt disastrous consequences for Singapore's economic growth and employment outlook. Faced with this pressing situation and realizing that the import substitution strategy would not provide a practical means of achieving efficient industrialization for employment and income growth because of the limited size of the domestic market after separation, Singapore switched her industrialization strategy from import substitution to export orientation in 1967.

In order to encourage export-oriented labour-intensive industries, the government introduced the Economic Expansion (Relief from Income Tax) Act in 1967. The Act provided, among other things, a reduction of the tax rate on profits earned by approved industries for exports. Other incentives were also provided, such as easier access to duty-free or intermediate products for exporters and greater discretion for employers in labour matters.

The Higher-technology Export-orientation Phase, 1970–1978

The problem of unemployment which had arisen from population growth and the British withdrawal had been sufficiently overcome by the end of the 1960s. In fact, the unemployment rate had dropped to 6.0 per cent by 1970, and in 1973, it was as low as 4.5 per cent—a situation of full employment in economic terms. Moreover, with the increased manpower requirements of expanding sectors, particularly in the commercial and service sectors and in National Service, a shortage of labour resulted, necessitating the inflow of thousands of foreign workers. This change in the labour market situation prompted a re-orientation of economic policy, the need for which was realized by the end of the 1960s.

The Economic-restructuring Phase, 1979 Onwards

The year 1979 saw the start of a 'Second Industrial Revolution' when the National Wages Council (NWC) launched its corrective wage policy of recommending a wage increase of about 20 per cent for three consecutive years. The higher cost of employing labour forced firms not to rely excessively on labour. This is consistent with the objective of encouraging high value-added and technologically sophisticated firms to set up plants in Singapore.

The corrective wage policy was necessary in the search for a higher level of industrialization. In the mid-1970s, Singapore was caught in a low-wage trap. The low level of wages caused labour-intensive industries to flourish in Singapore. Consequently, her exports relied on labour-intensive products. At the same time, she permitted many foreign workers into Singapore to ease the tight labour market situation created by the presence of a large number of labour-intensive industries. The influx of foreign workers further depressed wages, which in turn encouraged more labour-intensive industries to be set up. She was therefore caught in a vicious circle.

This situation gave rise to high turnover rates among the local workers and an over-dependence on foreign workers. Equally important, it also meant that Singapore would have had to compete with countries such as Malaysia, Thailand, and China in producing labour-intensive goods, and would have been at a disadvantage since wages in these countries are far below those in Singapore. Besides, labour-intensive products have often been the targets of rising trade protectionism in the industrial countries. On all accounts, it was not in the interest of Singapore to remain in the low-wage trap. She had to break out of the vicious circle by forcing her industries to export more technology-intensive products, which are subject to less restrictive measures in the industrial world.

The principal statistics of the manufacturing sector are reported in Table 2.3. The manufacturing sector has expanded very rapidly in terms of the number of establishments, employment, output, value-added, exports, and GDP contributions. However, during 1980–3, which is in the economic-restructuring phase, the manufacturing sector actually stagnated in terms of employment, output, value-added, and exports. This decline in manufacturing activity is not inconsistent with the aim of economic restructuring, which encourages manufacturing firms to produce selective high value-added and skill-intensive products. Given the small land size, the small labour force, and the reluctance to employ large numbers of foreign workers, the importance of the Singapore manufacturing sector must be preserved, not in terms of expanding industrial employment and output, but in terms of employing skilled workers and producing high value-added products.

Table 2.4 reports the characteristics of the manufacturing sector under different phases. The manufacturing sector had double-digit growth rates in output for 1960–6, 1967–9, 1970–8 and 1979–80. However, for the period 1981–3, the output growth rate was only 1.2 per cent. Similarly, the employment growth rate of the manufacturing sector was high for all the periods except 1981–3, when it registered −1.9 per cent employment growth. This was in line with the anticipated result of the successful economic restructuring through the NWC corrective wage policy. At the same time, the manufacturing sector has been investing in more capital per worker. The capital–labour ratio of the manufacturing sector rose from $6,600 per worker for the 1960–6 period to $38,500 per worker for the 1981–3 period.

Table 2.5 presents three indicators of production structural changes in the manufacturing sector. The capital–labour ratio increased from $5,900 in 1963 to $38,500 in 1983, representing an increase of over 500 per cent. Its value-added per worker also made an impressive improvement from $5,000 in 1960 to $36,200 in 1983. The labour skill coefficient of the manufacturing sector also increased from 0.03 in 1957 to 0.424 in 1983. In a country with limited natural resources and a labour-deficit economy, it is clear that the manufacturing sector has done its share in upgrading its industries with a continuous high capital–labour ratio, high value-added per worker, and a high labour skill coefficient. However, as was discussed in the previous section, the manufacturing sector is still labour intensive compared with other sectors. (Its GDP contribution in 1983 was 20 per cent but its share in employment was 27.8 per cent. See Tables 2.1 and 2.2.)

Other interesting aspects of the manufacturing sector are its capital and organization structures. In 1963, almost 90 per cent of the firms were wholly under local ownership (see Table 2.6). Foreign firms only accounted for 4.3 per cent of the total number of establishments. However, Singapore's industrialization was achieved to a great extent by MNCs. In 1975, foreign companies accounted for 12.4 per cent of the total number of establishments and their share rose to 15.4 per cent in 1980. There were, of course, many joint ventures which were encouraged by the government as an effective means of technology transfer from multinational to local companies. By 1980, the local companies in the manufacturing sector had decreased to 64.2 per cent while joint ventures accounted for 20.4 per cent.

The 1980–3 period saw an increase of 3 per cent in the local firms' contribution to the total number of establishments to 67.2 per cent. There were 2 per cent and 1 per cent decreases in the percentage of joint ventures and foreign firms in the manufacturing sector, respectively. The fall in the contribution to the number of establishments in the latter two groups could be attributed to the recent recession in the West.

Table 2.6 also reports the organization of firms in the manufacturing sector. Sole proprietorships and partnerships, which are suitable for small firms, accounted for 31.4 per cent and 37.8 per cent respectively of the total number of establishments in 1963. Public limited companies accounted for 3.6 per cent. However, the main disadvantage of sole proprietorships and partnerships is that it is difficult for them to secure loans. Consequently, by 1983, public limited companies accounted for 68.6 per cent of the total number of establishments while partnerships accounted for 17.4 per cent and sole proprietorships 11.5 per cent.

As will be discussed in Chapter 5, small firms are usually local firms and also sole proprietorships and partnerships. The preceding discussion indicates that small firms in Singapore experienced difficulties in the 1960s and 1970s.

The manufacturing sector has shown that it is dynamic enough to lead Singapore out of economic difficulties. Its work-force has shrunk, but it has managed to maintain a steady level of output, value-added, and exports with more capital per worker. As the manufacturing sector is comprised of small and large firms, it should be interesting to see whether small firms have responded in the same way.

Structural Changes in the Manufacturing Sector

The manufacturing sector has undergone extensive changes since 1960. Its level of output, direct domestic exports, and value-added rose steadily from 1960 to 1983 except for two years, 1975 and 1982, when it suffered a temporary reduction in output, exports, and value-added, mainly as a result of unfavourable international conditions (see Figure 2.1). The employment level of the manufacturing sector reached a peak in 1980. During the period 1981–3, the level of employment fell, and there seems to be a strong indication that the future level of employment in the manufacturing sector will be around the 1983 level.

The changes in the manufacturing sector at the aggregate level are inevitably brought about by changes in the various industries which comprise it. It is the purpose of this section to analyse the structural changes that have accompanied the changes at the aggregate level. The industrial changes will be examined in terms of output, value-added, capital stock, employment, and export–output ratio. To provide a consistent comparison with the phases considered in the above section, data for 1960, 1967, 1970, 1980 and 1983 will be analysed.

Changes by Contribution to Output

Table 2.7 shows the contribution to manufacturing output by industry groups in the manufacturing sector for the periods under consideration. In 1960, the major industries were beverages (15.8 per cent), food (15.2 per cent), chemical products and petroleum (12.7 per cent), paper and printing (9.3 per cent), and cigarettes (8.4 per cent). However, by 1967, petroleum and petroleum products had emerged as the most important industry, contributing 21.4 per cent of the total manufacturing output. Food, protected by the import-substitution strategy, contributed 18.3 per cent to remain as the second most important industry in the manufacturing sector. The third most important industry was beverages (7.7 per cent).

In 1970, petroleum and petroleum products remained the leading industry (31.4 per cent). However, food contributed only 13.2 per cent. The export-oriented strategy in the late 1960s gave rise to a few important intermediate goods industries, i.e. transport equipment (8.5 per cent), electrical/electronic products (7.3 per cent), and fabricated metal products (5.6 per cent).

A decade later, in 1980, petroleum still occupied the first place (34.4 per cent). But electrical/electronic products had emerged as the second most important industry (19.9 per cent). Food, which was dominant in the 1960s, contributed only 5.2 per cent in 1980. The structure was basically unchanged in 1983. The output contribution of the petroleum and petroleum products industry was around 35.3 per cent, and that of the electrical/electronic products industry rose to 22.1 per cent.

The share of consumer goods, such as food, beverages, and cigarettes, dominated the manufacturing sector in the early 1960s, but were replaced by intermediate goods, such as electrical/electronic products, non-electrical machinery, transport equipment, and fabricated metal products, in the 1980s. Over the 24-year period, the growth of the petroleum and petroleum products industry had been remarkable. Its growth was first sustained by demand arising from the Vietnam War and later by the surge of oil exploration.

Changes by Contribution to Value-added

As Singapore is a country with very limited resources, the importance of contribution to value-added by industries can never be over-emphasized. In 1960, the leading industries in terms of value-added contribution were beverages (18.3 per cent), paper and printing (16.2 per cent), food (10.7 per cent), and fabricated metal products (7.6 per cent) (see Table 2.8). However, by 1967, petroleum and petroleum products had emerged as the leading industry (14.3 per cent). Beverages fell to second position (11.7 per cent). Food (9.1 per cent), paper and printing (8.3 per cent), and transport equipment (7.9 per cent) were also industries important in contributing to Singapore's gross national product (GNP).

By 1970, the consumer goods sector was no longer important. Petroleum and petroleum products was again the most important industry (19.2 per cent), followed by transport equipment (14.6 per cent), and electrical/electronic products (11.7 per cent). With the emphasis on high value-added industries in the second industrial revolution, electrical/electronic products topped the list with 23.8 per cent in 1980. Petroleum and petroleum products was next (16.9 per cent), followed by transport equipment (12.4 per cent), and non-electrical machinery (8.7 per cent). The basic industrial structure remained the same in 1983 in terms of the ranking of the four industries mentioned above.

It is not surprising that petroleum and petroleum products has not been the leading industry since 1980 because the potential for further development of the industry is not as great as for other industries, such as the electrical and electronic industries, given Singapore's small land size and its lack of petroleum resources.

Changes by Contribution to Capital Assets

Capital-intensive industries dominate the manufacturing sector in terms of contribution to capital assets.[1] In 1963, petroleum and chemical products contributed 27.6 per cent (see Table 2.9). The other three important industries were cigarettes (15.1 per cent), beverages (10.9 per cent), and transport equipment (9.6 per cent). In 1967, petroleum and petroleum products continued to dominate the scene with 21.6 per cent. Food doubled its contribution from 5.5 per cent in 1963 to 10.6 per cent in 1967 to emerge as the second most important industry. The other two important industries were beverages (9.3 per cent) and transport equipment (9.2 per cent).

Both highly capital-intensive industries, petroleum and petroleum products and transport equipment increased their contribution to capital assets to 25.8 per cent and 15.3 per cent respectively in 1970. The consumer goods industries, such as food and beverages, were left far behind. A decade later, in 1980, in addition to the two most important industries, i.e. petroleum and petroleum products (32.5 per cent) and transport equipment (12.3 per cent), electrical/electronic products rose rapidly, from 3.0 per cent in 1970 to 11.3 per cent in 1980. By 1983, electrical/electronic products had surpassed transport equipment to be the second most important industry with 13.3 per cent. Petroleum and petroleum products was still the leading industry with 29.0 per cent.

Petroleum and petroleum products was consistently the main capital assets contributor. In 1983, other intermediate goods industries, such as electrical/electronic products, transport equipment, non-electrical machinery, and fabricated metal products, combined, were responsible for 38.8 per cent of capital assets. Foreign capital investment has been the main contributor in capital assets in the manufacturing sector.

Changes by Contribution to Employment

Table 2.10 shows the contribution of each industry to total employment. In 1960, paper and printing was the largest employer, accounting for 15.4 per cent of the total employment in the manufacturing sector. The other leading industries were food (12.4 per cent), wood and cork products (9.2 per cent), and beverages (8.6 per cent). The consumer goods industries, which include the above four mentioned industries, employed more than half of the working population in the early 1960s. The industrial structure in terms of employment altered in 1967 with apparel, footwear and leather products as the biggest employer (12.5 per cent), followed closely by paper and printing (10.5 per cent), transport equipment (10.3 per cent), wood and cork products (10.3 per cent), and food (10.2 per cent).

The success of the export-oriented strategy made the electrical/ electronic products the second largest employer (11.3 per cent) in 1970, next to transport equipment (13.5 per cent). The other leading industries were apparel, footwear and leather products (9.5 per cent), and paper and printing (7.9 per cent). A decade later, in 1980, electrical/ electronic products was the largest employer with 30.7 per cent. It continued to be the leading industry in 1983 with 30.0 per cent. Apparel, footwear and leather products occupied the second position with 10.9 per cent, and transport equipment the third with 10.0 per cent.

Petroleum and petroleum products, which dominated the industrial scene in terms of output, value-added and capital assets, played an insignificant role as an employer. It should be noted that apparel, footwear and leather products and transport equipment were the only two industries which consistently contributed around 10 per cent throughout the 24-year period.

Changes by Export–Output Ratio

It is interesting to examine the industrial structure by export–output ratio. In 1970, non-metallic mineral products had the highest export–

output ratio of 0.92 (see Table 2.11). It was followed by electrical/
electronic products (0.75), processing of gum (0.74), and apparel,
footwear and leather products (0.57). There was a tremendous change
in the industrial structure in terms of export–output ratio in 1980.
Structural cement and concrete products had the highest export–output
ratio of 0.95, followed by precision equipment and optics (0.88),
electrical/electronic products (0.81), and apparel, footwear and leather
products (0.67). By 1983, the high export performance industries were
precision equipment and optics (0.94), electrical/electronic products
(0.84), non-electrical machinery (0.81), and apparel, footwear and
leather products (0.68).

Judging by the industry contribution to output, value-added, capital
assets, employment, and export–output ratio, it is reasonable to conclude that there has been a drastic but favourable change in the industrial
structure. Petroleum and petroleum products will remain as an important main industry in terms of output, value-added capital assets,
and perhaps also export–output ratio. In the early 1960s, the manufacturing sector had to rely on food, beverages, cigarettes, and other
consumer goods industries for output, value-added and employment.
However, in the 1980s, the promising industries are electrical/electronic
products, transport equipment, non-electrical machinery, and fabricated
metal products.

Factors Affecting Industrial Growth

This section briefly discusses various factors that have contributed to
Singapore's growth as an industrial city-state.

The Role of the Government

The PAP government has played an indispensable role in the overall
development of Singapore since 1959. In the first place, it has provided
for the development of the industries and the infrastructure in public
utilities, industrial land development, transport, and communications.

Secondly, the PAP government has successfully convinced trade
union leaders that a peaceful and conducive industrial scene is in the
interest of both the workers and Singapore. Consequently, the government won the cooperation of the trade unions in instituting those
Industrial Relations Acts which have basically reduced the bargaining
power of the trade unions.[2]

Thirdly, the government has also spearheaded the drive for human
capital development through the adjustment and restructuring of the
formal education system, and the introduction of industrial training
schemes. The academically-biased educational programme was reformed
in 1968 to place greater emphasis on technical training; this was followed
by an expansion of skills-oriented courses in the tertiary institutions.
Assistance has also been provided for industries to train personnel both
locally and abroad in Joint Government–Industry training programmes.

Moreover, as human capital investment became increasingly crucial to Singapore in her higher technology industrialization drive, the Skills Development Fund (SDF) was set up to raise funds to upgrade workers.

Lastly, a number of institutional statutory authorities have been created to help in the implementation of industrial policies. Among these is the Economic Development Board, which was set up in 1961 for the purpose of facilitating industrialization through the promotion of investment, and the provision of technical and financial assistance for new and existing industries. Some of its functions were taken over in later years by the Development Bank of Singapore (1968), the Jurong Town Corporation (1968), the Singapore Institute of Standards and Industrial Research (1969), and the National Productivity Board (1973). An international study concluded that the 'very capable management of these institutions has been a significant contributing factor in the growth of manufacturing industries'.[3]

Foreign Investment

Foreign investment has undoubtedly contributed significantly to industrial development in Singapore. In the early 1960s, the economy was dominated by entrepôt trade, and there was an insignificant amount of manufacturing activity that could create jobs. Foreign investment was therefore regarded as the only way for industrial expansion to generate employment. At that time, the foreign firms were very labour intensive and catered for domestic markets as Singapore was encouraging import substitution.

When Singapore switched to the export-oriented strategy, foreign firms were even more indispensable to industrial progress. They brought in high technology, managerial skills, capital, and established world-wide markets. The contributions of foreign-owned firms and joint ventures were a major force behind the expansion of manufacturing output, value-added, employment, and exports. For instance, between 1966 and 1972, Singapore's industrial output from wholly-owned foreign firms increased eightfold, compared with a threefold increase in output from wholly-owned domestic firms.[4] During the same period, wholly-owned foreign firms increased their contribution from 12 per cent to 29 per cent in industrial employment, from 26 per cent to 43 per cent in manufacturing value-added, and from 40 per cent to 63 per cent in capital expenditure in manufacturing.[5] By 1983, wholly-owned foreign firms accounted for 39 per cent in industrial employment, 53 per cent in industrial output and value-added, and 47 per cent in industrial capital expenditure.

International Economic Conditions

The manufacturing markets were certainly less competitive in the 1960s than they are today. There was also very limited trade protectionism in the West. Moreover, Singapore attracted substantial capital inflow not only from Hong Kong but also from Malaysia and Indonesia in the 1960s and 1970s. The boom in oil exploration activities in South-East Asia and the Vietnam War in the 1960s created a strong demand for Singapore's products and services. The government of Singapore was able to capitalize on the favourable external conditions with excellent economic policies and domestic management.

The process of industrialization in Singapore has been comparatively rapid and changes in industrial structure have been substantial. Factors contributing to the economic performance have been identified as domestic government policies, foreign investment, and favourable external conditions.

Since the beginning of the industrialization programme, the role of local entrepreneurship has been a limited one, and industrial growth in the past two decades was fostered mainly by foreign investment. Local investment was usually on a small scale and was generally based on family enterprises in the early period of industrialization. However, there has been a growing trend towards joint ventures in recent years, indicating that substantial local capital can still play a significant role in the industrial development strategy in the future.

In Chapters 3 and 4, we will analyse the contribution of small firms in the Singapore economy.

1. Capital assets are defined here as the net value of fixed assets, which include land, buildings and structures, machinery equipment, vehicles, and office equipment.

2. For more discussion on the Industrial Relations Act, see the section, 'Workers' Health, Safety Regulations, Environmental Control and Labour Legislations', in Chapter 10.

3. International Bank for Reconstruction and Development, *Current Economic Position and Prospects of Singapore*, International Development Association, 1973, p. 9.

4. Pang Eng Fong and Augustine Tan, 'Employment and Export-led Industrialization: The Experience of Singapore', in Rashid Amjad (ed.), *The Development of Labour-Intensive Industry in ASEAN Countries*, Bangkok, Asian Regional Team for Employment Promotion, 1981, p. 147.

5. Kunio Yoshihara, *Foreign Investment and Domestic Response: A Study of Singapore's Industrialization*, Singapore, Eastern Universities Press, 1976.

TABLE 2.1

Percentage Distribution of Gross Domestic Product
by Industry Output, 1963–1983

Industry	Year				
	1963	1967	1970	1980	1983
Trade	36.0	32.5	30.0	26.5	24.0
Manufacturing	13.5	16.0	19.0	22.0	20.0
Transport & communications	13.0	12.0	12.0	19.0	21.0
Financial & business services	11.0	12.5	9.0	14.0	22.0
Construction	5.0	6.5	6.5	5.0	8.0
Utilities	2.5	3.0	2.5	3.0	3.0
Others	19.0	17.5	21.0	10.5	2.0
Total	100.0	100.0	100.0	100.0	100.0

Source: Singapore, Ministry of Trade and Industry, Economic Survey of Singapore, various
years.

TABLE 2.2

Percentage Distribution of Employment by Industry,
1963–1983

Industry	Year				
	1963	1967	1970	1980	1983
Agriculture/Fishing	1.2	0.9	0.6	1.3	1.0
Quarrying	0.6	0.9	0.4	0.2	0.2
Manufacturing	40.7	41.6	27.5	29.2	27.8
Utilities	6.4	6.6	3.3	0.9	0.7
Construction	11.7	12.7	5.3	5.4	7.2
Trade	7.9	7.5	22.4	22.9	22.7
Transport & communications	18.3	16.6	10.0	11.4	11.3
Financial & business services	13.2	13.2	30.5	28.2	28.9
Activities not adequately defined	0.0	0.0	0.0	0.5	0.2
Total	100.0	100.0	100.0	100.0	100.0

Sources: Singapore, Ministry of Labour, Report on the Labour Force Survey of Singapore,
various years; Singapore, Department of Statistics, Monthly Digest of Statistics, various
issues.

TABLE 2.3

Principal Statistics of Manufacturing, 1963–1983

Characteristics		Year				
		1963	1967	1970	1980	1983
Establishments	(number)	548	1,586	1,747	3,347	3,743
Employment	(number)	27,416	74,833	120,509	287,314	270,351
Output	($million)	466	2,176	3,891	34,285	34,679
Input	($million)	320	1,431	2,748	24,836	24,722
Value-added	($million)	142	612	1,094	8,842	9,049
Direct exports	($million)	164	598	1,523	22,578	21,017
GDP contribution (% at current factor cost)		13.2	17.0	19.7	22.7	18.2

Source: Singapore, Economic Development Board, Annual Report, various years.

TABLE 2.4

Indicators of Industrialization Process, 1960–1983

Indicators	1960–1966	1967–1969	1970–1978	1979–1980	1981–1983
1. Average manufacturing output growth rate (% p.a.)	19.3	34.7	23.8	26.9	1.2
2. Average manufacturing employment growth rate (% p.a.)	11.9	24.5	12.3	8.2	−1.9
3. Labour absorption coefficient (2 ÷ 1)	0.62	0.71	0.52	0.30	−1.58
4. Capital–labour ratio ($'000 per worker)	6.6*	8.1	15.1	22.0	38.5

Source: Singapore, Department of Statistics, Report on the Census of Industrial Production, various years.

Notes: 1. Figures are obtained by averaging the annual growth rates of employment and output for the periods under consideration.

2. Rubber processing is excluded for reasons explained in the first Report, 1959.

* Excludes period 1960–2 for which no figures for net assets are available.

TABLE 2.5

Indicators of Production Structural Changes, 1957–1983

Indicators	Year						
	1957	1960	1963	1967	1970	1980	1983
1. Capital–labour ratio (factor intensity, $'000)	–	–	5.9	8.6	8.9	22.7	38.5
2. Value-added per worker ($'000)	–	5.0	–	8.0	9.0	29.0	36.2
3. Labour skill coefficient	0.03	–	–	–	0.097	0.166	0.424

Sources: For (1) and (2), data are obtained from Singapore, Department of Statistics, *Report on the Census of Industrial Production*, various years; for (3), calculations are based on data from Singapore, Department of Statistics, *Report on the Census of Population*, 1957, 1970, and 1980, and Singapore, Department of Statistics, *Monthly Digest of Statistics*, various issues.

TABLE 2.6

Structure by Capital and Organization, 1963–1983
(By Percentage of Establishments)

Structure	Year					
	1963	1967	1970	1975	1980	1983
Capital						
Wholly local	89.3	80.5	–	66.9	64.2	67.2
More than half local	3.5	8.1	–	11.1	10.9	11.7
Less than half local	2.7	6.1	–	9.6	9.5	6.7
Wholly foreign	4.3	5.2	–	12.4	15.4	14.4
Ownership						
Sole proprietor	31.4	25.3	23.4	–	12.3	11.5
Partnership	37.8	34.4	29.8	–	19.5	17.4
Public limited company	3.6	3.0	3.9	–	2.0	68.6
Private limited company	27.2	37.3	42.8	–	65.8	1.7
Others	0.1	0.1	0.1	–	0.4	0.8

Source: See Table 2.4.

TABLE 2.7

Output of Industry Groups, 1960–1983
(As Percentage of Total Output)

Industry Group	Year				
	1960	1967	1970	1980	1983
Food	15.2	18.3	13.2	5.2	5.2
Beverages	15.8	7.7	3.2	1.3	0.9
Cigarettes and other tobacco products	8.4	5.5	2.51	0.54	0.6
Textiles and textile manufactures	} 2.3	0.5	1.2	1.5	0.7
Apparel, footwear & leather products		2.9	2.1	3.0	2.8
Wood & cork products	6.7	4.4	4.8	2.4	1.2
Furniture & fixtures	0.8	0.8	0.6	0.7	0.8
Paper & printing	9.3	5.1	3.5	2.6	3.1
Chemical products		6.5	2.11	2.9	3.4
Petroleum & petroleum products	12.7	21.4	31.4	34.4	35.3
Processing of gum	–	–	0.38	0.08	0.07
Rubber products	2.9	1.7	1.0	0.3	0.2
Plastic products	–	0.6	0.9	1.6	1.5
Pottery, china, glass products	–	–	0.46	0.02	0.25
Bricks, tiles, clay products	–	–	0.22	0.1	0.16
Cement	–	–	0.93	0.88	1.2
Structural cement & concrete products	–	–	0.29	0.49	1.6
Non-metallic mineral products	2.7	3.5	2.3	2.0	0.4
Basic metal	1.1	2.9	2.2	1.59	1.3
Fabricated metal products	6.1	5.1	5.6	3.9	4.9
Non-electrical machinery	3.6	1.8	1.9	5.3	5.5
Electrical/Electronic products	3.7	2.5	7.3	19.9	22.1
Transport equipment	6.7	5.6	8.5	6.5	5.0
Precision equipment & optics	–	–	0.3	1.4	0.7
Other manufacturing	2.0	3.2	3.1	1.4	1.2
Total	100.0	100.0	100.0	100.0	100.0

Source: See Table 2.4.

TABLE 2.8

Value-added by Industry Groups, 1960–1983
(As Percentage of Total Value-added)

Industry Group	Year				
	1960	1967	1970	1980	1983
Food	10.7	9.1	5.9	2.1	3.6
Beverages	18.3	11.7	4.5	1.9	1.5
Cigarettes and other tobacco products	5.4	6.5	2.26	0.62	0.9
Textiles and textile manufactures	3.1	0.7	1.2	1.8	1.0
Apparel, footwear & leather products		3.0	2.0	2.5	3.7
Wood & cork products	6.1	4.7	4.62	2.1	1.4
Furniture & fixtures	1.0	1.2	0.9	0.9	1.1
Paper & printing	16.2	8.3	5.8	4.4	6.2
Chemical products	6.8	5.5	4.5	4.9	6.5
Petroleum & petroleum products		14.3	19.2	16.94	14.9
Processing of gum	–	–	0.15	0.03	0.04
Rubber products	2.3	2.2	1.7	0.5	0.4
Plastic products	–	0.9	1.1	2.0	1.9
Pottery, china, glass products	–	–	0.91	0.29	0.35
Bricks, tiles, clay products	–	–	0.55	0.22	0.3
Cement	–	–	0.69	0.57	1.07
Structural cement & concrete products	–	–	0.32	0.63	1.34
Non-metallic mineral products	3.8	5.5	3.0	2.3	0.6
Basic metal	1.3	3.4	2.0	1.8	1.6
Fabricated metal products	7.6	6.7	6.6	4.9	7.0
Non-electrical machinery	4.6	3.0	2.6	8.7	8.8
Electrical/Electronic products	5.5	3.3	11.7	23.8	24.0
Transport equipment	6.0	7.9	14.6	12.4	9.4
Precision equipment & optics	–	–	0.6	2.1	1.2
Other manufacturing	1.3	2.2	2.6	1.6	1.2
Total	100.0	100.0	100.0	100.0	100.0

Source: See Table 2.4.

TABLE 2.9

Capital Assets by Industry Groups, 1963–1983

(As Percentage of Total Assets)

Industry Group	Year				
	1963*	1967	1970	1980	1983
Food	5.5	10.6	7.9	3.1	4.4
Beverages	10.9	9.3	5.3	1.3	1.48
Cigarettes and other tobacco products	15.1	3.0	0.2	0.57	0.52
Textiles and textile manufactures	0.9	0.6	6.1	2.6	1.2
Apparel, footwear & leather products		2.2	1.8	2.3	2.1
Wood & cork products	2.5	4.4	4.9	2.9	1.7
Furniture & fixtures	0.5	0.5	0.4	1.0	0.9
Paper & printing	8.4	5.1	4.4	3.2	4.8
Chemical products	27.6	5.9	4.7	3.5	5.32
Petroleum & petroleum products		21.6	25.8	32.5	29.0
Processing of gum	–	–	0.05	0.003	0.03
Rubber products	0.8	3.7	1.7	0.6	0.4
Plastic products	–	–	1.2	2.2	2.6
Pottery, china, glass products	–	–	0.69	1.56	0.69
Bricks, tiles, clay products	–	–	0.49	0.25	0.54
Cement	–	–	1.73	0.14	0.72
Structural cement & concrete products	–	–	0.46	0.42	0.9
Non-metallic mineral products	5.8	6.3	3.78	2.1	0.4
Basic metal	2.3	4.8	2.1	1.3	1.3
Fabricated metal products	5.2	6.4	5.4	5.2	7.4
Non-electrical machinery	1.5	3.3	1.2	6.7	7.2
Electrical/Electronic products	2.4	1.7	3.0	11.257	13.3
Transport equipment	9.6	9.2	15.3	12.3	10.9
Precision equipment & optics	–	–	0.4	1.9	1.4
Other manufacturing	1.0	1.4	1.0	1.1	0.8
Total	100.0	100.0	100.0	100.0	100.0

Source: See Table 2.4.

* Figures for net value of capital assets are available only for 1963 onwards.

TABLE 2.10

Employment by Industry Groups, 1960–1983
(As Percentage of Total Employment)

Industry Group	Year				
	1960	1967	1970	1980	1983
Food	12.4	10.2	6.5	2.5	3.8
Beverages	8.6	4.6	2.8	1.4	0.88
Cigarettes and other tobacco products	3.5	2.0	0.87	0.45	0.32
Textiles and textile manufactures	4.7	1.8	4.9	3.4	1.7
Apparel, footwear & leather products		12.5	9.5	9.83	10.9
Wood & cork products	9.2	10.3	7.11	3.6	2.2
Furniture & fixtures	1.6	2.2	1.5	2.2	2.5
Paper & printing	15.4	10.5	7.9	5.7	6.5
Chemical products	5.2	4.4	3.2	2.3	2.5
Petroleum & petroleum products		1.1	1.8	1.2	1.72
Processing of gum	–	–	0.20	0.05	0.06
Rubber products	3.2	2.8	1.4	0.7	0.5
Plastic products	–	1.4	1.8	3.2	3.2
Pottery, china, glass products	–	–	1.46	0.33	0.37
Bricks, tiles, clay products	–	–	0.1	0.17	0.25
Cement	–	–	0.36	0.16	0.21
Structural cement & concrete products	–	–	0.5	0.51	0.99
Non-metallic mineral products	8.2	5.4	4.0	1.6	0.6
Basic metal	1.7	2.9	1.2	0.8	0.8
Fabricated metal products	6.3	7.7	7.2	6.2	7.8
Non-electrical machinery	5.3	3.5	3.2	7.1	8.3
Electrical/Electronic products	4.6	3.2	11.3	30.7	30.0
Transport equipment	8.3	10.3	13.5	9.6	10.0
Precision equipment & optics	–	–	1.0	3.7	1.9
Other manufacturing	1.8	3.2	6.7	2.6	2.0
Total	100.0	100.0	100.0	100.0	100.0

Source: See Table 2.4.

TABLE 2.11

Export–Output Ratio for Manufacturing, 1970–1983

Industry Group	Year		
	1970	1980	1983
Food	0.34	0.53	0.55
Beverages	0.20	0.22	0.22
Cigarettes and other tobacco products	0.04	0.11	0.12
Textiles and textile manufactures	0.48	0.49	0.41
Apparel, footwear & leather products	0.57	0.67	0.68
Wood & cork products	0.46	0.55	0.48
Furniture & fixtures	0.10	0.43	0.41
Paper & printing	0.14	0.15	0.20
Chemical products	0.24	0.57	0.65
Petroleum & petroleum products	0.48	0.66	0.63
Processing of gum	0.74	0.62	0.58
Rubber products	0.38	0.52	0.50
Plastic products	0.29	0.22	0.24
Pottery, china, glass products	0.52	0.54	0.59
Bricks, tiles, clay products	0.014	0.02	0.008
Cement	0.04	0.27	0.16
Structural cement & concrete products	–	0.95	0.50
Non-metallic mineral products	0.92	0.21	0.63
Basic metal	0.21	0.41	0.21
Fabricated metal products	0.23	0.29	0.26
Non-electrical machinery	0.23	0.65	0.81
Electrical/Electronic products	0.75	0.81	0.84
Transport equipment	0.30	0.47	0.57
Precision equipment & optics	0.47	0.88	0.94
Other manufacturing	0.31	0.45	0.44
Total	100.0	100.0	100.0

Source: See Table 2.4.

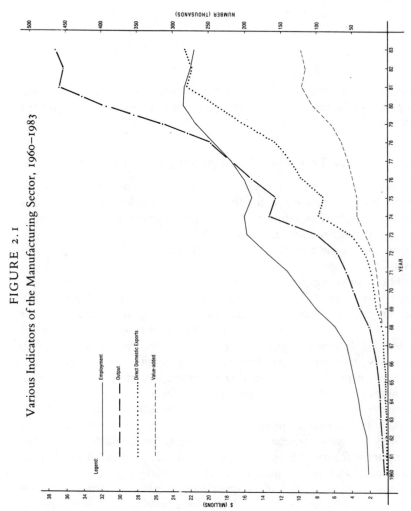

FIGURE 2.1

Various Indicators of the Manufacturing Sector, 1960–1983

Source: Singapore, Department of Statistics, *Report on the Census of Industrial Production,* various years.

3

THE CONCEPTUAL FRAMEWORK
OF SMALL FIRMS

IN this chapter, we aim to provide the analytical foundation for Chapter 4 in which the economic contribution of small industries in Singapore is examined.

The Theoretical Underpinning of Small Firms

In the literature on microeconomics, there does not seem to be any explicit theory to account for firm size. Nevertheless, firm size can be briefly explained in terms of the output-expansion path. As shown in Figure 3.1, the output-expansion path is a locus of points of tangencies between isoquants (I, II and III) and respective isocost lines (AA, BB and CC).

For a growing firm, firm size measured by capital, labour, and output will grow along the output-expansion path provided that there are no capital and labour constraints. Technological progress, which is likely to occur, will cause the output-expansion path to be more capital intensive. A firm will grow in size provided that its product or service is competitive. An efficient firm will enjoy certain degrees of economies of scale, depending on the market structure. In perfect competition and monopolistic competition, firm size is not likely to be large. However, in the case of an oligopoly or a monopoly, firm size is expected to grow rapidly in order for firms to reap the benefits of large-scale production.

Why are we interested in small firms? Is the smallness of a firm a temporary feature during its growth into a large firm? If small firms exist only as a phase, then it is not interesting to study them at all because most of them will eventually grow into large firms or simply die out. However, in view of the large number of small firms in existence and their persistence in the history of economic development of all countries, small firms are definitely not a passing phase. Indeed, small firms have contributed significantly to the economic development of most nations.[1]

How do we account for the existence of small firms? Small firms may exist under the following conditions:

1. Firm size cannot grow owing to a binding capital constraint (or a binding labour constraint). In Figure 3.2, KK is the binding capital constraint. A firm with KK capital constraint cannot produce an output

greater than 400 units in our example. Moreover, the firm under this capital constraint will have to produce 400 units at B rather than at C, which is on the output-expansion path. This indicates that the small firm under such a condition is more labour intensive. Since the firm does not produce along its output-expansion path, the cost of production will be higher than that of those firms without capital constraints which produce along the output-expansion path (at C in our example). This leads us to conclude that firms under capital constraints are intra-marginal firms.

2. Firm size cannot grow owing to an output constraint. In this case, the market for the product is small. If the demand for the firm's output is small, such as the 100 units in our example (see Figure 3.2), then the size of the firm is small. The firm, however, can and will produce on the output-expansion path. Thus, firms under this condition are efficient as they minimize the cost of production. Under what condition will the firm's demand for output be small? One classic example is *haute couture*, which cannot be mass-produced. For products like this, there will not be any economies of scale. Firms under output constraints are likely to be found in monopolistic competition, where product differentiation is very important to the survival of the firms.

3. Firm size cannot grow owing to an entrepreneur constraint. Many entrepreneurs operating small but not necessarily inefficient firms do not wish to expand the volume of their transactions beyond a point where they have to delegate most of their managerial functions to staff. Consequently, they do not want their firms to grow beyond certain limits. The size of the firm's operation and its efficiency can be maintained by only producing high value-added products. This is economic restructuring within the firm. Consequently, firms under entrepreneur constraints can be efficient in terms of producing along the output-expansion path. Of course, it is also very likely that firms under entrepreneur constraints may face labour constraints and/or capital constraints in their operation. In such cases, the firms will not be efficient as they do not produce along the output-expansion path.

Thus, firms under capital constraints are more labour intensive than those without capital constraints (see Figure 3.1). Firms under output or entrepreneur constraints are also likely to be labour intensive because the output expansion path is usually quite labour intensive at low levels of output, implying that the output-expansion path approaches the Y-axis as the level of output increases.

As stated, firms under capital constraints are inefficient, while firms under output and entrepreneur constraints may not be inefficient. This can be clearly explained in terms of average cost curves. In Figure 3.3, we present four different long-run average-cost (LAC) curves. Figure 3.3a shows a decreasing average-cost curve and Figure 3.3b shows a standard U-shaped average-cost curve. Firms with such LACs as in Figures 3.3a or 3.3b, whether they are under output or entrepreneur constraints, are definitely inefficient compared to large firms in terms of cost per unit of output. In the case of a constant-cost curve (see Figure

3.3c), firms under output and entrepreneur constraints are as efficient as big firms provided they are not under capital (or labour) constraints. Figure 3.3d presents a situation where efficiency is reached at a rather low level of output. In this case, firms under output or entrepreneur constraints are as efficient as large firms.

The preceding discussion clearly indicates that small firms may exist under any of the three conditions. We therefore expect small firms to be more labour intensive. There is little division of labour and specialization in management, and the entrepreneur performs most of the managerial functions. There is also close personal contact among staff and between staff and customers in small firms. There is very little red tape in administration. The rapidity of response to market changes is important to the survival of small firms. Most of all, small firms may not necessarily be inefficient compared to large firms.

Existing studies indicate that the economic contribution of small firms is very much related to the stage of development of an economy. We will examine how the three different types of small firms behave at different stages of industrial development.

The Pre-industrialization Era

During this period, there is no systematic plan to stimulate industrial development. The financial market is not developed, and banking facilities are totally absent. The government is not development oriented. The literacy rate of the population is low, and there is a sizeable amount of unemployment. The transportation system is very backward. Understandably, there is no substantial investment, local or foreign, in the country. International trade is mainly confined to entrepôt activities. The economy during this period is dominated by small firms. In other words, small firms usually account for more than 90 per cent or even 95 per cent of the number of establishments in the country.

Small firms in the pre-industrialization era are likely to be firms with an output constraint. With an inadequate transportation system, the low purchasing power of the population and a lack of the necessary facilities for international trade, the market for most products is understandably small. The level of technology of these firms is rather primitive. The business is operated and organized by family members.

As the financial market is underdeveloped, it is difficult for firms to raise capital for expansion. Sources of funds only come from family members. It is thus difficult for small firms to expand even if they want to. Consequently, many small firms also face a capital constraint during this pre-industrialization era.

The Planned Industrialization Era

The government in this era is development oriented, and there is a systematic approach towards industrialization. All possible resources are channelled into developing industrial infrastructure, banking facilities, foreign investment, technical training, industrial relations, capital markets, and political stability. The economy progresses rapidly during this era.

As the industrialization progress speeds up, the economy moves more and more towards big firms. The markets for products expand. With a better transportation network, good banking facilities, a rising standard of living, and more avenues for international trade, some small firms grow into big firms. Foreign investment is rapidly introduced into the domestic economy. Foreign firms are definitely big firms as they do not face capital, output or entrepreneur constraints.

The competition becomes keener as industrialization progresses. Many small firms die a natural death as they are not sufficiently competitive. Workers become more and more sophisticated. Most of them are attracted to big firms for better salaries and fringe benefits. Small firms often cannot afford the facilities and attractive wages necessary to retain good workers.

The absolute number of small firms, however, does not necessarily decline. With rapid economic progress, business opportunities multiply. There is also an increasing tendency among the people to make use of the improved facilities to become entrepreneurs. Consequently, the number of small firms increases as the economy develops although at a slower rate. The educational background of the entrepreneurs during this era is different from those of the pre-industrialization era. They are more educated and more professional in their operations.

Small firms during the planned industrialization era are dominated by firms with output and capital constraints. As competition, especially between small firms, is very keen, the market for products is quite limited. Most small firms also face a capital constraint because most banks and other financial institutions consider it too risky to extend a sizeable loan to them.

The importance of small firms in the economy declines during this planned industrialization era. The rate of increase in the number of large firms is higher than that in the number of small firms. Since big firms contribute more proportionately towards employment, output and value-added, the contribution of small firms towards the total number of establishments, total employment, total output, and total value-added decreases as industrialization advances.

The Era of Industrial Maturity

During this era, the economy reaches a certain degree of industrial maturity. There is considerable interdependence among the various sectors in the economy, but competition remains high. More and more channels of growth are exhausted, and business and investment opportunities become relatively limited. The rate of economic growth is not high but, rather, stable.

The population is more educated, voters are more sophisticated, workers are more demanding and, at the same time, management is more professional. Generally, there is an increasing tendency among different segments of the population to lobby for concessions from the government for their own benefit.

The economy is dominated by large firms in terms of employment, output, and value-added. There is a limit to which a large firm can grow. This is because, theoretically, as we have discussed earlier, LAC may take four different shapes depending on various types of returns to scale. Returns to scale simply means that if we double all inputs, we will then see whether output will increase proportionately or not. In practice, it is impossible to increase the quantity of all inputs simultaneously, especially in the same proportion. A classic example is the time and talent of the entrepreneur. A firm can double factors such as equipment, manpower, and capital; however, it cannot increase substantially the time and talent of the entrepreneur: This implies that the law of diminishing returns will eventually set in. Except for natural monopolies, all firms will have to operate with decreasing returns to scale like the LACs in Figures 3.3b and 3.3d.

What this means is that it is neither possible nor practicable for any firm to grow infinitely. The Law of Diminishing Returns will prevent firms from growing excessively large. Large firms must therefore subcontract some of their orders to small firms for production. Large and small firms are therefore interdependent, implying that a modern manufacturing sector is not complete and not as efficient as it should be unless it has both large and small units. There thus exists an important relation between small and large firms. While the former are capable of radical innovations in response to market conditions, the latter are able to develop large-scale projects.

As economic development progresses, people are more affluent. Consequently, consumers are more sophisticated. With a rising level of income, consumers are willing to pay more for certain types of products, for what is known as individuality. In other words, there is a demand for these products provided that they are in limited supply. These types of products range from drapery to dresses and accessories. As society matures and consumers are more sophisticated, there will be a greater demand for these products, and it is small firms rather than large ones which will be able to cater to the individual tastes of these consumers.

Thus, small firms can play an important role in satisfying the individualized tastes of consumers as well as in supplying the necessary production components or services to big firms. The rate of increase of small firms during this era is similar to that of big firms. More importantly, the contribution of small firms towards the number of establishments, employment, output and value-added does not decline but remains stable at a significant level in the economy.

Our theoretical analysis of small firms is therefore consistent with Staley and Morse's observation that 'once a critical minimum level of modern industry is established, the role of small factories does not decline with time but holds an equal position in the further development and expansion of the manufacturing economy'.

A Definition of Small Firms

Conceptually it is rather easy to define small firms as we have discussed in the above section. Firms which face capital, output or entrepreneur constraints can be classified as small firms. Apart from this, however, there is no clear-cut operational definition for classifying small firms. Small firms can be defined in various ways depending on the country's stage of development, policy objectives, and administrative pattern. The Georgia Institute of Technology has found at least sixty different definitions used in seventy-five countries.[2]

The most common way of classifying small firms is to employ some objective quantitative measures such as employment, fixed capital assets or the level of output. In Singapore, there is no official legislation to define small firms. But the government has used various criteria to classify small firms for the purpose of assistance. For example, in 1963, the EDB regarded a small firm as one employing less than 50 workers and having fixed capital assets of less than $250,000. Only firms which met the requirements were eligible for the Light Industries Services (LIS) Loan Scheme. In 1976, to qualify for the Small Industries Finance Scheme (SIFS), a small firm was defined as one with fixed productive assets of not more than $1 million inclusive of the loans incurred. The ceiling was raised to $2 million after 1979.

Lau Puay Choo[3] has made an interesting study on the development of small manufacturing firms in Singapore. In it, she examined the common criteria of classifying small firms as reported in Table 3.1. In the US, firms which employ less than 500 workers are considered small. In Japan, firms which have less than 300 workers are considered small for the manufacturing sector, less than 100 workers for the wholesale sector, and less than 50 workers for the retail and services trade sector. South Korea, Sweden, the Philippines, Malaysia, and Hong Kong use slightly different yardsticks. In the case of Singapore, Tan Thiam Soon suggested that small firms be defined according to industries as follows:

1. less than 100 workers for manufacturing, and
2. less than 50 workers for commerce and service industries.[4]

Of course, there are also various supplementary ways of classifying small firms in terms of value of fixed assets (see Table 3.1).

Lau defined small firms as establishments with less than 100 employees. She did not use fixed capital assets to categorize small firms because there are no published industrial statistics by size of fixed capital assets. Her criterion of using 100 workers as the upper limit of employment for small firms is supported by the following arguments:

1. Between 1968 and 1978, the net value of fixed assets for the manufacturing sector increased ninefold from $575 million to $5,200 million whereas the upper limit for the fixed assets criterion was raised eight times from $250,000 to $2 million.

2. Within the same period, the number of manufacturing establishments had almost doubled. By the principle of proportions, it is

reasonable to raise the employment limit of 50 workers (employed by the LIS Loan Scheme)[5] by two times to 100 workers.

In our study, we will adopt Lau's definition with some modifications. Small firms consist of three types of firms, namely, tiny establishments which employ 5–9 workers; small establishments which employ 10–49 workers; and medium establishments which employ 50–99 workers. The small firms sector therefore refers to all firms employing 5–99 workers.

As stated earlier, Staley and Morse have advanced the interesting hypothesis that once a critical minimum level of modern industries is established, the role of small firms does not decline with time.[6] We want to test this hypothesis at the tiny establishment level, at the small establishment level, at the medium establishment level and also at the combined small and medium establishments level.

The Competitive Bases of Small Firms

Staley and Morse made an in-depth study of small firms' contribution towards employment in six countries.[7] In the case of the US, they found that, in the initial period of industrialization, small firms dominated the industrial scene in terms of the percentage share of employment. As the American economy developed, the percentage share of employment in small firms decreased. However, the decreasing trend was arrested and consequently the percentage share of employment in small firms remained stable when the economy matured. They also found the percentage share of employment in small firms in Japan, Canada, Sweden, Brazil, and Argentina to be relatively constant too. This led them to conclude that small firms can coexist with large firms even in a modern manufacturing economy.

Based on this study, Staley and Morse highlighted certain factors which give competitive advantage to small firms:

1. Physical and engineering relationships—Products which are light and small, requiring only moderate precision, and frequently made with light equipment or by relatively simple assembly operations for which efficiency in terms of cost per unit is achieved at a low volume of output.

2. Production of specialized components—Division of tasks permits specialized small firms to concentrate on producing components for several large firms because the latter will find it uneconomical to produce these specialized components on their own.

3. Products made in small lots and short runs—Some products cannot be standardized or are varied to suit the tastes of different consumers. Consequently, the total market for these products is too small to bear the cost of large firm overheads.

4. Operating flexibility and lower overheads—The business operation of a small firm is generally more flexible and its overheads are lower. Consequently, small firms have a faster response to growth opportunities than large firms.

5. Selling services—Efficient small firms can provide better selling services, such as extra quality, speed, or provision of technical knowledge to customers who require special attention, than large firms.

They also identified the following four principal types of small-plant industry which are specially suited to small firms:

1. Separable manufacturing operations, producing specialized machine products, components, and tools.

2. Differentiated products, particularly women's and children's clothing.

3. Precision handwork, such as jewellery.

4. The service industries, including printing and the metal service trades.

Because of the advantages of their operations, small firms can act as a buffer to cushion sharp fluctuations in income and employment. For example, several reports on the Organization for Economic Cooperation and Development (OECD) countries indicated that the resilience of small firms during the current world economic crisis has been remarkable.[8] It has also been reported that small American firms laid off fewer workers and weathered the 1981/2 recession better than big firms. In fact, some people have even claimed that small firms are leading the way out of the recession in the US.[9] The small firms sector in Japan is also strong, healthy and vigorous.[10]

Among the NICs, small firms over the past two decades have contributed to their countries' industrial development. In South Korea and Taiwan, small firms flourished by playing the dual role of providing supportive services to large firms and exporting labour-intensive products. According to Al Youngson,[11] Hong Kong is an economy of small firms. About 96 per cent of manufacturing firms in Hong Kong employed less than 100 workers in 1980. The adaptability of small firms has contributed significantly to Hong Kong's economic success. In the 1960s and 1970s, when barriers were raised against Hong Kong's cotton textile exports in the British and American markets, firms in Hong Kong responded quickly by seeking new export outlets and by switching from the export of cheap clothing in bulk to the export of low-volume high-class garments.

Small firms are even important in the economic development of developing countries. As developing countries face unemployment, and a shortage of capital and technology, small firms, being more labour intensive, can be expected to play an important role in producing output and providing job opportunities.[12]

Small firms also have a favourable impact on income distribution and regional development. They provide income-earning opportunities for people in less developed parts of the country and consequently promote more equitable income distribution. Small firms are also the only means for financially weak but innovative entrepreneurs to enter the industrial sector and participate in the industrialization process. Small firms can survive in less developed parts of the country because of their locational flexibility, their lower requirement of infrastructure, their nature to serve small geographical markets, and their firm commitment to local development. By providing job opportunities and fulfilling people's aspiration for industrialization, and consequently preventing excessive migration from rural to urban areas, small firms are conducive to regional development. China, Indonesia, Thailand, and many other countries have been trying to set up small firms in the countryside to promote both industrialization and regional development as well as to reduce income inequality.

In the light of the above discussion, we can safely conclude that small firms are indispensable to the industrial growth of a country, regardless of whether it is a developing or a developed nation.

The Case for Small Firms in Singapore

In this section, we shall attempt to demonstrate that small firms are indispensable to Singapore's economic development. Small firms are desirable and important, and they also play a role in the growth of Singapore's manufacturing sector for the following reasons.

The Resilience of Small Firms in Economic Crises

Singapore is a small open economy and consequently her economic performance is largely dependent upon the world economic climate. Small firms, however, are able to withstand economic crises better than large firms. Small firms being small have low overheads. They are quick in responding to changes in market conditions and therefore are less vulnerable to external economic fluctuations than large firms. For instance, small firms performed better than large firms during the 1973–5 economic crisis. According to Lau, in 1975, while 9 large firms closed down due to the recession, 215 new small firms came into operation; while large firms retrenched some 20,000 workers, small firms took in more than 5,000 new employees; while the value of output for large firms fell by $810 million, that for small firms increased by $74 million; and while the value-added of large firms decreased by $216 million, that of small firms increased by $99 million.[13] It can thus be argued that the small firms sector cushioned the recessionary pressures. This implies that the resilience of the Singapore economy against future economic crises may be strengthened if the small firms sector is able to play a greater role in the industrialization process.

Infrastructural Support to Large Firms

Small firms provide essential infrastructural support to large firms through subcontracting. According to the United Nations Industrial Development Organization (UNIDO), 'A subcontracting relationship exists when a firm (the principal) places an order with another firm (the subcontractor) for the manufacture of parts, components, sub-assemblies or assemblies to be incorporated into a product which the principal will sell.'[14] The advantage of subcontracting is to enhance the efficient use of both capital and labour by means of external economies of scale. According to an EDB report, most of the supporting firms in Singapore are small.[15] A strong supporting sector to modern large firms is crucial to the restructuring process in Singapore for the following reasons:

1. A reliable supporting sector is as important as physical infrastructure and fiscal incentives in attracting 'high-technology' foreign investment to Singapore. Singapore's *Business Times* reported that a Japanese X-ray equipment manufacturer once decided against setting up a plant in Singapore simply because no local manufacturer could meet his welding requirements.[16]

2. Without the local supporting sector, the foreign firms may have to bring in their own subcontractors which will reduce the linkage effects on the one hand, and increase the need to import foreign workers on the other. The government wants neither of these to occur.

3. The competitiveness of goods produced by large firms actually depends upon the efficiency of small firms in supplying parts and components. A more efficient supporting small firms sector will mean a more efficient export sector.

Lau identified three ways in which small firms can complement large firms:[17]

SPECIALIZED SUBCONTRACTING

In this case, the principal firm entrusts the small subcontracting firm with the execution of certain manufacturing operations which it is unable to perform due to lack of specialized skills or facilities within its own manufacturing unit. According to Lau, the subcontractor thus possesses specialized machinery and equipment, or has acquired the skills and technologies to be a more efficient supplier of the product in question.

ECONOMIC SUBCONTRACTING

The principal firm has the necessary technology and equipment to produce all the parts and components it requires; but owing to the considerable variety and volume to be produced, the principal firm finds it uneconomical for in-house production. Hence, subcontractors are engaged.

CAPACITY SUBCONTRACTING

In this case, whenever the principal firm's production capacity is insufficient owing to sudden surges in orders, it relies on subcontractors to meet the demand.

From the above analysis, we can conclude that an efficient supporting sector is crucial to Singapore's restructuring effort.

Supplies of a Diversity of High Quality Consumer Products

With the growth in the economy, the average Singaporean has experienced a rising income level. Being in an international city-state, his consumption pattern tends to shift in favour of higher quality, more personalized products, as opposed to mass-produced ones. This means that small consumer goods industries have cost advantages in producing these individualized, often skill-intensive products. Lau identified three product categories in which small firms have cost advantages:[18]

1. Products made in small lots and short runs and which are highly differentiated. Examples include built-in furniture and personal accessories, such as wallets and belts. In these markets, product differentiation exists in the form of variation in size, quality, design, and style. By operating in small lots and multiple short runs, small firms are able to avail consumers with a wider choice in their consumption set.

2. Products requiring flexibility of operation and swift responses to market changes. High-fashion ladies' wear is a classic example in this category. These products call for quick responses to market changes and flexibility to switch from one line of production to another. With their lower overheads and shorter channel of communication, small firms are therefore better able to provide the fashion conscious with the latest styles.

3. Products requiring highly skilled labour and precision handwork. Examples in this category are antique reproductions, jewellery, and hand-sewn shoes. The value of these products lies in their scarcity.

As Singapore's GNP increases and her export potential increases due to more prosperous ASEAN and world economies, small firms will contribute more to the GDP in these product categories in the years to come.

Technology Transfer and Entrepreneurial Development

Singapore's industrialization process has been dominated by foreign investment. There has been a need for foreign investment because it provides capital inflow, transfer of technological know-how, and access to foreign markets. In this respect, small firms are important because technology transfer is determined by the absorptive capacity of small firms, as much as by the willingness to transfer on the part of foreign firms. Small firms are involved in the transfer of technology in three ways:

1. by joint ventures with foreign firms;
2. by subcontracting relationships with foreign firms; and
3. by being an alternative employer to former foreign-firm employees.

It is clear that technology transfer is absent unless skilled personnel trained by MNCs move to the domestic sector either by taking up employment with local small firms or by becoming entrepreneurs themselves.

Singapore must therefore help to promote local small firms in order to gain foreign technological know-how and develop her entrepreneurship.

New Technology Based Small Firms

Technological progress is generally capital intensive and also favours large firms. However, the recent technological progress in the microelectronics industry actually favours small firms. It can accommodate small firms in terms of capital outlay and the scale of production. Lau gives an example of the 'system house' industry which comprises small software and hardware manufacturers.[19] The Singapore computer industry only became competitive in the late 1970s. In recent years, many local professionals have set up software houses.

The software house essentially provides specialized manpower and computer services to help other industries automate or computerize. Because it is service and people oriented, the software house is small in terms of employment. It has been reported that the typical software house in Singapore employs between 1 to 50 professional staff.[20] In Australia, 75 per cent of the software houses in 1978 employed less than 20 staff.[21] A successful software house does not necessarily purchase computer hardware which is very expensive. It can gain access to the necessary equipment through vendors (suppliers), customers, or larger software firms.

Small software firms are essential to Singapore's industrialization for the following reasons:

1. They can stimulate regional demand and therefore the domestic production of hardware by MNCs in Singapore;

2. They can help other industries to automate and computerize, which is what economic restructuring is all about; and

3. They can help to develop Singapore as a regional 'brain centre'.

In conclusion, small firms are indispensable to Singapore's economic development. It is therefore not surprising to see that the government is trying its best to help small firms to develop.

A Survey of Existing Studies on Small Firms in Singapore

A few researchers have studied the role of small firms in Singapore's economic development. At the industrial level, using published data, Lau systematically examined the contributions of small firms towards employment, output, capital expenditure, exports, and linkage effects.[22] Lee Soo Ann examined in detail the viability of small firms in terms of whether young graduates could be encouraged to start small businesses instead of looking to a promising career in a large firm.[23] Both Lau and Lee concluded that small firms in Singapore will do better in the future.

At the firm level, researchers have had to resort to surveys to gather data and information concerning the various aspects of small firms. Singapore's Chinese Chamber of Commerce and Industry's

Training Centre carried out a survey in October 1984 to assess manpower training requirements for small Chinese firms in Singapore.[24] According to the Centre's Director, Louis Lim, about 18,145 people in Chinese small firms needed training, and at least 3,411 (or about 20 per cent) of them were entrepreneurs. The survey revealed that these entrepreneurs needed to attend financial management courses, as well as business decision-making and small business management programmes. The entrepreneurs would also like to see their managers improve their knowledge of marketing and commercial law, and learn to handle computer data processing. The need for inventory control courses was also indicated.

The survey discovered that the Chinese entrepreneurs were generally not overly enthusiastic about training, either for themselves or for their workers. About 40 per cent of the owners interviewed did not consider training beneficial. The survey also found that 17 per cent of the managers in small Chinese firms had university degrees. The response rate of the survey was 11 per cent, which was considered normal.

Amy Wong's study on small firms employing less than 10 workers found that 78.2 per cent of the 222 firms were organized as sole proprietorships and 21.7 per cent as partnerships.[25] The majority of the sole proprietorships had 1–4 workers while the majority of the partnerships had 5–9 workers. Chng Hak Kee also studied small firms in Singapore.[26] In 1978, he found that, of the 77 firms surveyed, 29 per cent were organized as sole proprietorships and partnerships, 68 per cent as private limited companies, and only 4 per cent as public limited companies. It was also found that small firms which were partnerships and sole proprietorships were more labour intensive (as in food, apparel, and printing and publishing), whereas those which were private limited companies were more capital intensive (as in plastic and fabricated metal products).

Chng also found that 31 per cent of the entrepreneurs were former commercial traders, 24 per cent were former employees of mercantile firms, 22 per cent were former engineers and technicians, and 9 per cent were former factory workers and artisans who had limited educational background. The other 5 per cent that were formerly engaged in other professions, were in such areas as journalism, maritime work, teaching and hawking. One common characteristic among all these entrepreneurs was that at one time they were employees in similar industries. Chng observed that small firms do provide an avenue for enterprising individuals from all walks of life.

It has been reported in *The Straits Times* that, in recent years, a new breed of small entrepreneurs—engineers and professionals between ages 27 to 35 who were once employed by MNCs—is emerging on the Singapore industrial scene.[27] Compared to the majority of the traditional entrepreneurs, who are less educated, the new entrepreneurs have the benefit of tertiary education, and tend to use more equipment, technology, and management methods. These entrepreneurs are mostly engaged in supporting industries, for example, those which supply printed circuit boards, plastic mouldings, and aircraft components for the electronics and aerospace industries, as well as manufacturing related services such as computer software and engineering consultancy services.

Nevertheless, there is still a long way to go before Singapore can develop a significant core of domestic industrial entrepreneurs. In 1978, Lee Kuan Yew, the Prime Minister of Singapore, made the following remark about entrepreneurship in Singapore. 'The failure rate for wholly foreign owned enterprises from US, Europe and Japan was 6%; that for wholly Singaporean owned enterprises was 38%. But when Singapore went into joint ventures with American, European or Japanese entrepreneurs, their casualty rate went down dramatically from 38% to 7%.'[28]

From this section, we can conclude that Singapore needs to develop her industrial entrepreneurs. Without dynamic entrepreneurs, small firms in Singapore will not be able to make an impact on Singapore's economic development. As has been discussed in the above section, a backward small firm sector may hinder Singapore's industrialization process in the future. It is thus absolutely essential that Singapore gives her young graduates the necessary orientation or motivation to start small businesses. As Lee Soo Ann puts it, the case for small firms as viable entities in an enlarged Singapore economy has to be put across to young Singapore graduates.[29]

In the next chapter we will examine the economic contribution of small firms and also ascertain their future role in the economic development of Singapore.

1. The section 'The Competition Bases of Small Firms' in this chapter discusses this point. See also E. Staley and R. Morse, *Modern Small Industry for Developing Countries*, New York, McGraw-Hill Book Company, 1965.

2. World Bank, *Employment and Development of Small Enterprises*, Sector Policy Paper, Washington DC, World Bank, February 1978.

3. Lau Puay Choo, 'The Role of Small Industries in Singapore's Economic Restructuring', Honours thesis, Department of Economics and Statistics, National University of Singapore, 1983/4.

4. Tan Thiam Soon, 'Management Guidance for Small and Medium Enterprises—Japan, Taiwan and Singapore', unpublished Asian Productivity Organization Report, 1983.

5. The LIS Loan Scheme was abolished in 1968.

6. See the discussion in Chapter 1.

7. Staley and Morse, op. cit., pp. 20–1.

8. R. Rothwell and W. Zegveld, *Innovation and the Small and Medium-Sized Firm*, Hingham, Massachusetts, Kluwer Nijhoff Publishing, 1981, p. 2.

9. '10th International Business Congress: Small But Tough', *The Straits Times*, 14 September 1983.

10. Rothwell and Zegveld, op. cit., p. 119.

11. Al Youngson, *Hong Kong: Economic Growth and Policy*, Hong Kong, Oxford University Press, 1982, pp. 21–3.

12. See World Bank, op. cit.

13. Lau, op. cit., pp. 28–9.

14. United Nations Industrial Development Organization, *Subcontracting for Modernizing Economies*, New York, United Nations, 1974, as quoted in Dimitir Germidis (ed.), *International Subcontracting: A New Form of Investment*, Paris, OECD, 1980, p. 12.

15. Singapore, Economic Development Board, 'Singapore Investment News', October 1982, p. 1.

16. 'Helping the Supporting Industries to Upgrade', *The Business Times*, 28 October 1982.

17. Lau, op. cit.

18. Ibid.

19. Ibid.

20. For more information, see the listing of Singapore software firms in *Asian Computer Yearbook, 1981–82*, Hong Kong, Computer Publications, 1982.

21. Anthony Benson, 'Transfer of Software Technology from the Developed Countries', in *Developing Singapore into a Software Centre*, Proceedings of a Data Processing Managers' Association Seminar, Singapore, 19 January 1982.

22. Lau, op. cit. Indeed, Lau's work has been widely cited in our discussion.

23. Lee Soo Ann, 'Export-Led Growth with Particular Reference to Small Industry Experiences of Singapore', Paper presented at Asian Productivity Organization Symposium on Export-Oriented Small Industries, Lahore, Pakistan, 10–14 November 1984.

24. *The Straits Times*, 29 January 1985.

25. Amy Wong, *A Study of Selected Small-Scale Manufacturing Industries in Singapore*, Singapore Economic Research Centre, University of Singapore, 1975.

26. Chng Hak Kee, 'A Study of the Characteristics of Local Small Industries and Entrepreneurs', Case Studies No. 3, Department of Industrial and Business Management, Nanyang University, July 1978.

27. 'Our New Breed of Young Entrepreneurs', *The Straits Times*, 1 December 1980.

28. Lee Kuan Yew, *Extrapolating from the Singapore Experience*, Singapore, Ministry of Culture, 1978, p. 14.

29. Lee Soo Ann, op. cit.

TABLE 3.1

Definition of Small Firms by Employment and Fixed Assets

Country	Definition		
	Number of Workers Employed	Fixed Assets	Qualifications
United States	1. Less than 500		If not dominant in its field of operation
Japan	1. Less than 300	and/or less than ¥100 m (S$0.95 m)	For manufacturing
	2. Less than 100	and/or less than ¥30 m (S$285,000)	For wholesaling
	3. Less than 50	and/or less than ¥10 m (S$95,000)	For retail and services trade
South Korea	1. 5–300	or less than 500 m won (S$2.2 m)	For manufacturing, mining and transportation
	2. 5–50	or less than 500 m won (S$2.2 m)	For construction
	3. 5–20	or less than 50 m won (S$220,000)	For the services trade
		or less than 20 m won (S$88,000)	For wholesale trade in particular
Sweden	1. Less than 200		
Philippines	1. Less than 100	15,000 Pesos (S$5,000) to 1 m Pesos (S$330,000)	

(continued)

TABLE 3.1 (*continued*)

Country	Number of Workers Employed	Definition Fixed Assets	Qualifications
Malaysia	1. Less than 25	Less than M$250,000	
Hong Kong	1. Less than 100		
	2.	Less than HK$200,000 (S$86,000)	
Singapore	1. Less than 100		For manufacturing
	2. Less than 50		For commerce and services
	3.	Less than S$2 m	

Sources: For the United States, see E. Staley and R. Morse, *Modern Small Industry for Developing Countries*, New York, McGraw-Hill Book Company, 1965; For Japan, see Hiroshi Tanaka, 'Position and Role of Small and Medium-Sized Enterprises in the Japanese Economy and their Overseas Investment', paper presented at a Conference on the Role of Small Industries in the ASEAN National Economies, Singapore, November 1978; For South Korea, see Yoon-Bae Ouh, *International Research Project on Korean Small Industry Development*, Seoul, Soong Jun University, 1978; For Sweden, see Helge Herzog, 'Small and Medium-Sized Firms in Sweden and Government Policy', *American Journal of Small Business*, Vol. VII, No. 2, December 1982; For the Philippines and Malaysia, see Hsuan Owjiang, 'Definition and Role of Small Industries in Singapore', paper presented at a Symposium on Small Industries in Singapore, Singapore, March 1977; For Hong Kong, see Victor Fung-Shuen Sit, *Small Scale Industries in a Laissez-Faire Economy*, Hong Kong, University of Hong Kong Press, 1980, p. 21; For Singapore, see Tan Thiam Soon, 'Management Guidance for Small and Medium Enterprises—Japan, Taiwan and Singapore', unpublished Asian Productivity Organization Report, 1983, p. 9.

Note: Conversion to Singapore dollars is based on average 1980 exchange rates.

FIGURE 3.1
Output-expansion Path

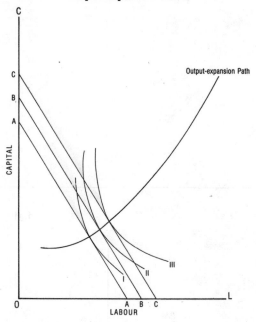

FIGURE 3.2
Output-expansion Path *vis-à-vis* Constraints

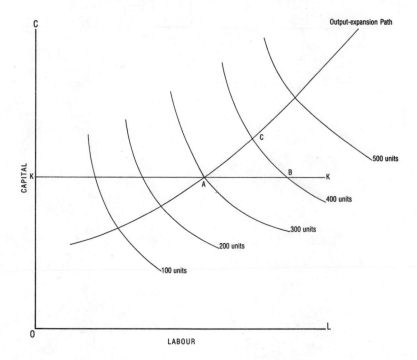

FIGURE 3.3

Long-run Average-cost Curves

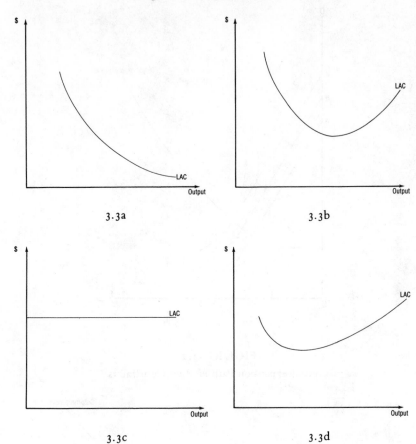

3.3a   3.3b

3.3c   3.3d

4

THE RELATIVE ECONOMIC
CONTRIBUTION OF SMALL FIRMS

IN this chapter we aim to assess the contribution of small firms *vis-à-vis* large firms with respect to the number of establishments, employment, output, and value-added of the manufacturing sector over the period 1963–83. Since the small firms in our study consist of tiny establishments, small establishments and medium establishments, we will examine each category in the first three sections respectively. In the fourth section, the economic contribution of large establishments is examined. In the last section, we will analyse the comparative economic contributions of small and large establishments.

Tiny Establishments

In our study, tiny establishments are, by definition, firms which employ only 5–9 workers. Data on tiny establishments are rather limited. The *Report on the Census of Industrial Production* contains data on tiny establishments only for 1963, 1968, 1973, 1978, and 1983. Consequently, the assessment of tiny establishments will be made only from the data for these five years.

First of all, let us find out which industries can accommodate such tiny enterprises. The majority of tiny establishments were concentrated in the textile, apparel and footwear industry (132 establishments) and the food manufacturing industry (120 establishments), in 1963 (see Table 4.1). The two industries combined accounted for 36.8 per cent of the total number of tiny establishments in the manufacturing sector in the same year. Moreover, the textiles, apparel and footwear industry consistently topped the list in terms of the number of establishments in 1963, 1973, and 1983. The food manufacturing industry, however, fell from the second position to the third position in 1983, having been overtaken by the machinery industry. It is rather interesting to learn that the number of tiny establishments in the machinery industry has grown rapidly, from 49 units in 1963 to 132 units in 1973 and 274 units in 1983. This shows that such tiny establishments have not only flourished in the household industries, such as textiles, food, furniture, and printing, but also in the machinery industry and the fabricated metal products industry (which held fourth position in terms of the number of establishments in 1983).

One would expect that, as the economy progressed in the period 1963–83, the industries would be more dominated by firms with 10 or more workers. This is true only for 14 of the 18 industries, for which the percentage of tiny establishments in the respective industries declined over the 21-year period.

However, for the food manufacturing industry, the printing and publishing industry, the non-metallic products industry, and the fabricated metal industry, the percentage of tiny establishments has significantly increased over time. This goes to show that tiny establishments have not flourished only in terms of absolute number of establishments, but also in terms of the relative contribution in the number of establishments in at least four industries.

We will now analyse the contribution of tiny establishments in terms of the number of establishments, employment, output and value-added in the whole manufacturing sector. Table 4.2 reports the distribution of manufacturing establishments for each of the five years. In 1963, there were 684 tiny establishments. Ten years later, the number of tiny establishments rose to 1,248 and, by 1983, there were 2,136 tiny establishments, representing an increase of more than 200 per cent over 1963.

In terms of the absolute number of establishments, the performance of tiny establishments has been very impressive. In terms of their contribution relative to the total number of establishments, however, their performance has been less spectacular. Between 1963 and 1978, while tiny establishments flourished, other establishments performed even better. In 1963, tiny establishments accounted for 44.4 per cent of the total number of establishments (see Table 4.2). The rate of increase in the number of establishments for tiny establishments was 55.1 per cent from 1963 to 1968, 17.6 per cent from 1968 to 1973, and 6.1 per cent from 1973 to 1978 while the rate of increase in the total number of establishments for the corresponding periods was 71.7 per cent, 25.7 per cent and 28.3 per cent. The relative contribution of tiny establishments in the number of establishments had therefore declined since 1963. It reached a trough at 31 per cent in 1978.

The 1983 figures, however, present a totally different picture for tiny establishments. The rate of increase in the number of tiny establishments from 1978 to 1983 was 61.3 per cent while the rate of increase in the total number of establishments for the same period was only 34.7 per cent. Consequently, the relative contribution of tiny establishments in the number of establishments increased to 37.1 per cent in 1983.

The employment situation of tiny establishments is presented in Table 4.3. In 1963, 4,754 workers were employed by tiny establishments. The rate of increase of the work-force of tiny establishments was 51.9 per cent from 1963 to 1968, 24.0 per cent from 1968 to 1973, and −1.7 per cent from 1973 to 1978. The work-force of tiny establishments was 8,805 persons in 1978. However, from 1978 to 1983, the rate of increase of the work-force of tiny establishments was spectacular at 66.2 per cent, bringing the total work-force to 14,636 in 1983.

By definition, the relative contribution of tiny establishments in employment must be smaller than that in the number of establishments. Tiny establishments accounted for as much as 11.5 per cent of the work-force in manufacturing in 1963. But it went down steadily to 3.5 per cent in 1978. However, due to the high rate of increase in employment by tiny establishments in 1983, the relative contribution of tiny establishments in employment rose to 5.1 per cent in the same year.

Table 4.4 shows the distribution of manufacturing output for the five years. In 1963, the total output of tiny establishments amounted to $45 million. The rate of increase in output of tiny establishments was 41.4 per cent from 1963 to 1968, 113.5 per cent from 1968 to 1973, and 64.5 per cent from 1973 to 1978. By 1978, the output by tiny establishments reached $223 million. From 1978 to 1983, the rate of increase of output by tiny establishments was 160.3 per cent, and the value of its output was $583 million, in 1983.

In terms of the relative contribution in output, tiny establishments did not perform as well as in their absolute contribution in output. In 1963, tiny establishments accounted for only 5.1 per cent of the total manufacturing output. It went down steadily to 1.1 per cent in 1978. In 1983, the contribution of the tiny establishments sector in output rose to 1.5 per cent.

Our theoretical analysis of small firms implies that small firms are more labour intensive. We can deduce that tiny establishments are indeed more labour intensive than the average establishment. In 1963, although tiny establishments accounted for 11.5 per cent of the work-force, they only accounted for 5.1 per cent of the total manufacturing output, implying that tiny establishments employed more labour per dollar's worth of output. In fact, comparing all the years, the relative contribution of tiny establishments in employment was consistently higher than that in output (11.5 per cent vs 5.1 per cent, 8.8 per cent vs 2.8 per cent, 4.3 per cent vs 1.7 per cent, 3.5 per cent vs 1.1 per cent, and 5.1 per cent vs 1.5 per cent (see Tables 4.3 and 4.4). The absolute differences between the two relative contribution percentages were 6.4 per cent, 6.0 per cent, 2.6 per cent, 2.4 per cent and 3.6 per cent for the years 1963, 1968, 1973, 1978 and 1983 respectively. The above figures show that over 1963–78, the gap in labour productivity between tiny establishments and the average establishment had narrowed but, in 1983, the gap widened again, implying that tiny establishments were more labour intensive in 1983, compared to 1978.

It is also important to examine the contribution of tiny establishments in value-added. The value-added by tiny establishments was $15 million in 1963 (see Table 4.5). Not surprisingly, it went up steadily to $213 million in 1983. In 1963, tiny establishments accounted for 5.7 per cent of the total manufacturing value-added but this declined steadily to 1.5 per cent in 1978. However, in 1983, the relative contribution in value-added by tiny establishments rose again to 2.1 per cent.

Again, in terms of value-added per worker, one can see that tiny establishments were more labour intensive than the average establishment. This is because the relative contribution in employment by tiny establishments was always greater than its relative contribution in value-added for the same period. In other words, tiny establishments employed more labour per dollar's worth of value-added.

An interesting and important aspect of tiny establishments is that they generated more value-added per dollar's worth of output, compared to the average establishment. This is because, for instance, in 1963, although tiny establishments only accounted for 5.1 per cent of the total manufacturing output, they accounted for 5.7 per cent of the total manufacturing value-added. Indeed, the relative contribution in value-added by tiny establishments was always greater than their relative contribution in output (5.7 per cent vs 5.1 per cent, 3.6 per cent vs 2.8 per cent, 1.8 per cent vs 1.7 per cent, 1.5 per cent vs 1.1 per cent and 2.1 per cent vs 1.5 per cent).

On the basis of the preceding discussion, the pattern of tiny establishments in terms of relative contribution in the number of establishments, employment, output, and value-added can be traced. As Figure 4.1 clearly shows, the four relative contributions by tiny establishments declined from 1963 to 1978 and then, without exception, rose rather significantly in 1983. Comparing the trends of the four relative contributions by tiny establishments suggests that they are indeed very tiny. They employ few workers, and produce much smaller output and value-added. The main contribution of tiny establishments does not therefore lie in their absolute contribution in terms of output and value-added, but rather in their industrial complementarity to other establishments.

Our empirical analysis with respect to tiny establishments therefore indicates that the role of tiny establishments will not decline as the economy progresses. This is because as the economy progresses, the interdependency between different sizes of firms becomes stronger.

Small Establishments

Firms with 10–49 workers are classified as small establishments. In 1963, the majority of small establishments was found in the food manufacturing industry (130), followed by the printing and publishing industry (101) (see Table 4.6). Small establishments were also found in the fabricated metal products industry (64), the machinery industry (50), and the textile, apparel and footwear industry (49). In 1973, these industries continued to dominate the small establishments sector with the textile, apparel and footwear industry ranking first, the food manufacturing industry ranking second, the printing and publishing industry ranking third, fabricated metal products ranking fourth, and the machinery industry ranking fifth.

In 1983, the textile, apparel and footwear industry continued to top the list with 424 small establishments. The fabricated metal products industry rose to the second position, followed by the printing and publishing industry, the machinery industry, the food manufacturing industry, and the transport equipment industry. Thus, small establishments not only dominated the traditional industries such as food, textiles, printing and publishing, but also the new industries such as fabricated metal, machinery, and transport equipment.

Tables 4.7–4.10 show the contribution of small establishments in the manufacturing sector in terms of the number of establishments employment, output and value-added. There were 693 small establishments in 1963 (see Table 4.7). Small establishments more than doubled in 1973 and, by 1983, the small establishments sector had 2,630 units, representing an increase of 261 per cent over 1963. The rate of increase of small establishments has been rather impressive over the years. In contrast, the importance of small establishments relative to the total number of establishments has not been as significant. In 1963, small establishments accounted for 81 per cent of the total number of establishments. The relative contribution of small establishments fell to 78.6 per cent in 1964 and then fluctuated around 77 per cent until 1969. However, after 1969, the relative contribution of small establishments declined to 69.8 per cent in 1973. Surprisingly, small establishments managed to arrest the declining trend and to increase their relative contribution to 73 per cent by 1976. Since then, the relative contribution of small establishments to the total number of establishments has stabilized at around 72–73 per cent.

The employment aspect of small establishments is given in Table 4.8. There were 15,032 workers employed by the small establishments sector in 1963. The number increased to 30,757 in 1973 and, by 1983, it had 52,589 workers, representing an increase of 250 per cent over 1963. Although the small establishments sector accounted for 74 per cent of the total number of establishments in 1963, it only accounted for 41.1 per cent of the total work-force in the manufacturing sector. The relative contribution of small establishments to the total employment also declined steadily and reached the lowest level at 15.5 per cent in 1973. Since then, the small establishments sector has managed to stabilize its relative contribution and, for 1975–83, it was around 18–19 per cent.

With respect to output, the small establishments sector exhibited the same trend. In 1963, the output of small establishments amounted to $248 million and, in 1973, the output increased to $1,053 million. By 1983, the small establishments sector produced an output worth $4,313 million, representing an increase of 17 times over 1963.

In terms of its relative contribution in the entire manufacturing sector, the small establishments sector did not do well in output either. It only managed to account for 29.4 per cent of the total manufacturing output in 1963 (see Table 4.9), although it accounted for 41.1 per cent of the total manufacturing employment in the same year. This implies that small establishments, like tiny establishments, were more labour intensive than the average establishment. This is consistent with our theoretical discussion in Chapter 3. In fact, the relative contribution of the small establishments sector in employment has always been larger than its relative contribution in output for every year. However, it should be noted that the absolute difference between the two relative contributions has been smaller in the 1980s than in the 1960s, implying that the small establishments sector has slowly narrowed the gap between its labour productivity and that of the average establishment.

The contribution of small establishments in value-added is reported in Table 4.10. In 1963, the small establishments sector contributed value-added worth $62 million. It went up to $307 million in 1973 and, by 1983, it reached $1,317 million. In terms of relative contribution, the small establishments sector accounted for 24.9 per cent of the total manufacturing value-added in 1963. Its relative contribution in value-added then declined steadily to 10.7 per cent in 1974. From 1974 onwards, the small establishments sector slowly increased its relative importance, which stabilized at around 12–13 per cent for 1975–83.

The small establishments sector has not performed well when its relative contribution in employment is compared with its relative contribution in value-added. For instance, in 1963, the small establishments sector accounted for 41.1 per cent of the total manufacturing employment but only contributed 24.9 per cent of the total manufacturing value-added. In fact, for this sector, its relative contribution in employment was always higher than its relative contribution in value-added for 1963–83, implying that small establishments, like tiny establishments, were more labour intensive relative to the average establishment.

For the tiny establishments sector, we discovered that its relative contribution in value-added has always been larger than its relative contribution in output. This is not true for the small establishments sector. Although the small establishments sector accounted for 29.4 per cent of the total manufacturing output in 1963, it only accounted for 24.9 per cent of the total manufacturing value-added. This shows that small establishments are less value-added oriented, compared to the average establishment. Fortunately for the small establishments sector, the relative contribution of small establishments in value-added was consistently larger than the relative contribution in output for the period 1975–83.

The four relative contributions of small establishments are presented in Figure 4.2. Each of the four trends of small establishments exhibits the same pattern, i.e. the relative importance of small establishments in the number of establishments, employment, output, and value-added, declined steadily from 1963 to 1973–4, and then increased slightly and stabilized around that level. This pattern is remarkably similar to that of tiny establishments.

This shows that both tiny and small establishments may lose some of their relative importance during the rapid process of initial industrial growth. But, once the economy matures, both tiny and small establishments certainly have an important role to play in the industrial process.

Medium Establishments

Medium establishments refer to firms which employ 50–99 workers. In the two sections above, we have discovered that tiny and small establishments are generally concentrated in the food, textiles, printing and publishing, fabricated metal, and machinery industries. It will be interesting to see whether medium establishments exhibit a similar pattern of distribution across industries.

In 1963, the food manufacturing industry topped the list with 28 medium establishments (see Table 4.11). The wood products industry occupied the second position with 26 medium establishments, followed by the transport equipment industry (16), and the printing and publishing industry (15). The distribution of medium establishments was slightly different in 1973. Textiles, apparel and footwear topped the list with 39 medium establishments, followed by the food manufacturing industry (38), the wood products industry (30), and the fabricated metal products industry (also 30).

The 1970s was an era dominated by the rapid growth of the electrical/electronic products industry. As Table 4.11 shows, this industry dominated the medium establishments sector with 66 firms in 1983. The fabricated metal products industry took the second place with 61 firms, and the textile, apparel and footwear industry occupied the third place with 59 firms. The industrial distribution of medium establishments is not the same as those of tiny and small establishments. Medium establishments tend to concentrate on electrical/electronic products, fabricated metal products, and machinery industries, more so than tiny and small establishments.

Tables 4.12–4.15 show the contribution of medium establishments in the manufacturing sector in terms of number of establishments, employment, output and value-added. In 1963, there were 106 medium establishments (see Table 4.12). By 1973, the number of medium establishments had increased almost three times—to 296—and, by 1983, there were 483 medium establishments. Thus medium establishments accounted for 12.4 per cent of the total number of industrial establishments in 1963. Over the period 1964–83, the percentage of medium establishments over the total number of industrial establishments was stable at 13–14 per cent, indicating that the rate of increase in medium establishments was similar to that of the total industrial establishments.

The medium establishments sector employed 7,334 workers in 1963 (see Table 4.13). The employment figure grew almost three times to 20,443 in 1973 and, by 1983, there were 33,284 workers employed by medium establishments. Medium establishments accounted for 20 per cent of the manufacturing work-force in 1963. The contribution of the medium establishments sector in employment fluctuated around 20–21 per cent between 1963 and 1966. Its relative importance then declined steadily from 1966 to 1974. However, the relative contribution of the medium establishments sector rose from 10.2 per cent in 1974 to 11.7

per cent in 1975 and, from 1975 to 1983, it fluctuated around 10.5 per cent to 12.5 per cent.

The output of the medium establishments sector was $269.8 million, $752 million, and $3,389.6 million in 1963, 1973, and 1983 respectively (see Table 4.14). In 1963, the medium establishments sector contributed 32 per cent of the total manufacturing output. Its relative contribution in employment declined rather significantly from 32.4 per cent in 1964 to only 6.8 per cent in 1978. However, the medium establishments sector managed to maintain its relative position at around 9 per cent during 1980–3.

In our discussions in the two sections above, we discovered that tiny and small establishments were more labour intensive than the average establishment. However, medium establishments were exceptional. Although the medium establishments sector accounted for 20 per cent of the total manufacturing employment in 1963, it contributed 32 per cent of the total manufacturing output, implying that medium establishments were less labour intensive than the average establishment. Unfortunately, the relative contribution of the medium establishments sector in output was consistently lower than its relative contribution in employment from 1969 to 1983, implying that medium establishments became labour intensive, compared to the average establishment during this period.

The value-added of medium establishment was $61 million, $238 million, and $1,137 million in 1963, 1973, and 1983 respectively (see Table 4.15). The medium establishments sector contributed 24.4 per cent of the total manufacturing value-added in 1963. Since then, its relative contribution in value-added declined rather steadily to 7.4 per cent in 1974. From 1974 to 1983, the relative contribution of the medium establishments sector in value-added increased slightly and stabilized around 11–12 per cent in the early 1980s.

In terms of value-added per worker, the medium establishments sector was again less labour intensive than the average establishment during 1963–8 because its relative contribution in employment was less than its relative contribution in value-added. However, the reverse holds for the latter part of the sample period as its relative contribution in employment was higher than its relative contribution in value-added.

It is also interesting to see whether medium establishments are more value-added oriented than the average establishment. From 1963 to 1968, the relative contribution of the medium establishments sector in output was higher than its relative contribution in value-added. However, from 1969 onwards, its relative contribution in output was marginally lower than its relative contribution in value-added, implying that medium establishments have been more value-added oriented in the 1970s and 1980s.

The preceding discussion clearly shows that tiny, small and medium establishments have been more service oriented and thereby employ more labour per unit of output and value-added.

The trends in the relative contributions of medium establishments in the number of establishments, employment, output, and value-added are presented in Figure 4.3. The relative contributions of the medium establishments sector in the number of establishments have fluctuated rather drastically. However, generally, one can conclude that the relative contributions of the medium establishments sector in the number of establishments, employment, output, and value-added have exhibited the same pattern, i.e. they declined from the 1960s to the mid-1970s, rose in the late 1970s, and stabilized in the early 1980s.

It should be highlighted that tiny, small, and medium establishments have exhibited the same pattern in their relative contributions in the four aspects of firms. Figure 4.4 presents the trends of the four relative contributions of small and medium establishments combined and they too expectedly exhibited the same pattern.

Large Establishments

Large establishments refer to firms which employ 100 workers or more. As Table 4.12 shows, there were only 59 large establishments in 1963. Over the ten-year period from 1963 to 1973, the growth of the large establishments sector was spectacular with an average annual growth of 19 per cent. However, since 1980, the rate of increase of large establishments has been declining. In fact, there were negative growth rates in 1982 and 1983.

The large establishments sector employed 14,220 workers in 1963 (see Table 4.13). Not surprisingly, the employment of large establishments grew more than ten times in the next twenty years, to 147,374 workers and, by 1983, had reached 185,233 workers.

The employment contribution of large establishments in the manufacturing sector rose steadily from 38.9 per cent in 1963 to 74.2 per cent in 1973 (see Table 4.13). Subsequently, the relative contribution of large establishments in employment began to fall slightly until it stabilized around 68 per cent in 1982–3.

The output of the large establishments sector was $325 million, $6,132 million, and $29,518 million in 1963, 1973, and 1983 respectively (see Table 4.14). The contribution of large establishments in industrial output rose from 38.6 per cent in 1963 to 77.3 per cent in 1973. It reached a peak in 1978 with 81.8 per cent. It is not surprising that the relative contribution of large establishments in industrial output did not grow after 1978, since the relative contribution of tiny, small, and medium establishments in industrial output had stabilized during 1978–83. In fact, the share of output by large establishments declined slightly from 81.1 per cent in 1981 to 79.3 per cent in 1983.

The value-added of the large establishments sector was $128 million, $1,995 million, and $7,366 million in 1963, 1978, and 1983 respectively (see Table 4.15). The contribution of large establishments in industrial value-added rose from 50.7 per cent in 1963 to 78.5 per cent in 1973. It reached a peak in 1974 with 81.9 per cent. However, since 1975–81, its relative importance in industrial value-added stabilized around 77 per cent and declined to 75 per cent in 1982–3.

In the earlier sections, it has been suggested that small firms consisting of tiny, small, and medium establishments have been more labour intensive and more value-added oriented. The reverse must naturally hold for the relative contribution of large establishments which constitute the remainder of the establishments under study. Large establishments have been less labour intensive because the relative contribution of large establishments in output and value-added has been consistently higher than their relative contribution in employment. Similarly, large establishments have been less value-added oriented because, except from 1963 to 1968, the contribution of large establishments in value-added has been lower than their relative contribution in output.

Figure 4.5 presents the trends of the four relative contributions of large establishments. The trends conform with the expectations that they would first rise and then level off in the 1980s.

Generally speaking, our analysis suggests that, prior to an industrialization era, the manufacturing sector is heavily dominated by small firms. However, during a planned industrialization era, when the government systematically promotes industrial activities, the importance of small firms is reduced and the role of large firms grows. The declining trend in the importance of small firms is arrested when the economy reaches a certain level of industrialization, where interdependence among firms is indispensable. Thus, small firms in the modern economy can still play an important role and their relative contributions in employment, output, and value-added will not decline as the economy matures.

An Analysis of the Economic Contribution of Small and Large Firms

In the earlier three sections we analysed the economic contributions of Singapore industries in terms of the number of establishments, employment, output, and value-added. With respect to the tiny establishments sector, as Figure 4.1 shows, its relative contributions declined from 1963 to 1978 and then increased in 1983. The small establishments sector also exhibited the same trend except that it reached a trough in 1973, five years earlier than the tiny establishments sector (Figure 4.2). The medium establishments sector and the small and medium establishments sector also exhibited the same pattern, i.e. their relative contributions declined from 1963 to 1973/4 and then rose slightly and stabilized in the early 1980s (Figures 4.3 and 4.4). For the large establishments sector, its relative importance at first increased from 1963 to 1973 and then levelled off in the early 1980s (Figure. 4.5).

Generally speaking, we can identify three periods of development in Singapore in relation to our theoretical analysis for small firms: (i) the pre-industrialization era, the period 1959–63, during which the industrial sector was dominated by small firms in terms of the number of establishments, employment, output, and value-added; (ii) the planned industrialization era, the period 1963–73/4, during which small firms lost their relative importance to large establishments; and (iii) the era of industrial maturity, the period 1973/4–1983, during which small firms managed to consolidate their relative importance in the economy.

In the 1959–63 period, as we have discussed in Chapter 1, the industrial activities involved mainly the processing of imported raw materials and the manufacturing of simpler consumer goods. Most industrial establishments were small and were generally found in the food manufacturing, printing and publishing, and engineering industries. They were household units or backyard repair and service units using little capital equipment. The economy was dominated by such small firms as the strategy for industrialization was being formulated and implemented.

During the 1963–73/4 period, the relative importance of the small firm sector declined considerably. Several factors can account for this dramatic drop. First, as the PAP government was determined to embark on a deliberate strategy for industrialization, foreign investment was encouraged. Foreign investment provided technology, capital, and markets, which were the necessary ingredients for industrialization. As foreign firms were generally large, a larger role for foreign investment necessarily implied a smaller role for small firms. Secondly, some successful small firms grew larger and consequently were not classified as small firms. Thus, the declining share of small firms could also be due to the growth of small firms into large firms. Thirdly, the small domestic market posed a constraint on the rate of growth of small firms. Foreign investment was attracted to Singapore by her excellent infrastructure, good industrial relations, and trainable work-force. Consequently, foreign firms used Singapore as a production base for export to countries outside Singapore, a situation which exists to this day. During this period, international trade rapidly expanded and the rate of growth of foreign firms (which were generally large) was therefore high. Since small firms mainly catered for the domestic market, the rate of growth of small firms was lower than that of large firms.

In the 1974–83 period, the decline of small firms in the national economy was arrested and the rate of growth of small firms was higher than that of large firms. Apparently, the two oil crises hurt the large firms far more than they did the small firms. The rate of growth of large firms in terms of the number of establishments, employment, output, and value-added was negative in both 1975 and 1982. Since large firms in Singapore have always been export oriented, it is not surprising that the stagflation that plagued the Western world has had a significant impact on their rate of growth. Small firms were also affected by the rising oil prices but only in terms of a lower rate of growth. By and large, the growth rate of small firms in terms of the number of establishments, employment, output, and value-added was positive during 1973–83, reflecting the resilience of small firms in economic crises.

It is interesting to see the areas of growth of small firms. For tiny establishments, the areas of growth were the textiles industry (an increase of 210 tiny establishments in 1983 over 1973, see Table 4.1), the machinery industry (142 firms), the furniture and fixtures industry (123 firms), and the food manufacturing industry (90 firms). For small establishments, the leading growing industries were textiles (196 firms), machinery (152 firms), transport equipment (151 firms), and fabricated metal products (177 firms) (see Table 4.6). For medium establishments, the increase in the number of establishments was 53 for the electrical/electronic products industry, 31 for the fabricated metal products industry, and 20 for the textiles industry, the machinery industry and for the transport equipment industry (see Table 4.11).

In Chapter 2 we discussed the structural changes in the manufacturing sector and discovered that the promising industries in the 1980s are electrical/electronic products, transport equipment, machinery, and fabricated metal products. These promising industries are also the same industries in which small firms have flourished. It explains why small firms have played an important role in the manufacturing sector in the late 1970s and early 1980s.

Our analysis therefore implies that Singapore is now in the era of industrial maturity where industrial complementarity among different sizes of firms is very strong. Small firms are expected to continue to play an important role in the economy in the future.

TABLE 4.1

Number of Tiny Establishments by Industry Group, 1963–1983

Major Industry Group	1963				1973				1983				
	No.	Rank	X^a	Y^b	No.	Rank	X	Y	No.	Rank	No. of Increase over 1973	X	Y
Food manufacturing	120	2	41.2	17.5	169	2	40.3	13.5	259	3	90	45.4	12.1
Textiles, apparel, footwear	132	1	68.8	19.3	378	1	52.6	30.3	588	1	210	51.0	27.5
Wood products (except furniture)	47	6	36.4	6.9	50	8	22.5	4.0	46	11	−4	29.5	2.2
Furniture & fixtures	28	9	60.8	4.1	52	7	52.5	4.2	175	5	123	57.9	8.2
Paper products	22	10	50.0	3.2	28	11	29.2	2.2	30	13	2	25.4	1.4
Printing & publishing	40	8	24.4	5.8	88	5	32.4	7.1	161	6	73	33.4	7.5
Chemicals & chemical products	15	14	25.4	2.2	41	9	29.1	3.3	32	12	−9	19.2	1.5
Petroleum & petroleum products	—	—	—	—	—	—	—	—	—	—	—	—	—
Rubber products	17	11	48.6	2.5	5	16	15.2	0.4	4	16	−1	12.1	0.2
Plastic products	—	—	—	—	23	12	18.5	1.8	56	10	33	20.7	2.6
Non-metallic products	17	11	33.3	2.5	7	15	25.9	0.6	18	14	11	41.9	0.8
Basic metal	4	15	44.4	0.6	5	16	19.2	0.4	3	17	−2	8.3	0.1
Fabricated metals products	68	3	45.9	9.9	131	4	39.7	10.5	233	4	102	35.4	10.9
Machinery (except electrical/electronics)	49	5	45.8	7.2	132	3	47.8	10.6	274	2	142	44.6	12.8
Electrical/Electronic products	17	11	42.5	2.5	16	13	13.0	1.3	58	9	42	15.5	2.7
Transport equipment	63	4	47.7	9.2	40	10	26.3	3.2	103	7	63	26.1	4.8
Instrumentation equipment	—	—	—	—	8	14	25.0	0.6	10	15	2	17.9	0.5
Other manufacturing	45	7	47.4	6.6	75	6	34.6	6.0	86	8	11	27.6	4.0
All industry groups	684	—	44.4	100.0	1248	—	35.3	100.0	2136	—	888	37.1	100.0

Source: Singapore, Department of Statistics, *Report on the Census of Industrial Production*, various years.

Note: Food manufacturing includes manufacture of beverage and tobacco.

a Represents percentage of tiny establishments over the total number of establishments in the particular industry group.

b Represents percentage of tiny establishments in industry group over the total number of tiny establishments in all industries.

TABLE 4.2

Number of Tiny Establishments, 1963–1983

Year	Tiny (5–9 Workers)			Total (5 & above Workers)	
	Number	Per Cent of Total[a]	Per Cent Increase	Number	Per Cent Increase
1963	684	44.4	—	1,542	—
1968	1,061	40.1	55.1	2,647	71.7
1973	1,248	37.5	17.6	3,327	25.7
1978	1,324	31.0	6.1	4,270	28.3
1983	2,136	37.1	61.3	5,752	34.7

Source: See Table 4.1.
[a] Total refers to firms which employ 5 workers or more.

TABLE 4.3

Employment of Tiny Establishments, 1963–1983

Year	Tiny (5–9 Workers)			Total (5 & above Workers)	
	Number	Per Cent of Total[a]	Per Cent Increase	Number	Per Cent Increase
1963	4,754	11.5	—	41,340	—
1968	7,222	8.8	51.9	82,055	98.5
1973	8,958	4.3	24.0	207,532	152.9
1978	8,805	3.5	−1.7	252,529	21.7
1983	14,636	5.1	66.2	285,739	13.2

Source: See Table 4.1.
[a] Total refers to firms which employ 5 workers or more.

TABLE 4.4
Output of Tiny Establishments, 1963–1983

| Year | Tiny (5–9 Workers) | | | Total (5 & above Workers) | |
	$'ooo	Per Cent of Total[a]	Per Cent Increase	$'ooo	Per Cent Increase
1963	45,088	5.1	—	888,839	—
1968	63,776	2.8	41.4	2,239,444	152.0
1973	136,153	1.7	113.5	8,074,227	260.5
1978	223,964	1.1	64.5	19,890,648	146.3
1983	583,007	1.5	160.3	37,804,526	90.1

Source: See Table 4.1.
[a] Total refers to firms which employ 5 works or more.

TABLE 4.5
Value-added of Tiny Establishments, 1963–1983

| Year | Tiny (5–9 Workers) | | | Total (5 & above Workers) | |
	$'ooo	Per Cent of Total[a]	Per Cent Increase	$'ooo	Per Cent Increase
1963	15,404	5.7	—	267,969	—
1968	22,959	3.6	49.0	634,717	136.9
1973	46,720	1.8	103.5	2,587,315	307.6
1978	78,046	1.5	67.1	5,240,968	102.6
1983	213,276	2.1	173.3	10,035,367	91.5

Source: See Table 4.1.
[a] Total refers to firms which employ 5 workers or more.

TABLE 4.6

Number of Small Establishments by Industry Group, 1963–1983

Major Industry Group	1963				1973				1983				
	No.	Rank	X^a	Y^b	No.	Rank	X	Y	No.	Rank	No. of Increase over 1973	X	Y
Food manufacturing	130	1	44.7	20.5	185	2	44.2	12.7	251	5	66	44.0	9.5
Textiles, apparel, footwear	49	6	24.7	7.7	228	1	31.8	15.7	424	1	196	36.7	16.1
Wood products (except furniture)	52	4	40.3	8.2	124	5	55.9	8.5	84	12	−40	53.8	3.2
Furniture & fixtures	12	13	26.1	1.9	38	12	38.4	2.6	103	10	65	34.1	3.9
Paper products	17	11	38.6	2.7	43	11	44.8	3.0	63	13	20	53.4	2.4
Printing & publishing	101	2	61.6	15.9	158	3	58.1	10.9	274	3	116	56.8	10.4
Chemicals & chemical products	30	9	16.9	4.7	73	8	51.8	5.0	91	11	18	54.5	3.5
Petroleum & petroleum products	—	—	—	—	3	18	30.0	0.2	2	18	−1	18.2	0.1
Rubber products	10	14	28.6	1.6	21	14	63.6	1.4	20	16	−1	60.6	0.8
Plastic products	—	—	—	—	70	9	56.5	4.8	168	8	98	62.0	6.4
Non-metallic products	18	10	35.3	2.8	13	16	48.1	0.9	15	17	2	34.9	0.6
Basic metal	2	15	22.2	0.3	14	15	53.8	1.0	22	14	8	61.1	0.8
Fabricated metal products	64	3	43.2	10.1	146	4	44.2	10.1	323	2	177	49.0	12.3
Machinery (except electrical/electronics)	50	5	46.7	7.9	115	6	41.7	7.9	267	4	152	43.4	10.2
Electrical/Electronic products	17	11	42.5	2.7	35	13	28.5	2.4	119	9	84	31.9	4.5
Transport equipment	43	7	32.6	6.8	62	10	40.8	4.3	213	6	151	54.1	8.1
Instrumentation equipment	—	—	—	—	10	17	31.3	0.7	21	15	11	37.5	0.8
Other manufacturing	40	8	46.1	6.3	113	7	52.7	7.8	170	7	57	54.5	6.5
All industry groups	635	—	40.3	100.0	1,451	—	41.1	100.0	2,630	—	1,179	45.7	100.0

Source: See Table 4.1.

Notes: 1. In this table only, small establishments in 1963 consist of firms with 10–39 workers instead of 10–49 workers.

2. Food manufacturing includes manufactures of beverage and tobacco.

[a] Represents percentage of small establishments over the total number of establishments in the particular industry group.

[b] Represents percentage of small establishments in industry group over the total number of small establishments in all industries.

TABLE 4.7
Number of Small Establishments, 1963–1983

Year	Small (10–49 Workers)			Total (10 & above Workers)	
	Number	Per Cent of Total[a]	Per Cent Increase	Number	Per Cent Increase
1963	693	80.8	—	858	—
1964	731	78.6	15.1	930	8.4
1965	772	77.2	5.6	1,000	7.5
1966	874	77.8	13.2	1,123	12.3
1967	921	77.1	5.4	1,195	6.4
1968	1,248	78.7	35.5	1,586	32.7
1969	1,309	76.4	4.9	1,714	8.1
1970	1,284	73.5	−1.9	1,747	1.9
1971	1,288	71.0	0.3	1,813	3.8
1972	1,365	70.7	6.0	1,931	6.5
1973	1,451	69.8	6.3	2,079	7.7
1974	1,528	70.1	5.3	2,179	4.8
1975	1,727	72.4	13.0	2,385	9.5
1976	1,829	73.0	5.9	2,505	5.0
1977	1,900	72.0	3.9	2,638	5.3
1978	2,133	72.4	12.3	2,946	11.7
1979	2,231	71.5	4.6	3,122	6.0
1980	2,407	71.7	7.9	3,355	7.5
1981	2,475	72.0	2.8	3,439	2.5
1982	2,596	72.4	4.9	3,586	4.3
1983	2,630	72.7	1.3	3,616	0.8

Source: See Table 4.1.
[a] Total refers to firms which employ 10 workers or more.

TABLE 4.8

Employment of Small Establishments, 1963–1983

Year	Small (10–49 Workers)			Total (10 & above Workers)	
	Number	Per Cent of Total[a]	Per Cent Increase	Number	Per Cent Increase
1963	15,032	41.1	—	36,586	—
1964	15,731	37.9	4.7	41,488	13.4
1965	16,829	35.6	7.0	47,334	14.1
1966	19,208	36.4	14.1	52,807	11.6
1967	20,940	35.9	9.0	58,347	10.5
1968	26,454	35.4	26.3	74,833	28.3
1969	28,609	28.4	8.1	100,758	34.6
1970	28,584	23.7	−0.1	120,509	19.6
1971	28,454	20.2	−0.5	140,543	16.6
1972	29,658	17.4	4.2	170,352	21.2
1973	30,757	15.5	3.7	198,574	16.6
1974	32,197	15.6	4.7	206,067	3.8
1975	35,903	18.7	11.5	191,528	−7.1
1976	37,936	18.3	5.7	207,234	8.2
1977	39,689	18.1	4.6	219,112	5.7
1978	44,261	18.2	11.5	243,724	11.2
1979	46,260	17.2	4.5	269,334	10.5
1980	49,270	17.3	6.5	285,250	5.9
1981	50,864	18.1	3.2	281,675	−1.3
1982	53,117	19.3	4.4	275,450	−2.2
1983	52,589	19.4	−1.0	271,103	−1.6

Source: See Table 4.1.

[a] Total refers to firms which employ 10 workers or more.

TABLE 4.9
Output of Small Establishments, 1963–1983

Year	Small (10–49 Workers)			Total (10 & above Workers)	
	$'000	Per Cent of Total[a]	Per Cent Increase	$'000	Per Cent Increase
1963	248,314	29.4	—	843,751	—
1964	254,384	27.4	2.4	927,928	10.0
1965	284,014	26.1	11.6	1,086,364	17.1
1966	342,091	25.8	20.4	1,325,782	22.0
1967	383,658	22.7	12.2	1,687,234	27.3
1968	484,953	22.3	26.4	2,175,668	28.9
1969	571,486	17.8	17.8	3,213,900	47.7
1970	659,641	17.0	15.4	3,891,012	21.1
1971	693,783	14.8	5.2	4,699,245	20.8
1972	750,746	13.1	8.2	5,722,225	21.8
1973	1,053,046	13.3	40.3	7,938,074	38.7
1974	1,517,768	11.4	44.1	13,346,912	68.1
1975	1,510,924	12.0	−0.5	12,610,144	−5.5
1976	1,980,435	12.9	31.1	15,317,439	21.5
1977	2,047,093	11.7	3.4	17,518,150	14.4
1978	2,234,245	11.4	9.1	19,666,684	12.3
1979	2,763,985	10.9	23.7	25,296,636	28.6
1980	3,450,135	10.9	24.8	31,657,894	25.1
1981	3,630,902	9.9	5.2	36,787,096	16.2
1982	3,965,928	10.9	9.2	36,467,443	−0.9
1983	4,313,819	11.6	8.8	37,221,519	2.1

Source: See Table 4.1.
[a] Total refers to firms which employ 10 workers or more.

TABLE 4.10

Value-added of Small Establishments, 1963–1983

Year	Small (10–49 Workers)			Total (10 & above Workers)	
	$'000	Per Cent of Total[a]	Per Cent Increase	$'000	Per Cent Increase
1963	62,891	24.9	—	252,565	—
1964	66,355	23.5	5.5	282,462	11.8
1965	78,170	22.4	17.8	348,362	23.3
1966	91,815	22.1	17.5	415,043	19.1
1967	105,118	22.0	14.5	478,646	15.3
1968	141,015	23.1	34.1	611,758	27.8
1969	161,475	18.9	14.5	856,630	40.0
1970	175,719	16.1	8.8	1,093,721	27.7
1971	192,133	14.1	9.3	1,366,472	24.9
1972	225,154	12.6	17.2	1,782,278	30.4
1973	307,063	12.1	36.4	2,540,595	42.5
1974	378,347	10.7	23.2	3,528,219	38.9
1975	448,388	13.1	18.5	3,411,129	−3.3
1976	549,787	13.9	22.6	3,961,812	16.1
1977	602,662	13.5	9.6	4,475,458	13.0
1978	674,207	13.1	11.9	5,162,922	15.4
1979	784,351	11.7	16.3	6,703,377	29.8
1980	1,023,446	12.0	30.5	8,521,888	27.1
1981	1,133,668	11.7	10.8	9,720,545	14.1
1982	1,204,132	12.9	6.2	9,355,941	−3.8
1983	1,317,310	13.4	9.4	9,822,091	5.0

Source: See Table 4.1.
[a] Total refers to firms which employ 10 workers or more.

Number of Medium Establishments by Industry Group, 1963–1983

Major Industry Group	1963				1973				1983				
	No.	Rank	X[a]	Y[b]	No.	Rank	X	Y	No.	Rank	No. of Increase over 1973	X	Y
Food manufacturing	28	1	9.6	17.1	38	2	9.1	12.8	32	7	-6	5.6	6.6
Textiles, apparel, footwear	9	8	4.7	5.5	39	1	5.4	13.2	59	3	20	5.1	12.2
Wood products (except furniture)	26	2	20.2	15.9	30	3	13.5	10.1	13	12	-17	8.3	2.7
Furniture & fixtures	5	12	10.9	3.0	4	15	4.0	1.4	11	14	7	3.6	2.3
Paper products	5	12	11.4	3.0	15	11	15.6	5.1	13	12	-2	11.0	2.7
Printing & publishing	15	4	9.1	9.1	16	8	5.9	5.4	28	9	12	5.8	5.8
Chemicals & chemical products	10	7	16.9	6.1	16	8	11.3	5.4	27	10	11	16.2	5.6
Petroleum & petroleum products	—	—	—	—	—	—	—	—	3	18	3	27.3	0.6
Rubber products	6	11	17.1	3.7	5	14	15.2	1.7	8	15	3	24.2	1.7
Plastic products	—	—	—	—	22	5	17.7	7.4	34	6	12	12.5	7.0
Non-metallic products	11	6	21.6	6.7	4	15	14.8	1.4	6	17	2	14.0	1.2
Basic metal	2	15	22.2	1.2	3	17	11.5	1.0	7	16	4	19.4	1.4
Fabricated metal products	12	5	8.1	7.3	30	3	9.1	10.1	61	2	31	9.6	12.6
Machinery (except electrical/electronics)	7	10	6.5	4.3	16	8	5.8	5.4	36	5	20	5.9	7.5
Electrical/Electronic products	4	14	10.0	2.4	13	12	10.6	4.4	66	1	53	17.7	13.7
Transport equipment	16	3	12.1	9.8	17	7	11.2	5.7	37	4	20	9.4	7.7
Instrumentation equipment	—	—	—	—	6	13	18.8	2.0	13	12	7	23.2	2.7
Other manufacturing	8	9	8.4	4.9	22	5	10.1	7.4	29	8	7	9.3	6.0
All industry groups	164	—	10.6	100.0	296	—	8.9	100.0	483	—	187	8.4	100.0

Source: See Table 4.1.

Notes: 1. In this table only, medium establishments in 1963 consist of firms with 40–99 workers instead of 50–99 workers.

2. Food manufacturing includes manufacture of beverage and tobacco.

[a] Represents percentage of medium establishments over the total number of establishments in the particular industry group.

[b] Represents percentage of medium establishments in industry group over the total number of medium establishments in all industries.

TABLE 4.12

Number of Medium and Large Establishments, 1963–1983

Year	Medium (50–99 Workers)			Large (100 & over Workers)		
	Number	Per Cent of Total[a]	Per Cent Increase	Number	Per Cent of Total[a]	Per Cent Increase
1963	106	12.4	—	59	6.8	—
1964	127	13.7	19.8	72	7.7	22.0
1965	145	14.5	14.2	83	8.3	15.3
1966	158	14.1	9.0	91	8.1	9.6
1967	169	14.1	7.0	105	8.8	15.4
1968	206	13.0	21.9	132	8.3	25.7
1969	232	13.5	12.6	173	10.1	31.1
1970	250	14.3	7.8	213	12.2	23.1
1971	265	14.6	6.0	260	14.3	22.1
1972	267	13.8	0.8	299	15.5	15.0
1973	296	14.2	10.9	332	16.0	11.0
1974	308	14.1	4.1	343	15.7	3.3
1975	324	13.6	5.2	334	14.0	−2.6
1976	333	13.3	2.8	343	13.7	2.7
1977	356	13.5	6.9	382	14.5	11.4
1978	386	13.1	8.4	427	14.5	11.8
1979	410	13.1	6.2	481	15.4	12.6
1980	438	13.1	6.8	510	15.2	6.0
1981	450	13.1	2.7	514	14.9	0.8
1982	486	13.6	8.0	504	14.1	−1.9
1983	483	13.4	−0.6	503	13.9	−0.2

Source: See Table 4.1.
[a] Total refers to firms which employ 50 workers or more.

TABLE 4.13
Employment of Medium and Large Establishments, 1963–1983

Year	Medium (50–99 Workers)			Large (100 & over Workers)		
	Number	Per Cent of Total[a]	Per Cent Increase	Number	Per Cent of Total[a]	Per Cent Increase
1963	7,334	20.0	—	14,220	38.9	—
1964	8,835	21.3	20.5	16,922	40.8	19.0
1965	10,058	21.2	13.8	20,447	43.2	20.8
1966	10,612	20.1	5.5	22,987	43.5	12.4
1967	11,538	19.8	8.7	25,869	44.3	12.5
1968	13,963	18.7	21.1	34,416	46.0	33.0
1969	15,816	15.7	13.2	56,333	55.9	63.7
1970	16,975	14.1	7.3	74,950	62.2	33.0
1971	17,779	12.7	4.7	94,310	67.1	25.8
1972	18,465	10.8	3.9	122,229	71.8	29.6
1973	20,443	10.3	10.7	147,374	74.2	20.6
1974	20,952	10.2	2.5	152,918	74.2	3.8
1975	22,395	11.7	6.9	133,230	69.6	−12.9
1976	23,136	11.2	3.3	146,162	70.5	9.7
1977	24,866	11.3	7.5	154,557	70.5	5.7
1978	26,961	11.1	8.4	172,502	70.8	11.6
1979	28,568	10.6	6.0	194,506	72.2	12.8
1980	30,134	10.6	5.5	205,846	72.2	5.8
1981	31,331	11.1	4.0	199,480	70.8	−3.1
1982	34,300	12.5	9.5	188,033	68.3	−5.7
1983	33,284	12.3	−3.0	185,233	68.3	−1.5

Source: See Table 4.1.
[a] Total refers to firms which employ 50 workers or more.

TABLE 4.14

Output of Medium and Large Establishments, 1963–1983

Year	Medium (50–99 Workers)			Large (100 & over Workers)		
	$'000	Per Cent of Total[a]	Per Cent Increase	$'000	Per Cent of Total	Per Cent Increase
1963	269,799	32.0	—	325,638	38.6	—
1964	300,912	32.4	11.5	372,632	40.2	14.4
1965	330,742	30.4	9.9	471,608	43.5	26.6
1966	363,215	27.4	9.8	620,476	46.8	31.6
1967	472,909	28.0	30.2	830,667	49.2	33.9
1968	694,078	31.9	46.8	996,637	45.8	20.0
1969	420,203	13.1	−39.5	2,222,211	69.1	123.0
1970	457,668	11.8	8.9	2,773,703	71.3	24.8
1971	478,766	10.2	4.6	3,526,696	75.0	27.1
1972	531,160	9.3	10.9	4,440,319	77.6	25.9
1973	752,047	9.5	41.6	6,132,981	77.3	38.1
1974	968,899	7.3	28.8	10,860,245	81.4	77.1
1975	1,049,785	8.3	8.3	10,049,435	79.7	−7.5
1976	1,189,543	7.8	13.3	12,147,461	79.3	20.9
1977	1,345,890	7.7	13.1	14,125,267	80.6	16.3
1978	1,344,173	6.8	−0.1	16,088,266	81.8	13.9
1979	1,937,958	7.7	44.2	20,594,693	81.4	28.0
1980	2,778,280	8.8	43.4	25,429,479	80.3	23.5
1981	3,323,680	9.0	19.6	29,832,514	81.1	17.3
1982	3,319,532	9.1	−0.1	29,181,983	80.0	−2.2
1983	3,389,551	9.1	2.1	29,518,149	79.3	1.2

Source: See Table 4.1.
[a] Total refers to firms which employ 50 workers or more.

TABLE 4.15
Value-added of Medium and Large Establishments, 1963–1983

Year	Medium (50–99 Workers)			Large (100 & over Workers)		
	$'000	Per Cent of Total[a]	Per Cent Increase	$'000	Per Cent of Total	Per Cent Increase
1963	61,661	24.4	—	128,013	50.7	—
1964	66,269	23.5	7.5	149,838	53.0	17.0
1965	81,911	23.5	23.6	188,281	54.0	25.7
1966	89,025	21.4	8.7	234,203	56.4	24.4
1967	104,747	21.9	17.7	268,781	56.2	14.8
1968	145,139	23.7	38.6	325,604	53.2	21.1
1969	116,597	13.6	−19.7	578,558	67.5	77.7
1970	128,041	11.7	9.8	789,961	72.2	36.5
1971	138,996	10.2	8.6	1,035,343	75.8	31.1
1972	173,167	9.7	24.6	1,383,957	77.7	33.7
1973	238,041	9.4	37.5	1,995,491	78.5	44.2
1974	259,551	7.4	9.0	2,890,321	81.9	44.8
1975	288,408	8.5	11.1	2,674,333	78.4	−7.5
1976	354,070	8.9	22.8	3,057,955	77.2	14.3
1977	412,374	9.2	16.5	3,460,422	77.3	13.2
1978	459,558	8.9	11.4	4,029,157	78.0	16.4
1979	646,937	9.7	40.8	5,272,089	78.6	30.8
1980	807,409	9.5	24.8	6,691,033	78.5	26.9
1981	1,027,879	10.6	27.3	7,558,998	77.8	13.0
1982	1,106,837	11.8	7.7	7,044,172	75.3	−6.8
1983	1,137,818	11.6	2.8	7,366,963	75.0	4.6

Source: See Table 4.1.
[a] Total refers to firms which employ 50 workers or more.

72

FIGURE 4.1

Trends of the Relative Contributions of Tiny Establishments, 1963–1983

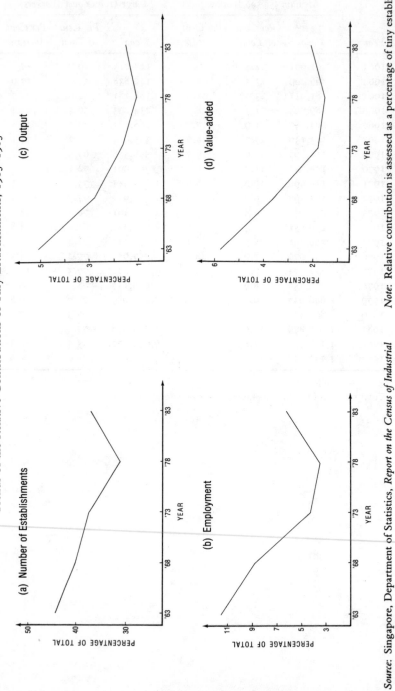

Source: Singapore, Department of Statistics, *Report on the Census of Industrial Production,* various years.

Note: Relative contribution is assessed as a percentage of tiny establishments over total. Total refers to firms which employ 5 workers or more.

FIGURE 4.2

Trends of the Relative Contributions of Small Establishments, 1963–1983

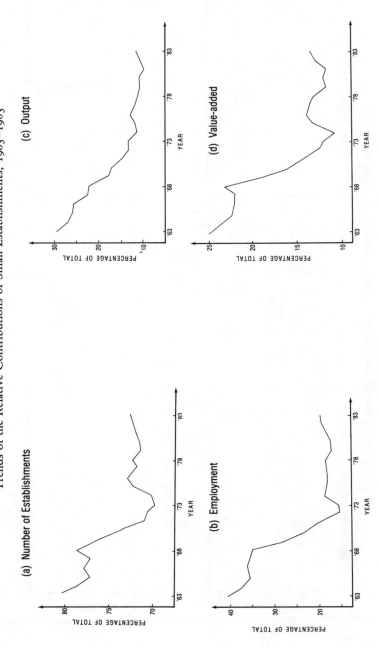

Source: See Figure 4.1.

Note: Relative contribution is assessed as a percentage of small establishments over total. Total refers to firms which employ 10 workers or more.

FIGURE 4.3

Trends of the Relative Contributions of Medium Establishments, 1963–1983

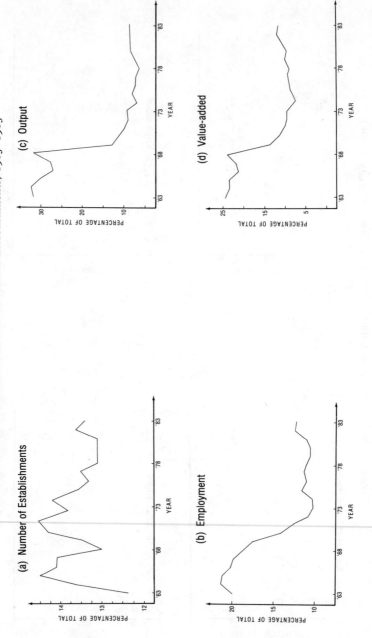

Source: See Figure 4.1.

Note: Relative contribution is assessed as a percentage of medium establishments over total. Total refers to firms which employ 10 workers or more.

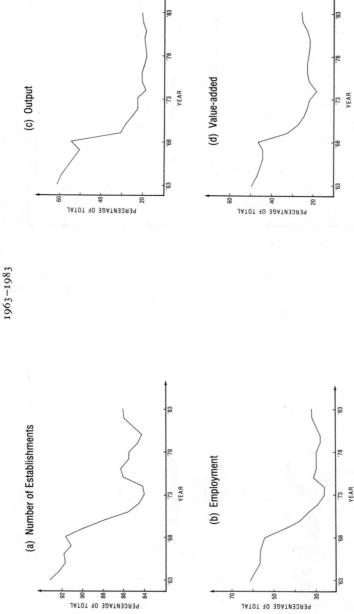

FIGURE 4.4

Trends of the Relative Contributions of Small and Medium Establishments,
1963–1983

Source: See Figure 4.1.

Note: Relative contribution is assessed as a percentage of small and medium establishments over total. Total refers to firms which employ 10 workers or more.

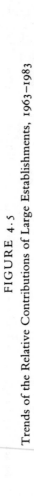

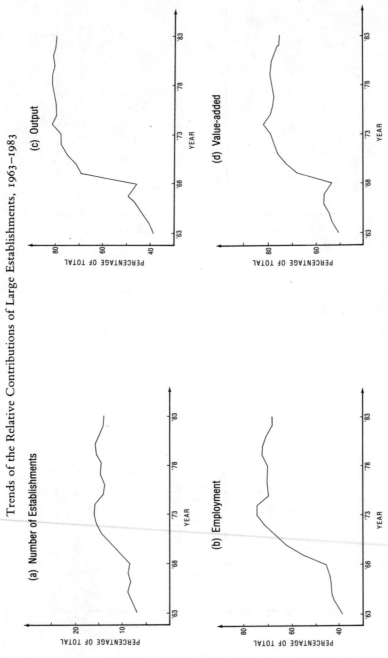

FIGURE 4.5

Trends of the Relative Contributions of Large Establishments, 1963–1983

(a) Number of Establishments

(b) Employment

(c) Output

(d) Value-added

Source: See Figure 4.1.

Note: Relative contribution is assessed as a percentage of large establishments over total. Total refers to firms which employ 10 workers or more. .

5

THE CHANGING STRUCTURE
OF SMALL FIRMS

In Chapter 4 we analysed the economic contribution of small firms in Singapore. In particular, we noticed that small firms have contributed positively to the industrial development of Singapore. Although the relative importance of small firms has been reduced since the period of initial rapid industrialization, they still play an indispensable role in the industrial process.

In order to understand how and why small firms change over time, Chapter 5 analyses the essential structural features of small firms in Singapore in terms of factor intensity, labour productivity, market orientation, extent of linkages, legal organization, and capital structure. An empirical analysis of the relationship between small firms and unionization is also presented in this chapter.

Factor Intensity

As is obvious from our discussion in Chapter 3, small firms are more labour intensive than large firms. The empirical analysis of Chapter 4 also confirms that tiny, small and medium establishments in Singapore have been more labour intensive than large establishments.

In this section, we want to examine the factor intensity of both small and large firms over a number of years. Table 5.1 contains data on capital expenditure per establishment. In 1968, the capital expenditure per establishment was $18,200 for small establishments, $76,806 for medium establishments, and $386,652 for large establishments. As has been predicted by our theoretical discussion in Chapter 3, capital expenditure per large firm is always greater than that for a smaller firm.

Both small and medium establishments have invested a considerable amount of capital in their operations. The average rate of increase in capital expenditure per establishment for 1968–83 was 44.2 per cent and 19.5 per cent for small and medium establishments respectively. However, they still lagged behind large establishments, which had an average rate of increase of 68.9 per cent.

A better indicator of capital intensity is capital expenditure per worker. In 1968 the capital expenditure per worker was $859, $1,133, and $1,483 for small, medium, and large establishments respectively (see Table 5.1). Again, large establishments invested more capital

expenditure per worker than small and medium establishments. However, both small and medium establishments had narrowed the gap.
The average rate of increase in capital expenditure per worker for
1968–83 was 44.5 per cent and 19.2 per cent for small and medium
establishments respectively while the corresponding figure for large
establishments was 19.1 per cent. Consequently, in 1983, the capital
expenditure per worker of small establishments was $6,747, which was
not far behind that of medium establishments ($7,792) and large estab-
lishments ($8,094).

The above discussion seems to suggest that there has been a growing
awareness among small firms, especially small establishments, to
mechanize their operations.

Labour Productivity

As discussed in Chapter 3, small firms are labour intensive and have
lower output and value-added per worker. The value-added per worker
for small and large firms is reported in Table 5.2. In 1963, the value-
added per worker was $3,240, $4,184, $8,408, and $9,002 for tiny,
small, medium, and large establishments respectively. Our findings
thus confirm our theoretical discussion that the value-added per worker
is higher for larger firms.

Productivity performance defined in terms of labour productivity has
been quite impressive for all types of establishments. For 1963–83, the
average increase in labour productivity was 10.9 per cent, 13.2 per cent,
10.6 per cent, and 11.1 per cent for tiny, small, medium, and large
establishments respectively. This shows that most firms have upgraded
their operations but relative productivity performance still remains the
same, i.e. the value-added per worker is still higher for larger firms.

Another indicator of labour productivity is value-added per unit of
labour cost. Value-added per unit of labour cost is a better indicator
than value-added per worker because it takes into account the number
of hours worked. In 1963, medium establishments had the highest
value-added per unit of labour cost of $3.1 million. The corresponding
figures for tiny, small, and large establishments were $2.5 million, $2.1
million, and $2.7 million respectively. Thus, in terms of efficiency
measured by value-added per unit of labour cost, medium establishments ranked first, large establishments second, followed by tiny and
small establishments. By 1983, tiny establishments ranked first in terms
of value-added per unit of labour cost, followed by large establishments, small establishments, and medium establishments.

It is rather surprising to learn that tiny establishments were even
more efficient than large establishments. There are two factors which
can account for a high ratio of value-added per unit of labour cost. The
first factor relates to the firm's effectiveness in the utilization of its
employees. If a firm is efficient in using its workers, it can increase
value-added and at the same time cut labour cost. Unfortunately, we do
not have data on this aspect of Singapore's establishments. The second

factor which also affects value-added per labour cost is wages. If an establishment pays its employees lower wages, *ceteris paribus*, its value-added per unit of labour cost will be higher.[1] We can examine this hypothesis using data from Table 5.2.

In 1963, the remuneration per worker was $1,295, $1,968, $2,715, and $3,380 for tiny, small, medium, and large establishments respectively. This shows that the remuneration per worker was higher for larger establishments. It also shows that tiny establishments had a high ratio of value-added per unit of labour cost because they paid their employees lower wages.

In 1983, medium establishments had the highest remuneration per worker ($15,201), followed by large establishments ($13,717), small establishments ($10,969), and tiny establishments ($4,735). This explains why medium establishments had the lowest value-added per unit of labour cost ($2.2 million) in 1983. It also indicates that large establishments had a higher value-added per unit of labour cost than medium establishments because the former had a lower remuneration per worker.

Market Orientation

The theoretical analysis in Chapter 3 indicates that we have three types of small firms, one under capital constraints, one under output constraints, and one under entrepreneur constraints. In view of the three types of constraints, we do not expect small firms to be highly export oriented because it takes considerable financial and manpower resources to sell in foreign markets.

Table 5.3 shows the sales and exports of manufacturing establishments in Singapore. In 1973, both small and medium establishments contributed about 5 per cent each to the total direct exports. In 1983, both small and medium establishments only managed to increase their relative contributions to the total direct exports by 1 per cent, to 6 per cent each. Needless to say, large establishments contributed almost 90 per cent of the total direct exports.

It is also important to examine the propensities of small firms to export, defined as the ratio of direct exports over sales. In 1973, the propensity to export was 21.5 per cent for small establishments and 30.3 per cent for medium establishments. Over the subsequent ten-year period, small and medium establishments successfully managed to export more. By 1983, the propensity to export had increased to 29.7 per cent and 37.2 per cent for small and medium establishments respectively. However, the degree of propensity to export was still low, especially compared to that of large establishments, which exported 67.6 per cent of their total sales in 1983.

Extent of Linkages

The extent of linkages can be measured in terms of the volume of subcontracting among firms in the manufacturing sector. However, we do not have data on subcontracting. Fortunately, we do have data on work given out to other firms. 'Work given out' is defined in the *Report on the Census of Industrial Production* as payment to other firms or persons, either for work performed on raw materials supplied or for the servicing work farmed out by the reporting establishment.[2]

In our theoretical analysis in Chapter 3, we did not discuss small firms playing the role of subcontractors. However, we still can relate the role of subcontractors to the three types of small firms operating under the three types of constraints. What usually prevents a subcontractor from growing is capital, output, and entrepreneur constraints. A subcontractor receives order from a few large establishments. The demand for the subcontractor's product is usually unstable. Because of the unstable demand, and also due to lack of funds and manpower, the subcontractor, upon receiving an excessive order, will not expand his volume of operation but subcontract to another level of subcontractors, who will operate in the same manner as the first subcontractor. We therefore expect that many small firms are subcontractors and small firms have stronger linkage effects than large firms.

Table 5.4 reports output and work given out by manufacturing establishments. In 1973, small establishments accounted for 14 per cent of total work given out, while medium establishments contributed 13 per cent. In 1983, when the industrial structure had become more interdependent, the relative contribution of small establishments increased to 29 per cent, while that of medium establishments increased slightly to 16 per cent. Owing to their sheer size in volume of output and value-added, large establishments still accounted for 55 per cent of the total work given out in 1983.

In order to assess the linkage effect, one has to look at the linkage ratio, which is the ratio of work given out to the total output. In 1973, the linkage ratio was 1.8 per cent for small establishments, 2.3 per cent for medium establishments, and only 1.5 per cent for large establishments. In 1983, the disparity in the linkage ratio between small and large firms had widened. The linkage ratio of small establishments was 6.6 per cent, while that of medium establishments was 4.8 per cent. The linkage ratio of large establishments was only 1.9 per cent.

The above discussion clearly indicates that small firms subcontract much more than big firms relative to their levels of output.

Legal Organization

There are four major forms of business organization, namely sole proprietorship, partnership, private limited company and public limited company. There are, of course, many differences between the four forms of business organization, but the most important difference is that there is a trade-off between flexibility in management and ability to raise funds:

Business Organization	Flexibility in Management and Operation by the Entrepreneur	Ease in Raising Funds for Business Expansion
Sole proprietorship	greatest	least
Partnership	great	some
Private limited company	some	great
Public limited company	least	greatest

For firms with entrepreneur constraints, the entrepreneurs will find sole proprietorships the most suitable form of business organization because, by definition, they want to have perfect control in management and operation. For firms with output constraints, the entrepreneurs will find sole proprietorships and even partnerships useful because the scope of their business is still manageable with their own manpower and financial resources.

Firms with capital constraints face a dilemma. Since they face capital constraints, the company form of business organization, such as public limited companies, suits them best. However, firms with capital constraints must demonstrate to the general public that they are capable of making profit, or else they will have problems in raising funds through issuing company shares. But, as we have discussed in Chapter 3, firms with capital constraints are inefficient because they do not produce along the output expansion path. Firms under capital constraints are therefore caught in this vicious circle and are consequently organized as sole proprietorships and partnerships. The government can help them by offering loans at low interest rates. We will discuss the issue in Chapter 9.

The above discussion indicates that small firms are more likely to be organized along the lines of sole proprietorships and partnerships than large firms. But, over time, it is also expected that more and more small firms will be organized along the lines of private and public limited companies. This is because the financial commitment of today's manufacturing operation, however small, usually goes beyond the financial ability of individuals and will have to be met by funds raised through issuing company shares.

Unfortunately, we do not have data correlating firm size and legal organization in Singapore. Nevertheless, we still can examine whether those industries in which small firms were concentrated had a higher percentage of sole proprietorships and partnerships. Table 5.5 gives the number of manufacturing firms by legal organization for the manufacturing sector as a whole as well as for each industry in 1968 and 1983. In 1968, the average percentage of sole proprietorships for the manufacturing sector as a whole was 28 per cent. As is obvious from Table 5.5, those industries which were dominated by small firms, such as the textiles, apparel and footwear industry, the furniture and fixtures industry, the paper products industry, the printing and publishing industry, the fabricated metal industry, and the machinery industry, had more than 30 per cent of sole proprietorships in their respective industries. Similarly, the industries which had a high concentration of small firms also had more than the average percentage of partnerships. On the other hand, the capital-intensive industries, such as the petroleum and petroleum products industry, the chemical and chemical products industry, and the basic metal industry, in which large firms dominate, had a very low percentage of sole proprietorships and partnerships. The same findings are observed for 1983 as well.

From 1968 to 1983, the percentage of private limited companies in the manufacturing sector increased from 36 per cent to 69 per cent at the expense of sole proprietorships and partnerships. The percentage of sole proprietorships declined from 28 per cent to 12 per cent, while that of partnerships fell from 34 per cent to 17 per cent. There has clearly been a tendency for establishments in Singapore to favour private limited companies instead of sole proprietorships and partnerships. This trend of favouring private limited companies is evident in those industries which have a high concentration of small firms. For instance, the percentage of sole proprietorships in the textiles, apparel and footwear industry fell from 44.6 per cent in 1968 to 21.7 per cent in 1983. The percentage of partnerships in the food manufacturing industry also decreased from 36.8 per cent to 24.4 per cent. The trend in favour of private limited companies also reflects the entrepreneurs' preference for ease in raising funds over flexibility in management.

Capital Structure

There are four categories of establishment with respect to capital structure in Singapore, namely, 'wholly local', 'more than half local', 'less than half local', and 'wholly foreign'. The relative advantages of the four categories of establishment are:

	Flexibility in Management and Operation by the Local Entrepreneur	Access to Foreign Capital, Technology and Markets
Wholly local	greatest	none
More than half local	great	limited
Less than half local	limited	great
Wholly foreign	none	greatest

Thus, to the local entrepreneur, there is a trade-off between control on the one hand and technology, capital, and markets on the other. A firm operating in a foreign country does not generally face output, capital or entrepreneur constraints. Foreign firms are mostly large firms. Consequently, we expect that most small firms are local as they, rather than the foreign ones, are likely to meet those constraints in their operations.

Most local entrepreneurs, typically, would like to have greater control over the management and operation of their establishments. However, in joint ventures with foreign entrepreneurs, they may gain access to technology, capital, and markets. In other words, firms under capital and output constraints may remove these two types of constraint through joint ventures with foreigners. In this case, they can either opt for becoming 'more than half local' or 'less than half local'. Firms with entrepreneurial constraints are not likely to opt for joint ventures with foreigners and therefore remain local.

As business becomes more competitive, firms under the three types of constraint might put less emphasis on control and more on capital, technology, and markets. We will therefore expect to see more joint ventures as the pace of the industrialization process increases.

Again, we do not have data correlating firm size and capital structure in Singapore. Table 5.6 presents the number of manufacturing establishments by capital structure for the manufacturing sector as well as for each industry. From 1968 to 1983, the share of wholly local firms decreased from 80.5 per cent to 67.2 per cent. For the same period, the shares of 'more than half local', 'less than half local' and wholly foreign firms increased from 7.8 per cent to 11.8 per cent, 5.7 per cent to 6.7 per cent, and 6.1 per cent to 14.4 per cent, respectively. There is therefore a clear tendency for local entrepreneurs to form joint ventures with foreigners instead of operating on their own. This trend in favour of joint ventures indicates the local entrepreneurs' preference for capital, technology, and markets over business control.

Our theoretical discussion with respect to capital structure indicates that small firms are local firms. Firms which are 'more than half local' and 'less than half local' may or may not be small depending on whether they can remove output and capital constraints through joint ventures. In 1968, the percentage of wholly local firms for the entire manufacturing sector was 80.5 per cent. Those industries in which small firms dominated, such as the food manufacturing industry, the textile, apparel and footwear industry, and the printing and publishing industry, had more than 80 per cent of wholly local firms in the same year. In 1983, while the percentage of wholly local firms fell for each industry, these industries still had a greater percentage of wholly local firms than the entire manufacturing sector.

Small Firms and Unionization

As in many countries, trade unions have played a decisive role in the economic development of Singapore. Singapore could not have achieved her present level of economic development without the cooperation of her trade unions. Even though Singapore has been very successful economically, the trade unions in Singapore have faced declining membership in the last few years. Between 1978 and 1984, the proportion of union members to total bargainable workers dropped from 31.3

per cent to 21.9 per cent. The National Trades Union Congress (NTUC), which is the national body of trade unions in Singapore, is fully aware of the problem and is confident that the declining membership will be arrested, if not reversed. The purpose of this section is to examine the relationship between small firms, unionization and capital structure.

Union membership and union density are commonly used as measures of union strength and success in an occupation, an industry or a country. Union membership indicates the total number of unionized workers at the place of work, while union density refers to the percentage of all workers who are unionized. Trade union membership is determined by various factors, such as industry-mix, worker–sex ratio, race ratio, and, of course, the effective organization of the union.[3] However, membership is also influenced by firm size. Because labour conditions in smaller firms tend to be inferior to those in large firms, employers in smaller firms are more likely to resist their employees' desire to form a union.

Employees in smaller firms are generally also less eager to form a union. Small firms are commonly run along family traditions. There is usually no explicit contract between the employer and the employee on increments, working conditions, duties, and retrenchment benefits. Thus, workers can be easily victimized if they go against their employers' wishes regarding the forming of a union. Besides, many of the workers in small firms are relatives of the employers, and so will not support any initiative to organize a union in the establishment.

It is also difficult for unions to organize and operate within small firms due to a lack of economies of scale in union activities. For instance, it is time-consuming to negotiate a collective agreement with management. A collective agreement in a large firm may cover 2,000 unionized members. While requiring almost the same effect, a collective agreement in a small firm only applies to, say, 20–50 workers. From an economic point of view, it is rational for the union, especially if they are understaffed and operating on a tight budget, to concentrate on large firms.

Thus, unionization among small firms is limited, regardless of the organization of the union. This is an important point to note, especially when we want to compare union density over time and across nations.

For example, it is not exactly suitable to compare union density in the US with that in Singapore. Obviously, other things being equal, the US will have a higher union density than Singapore if the percentage of firms employing less than, say, 50 is much smaller than that in Singapore. To have a meaningful comparison, we should measure union density as the percentage of union membership over the total number of employees of all firms which have more than, say, 50 workers in an industry, a sector or the whole economy.[4]

Thus our theoretical discussion clearly indicates that the percentage of unionization in small firms is low. As will be shown below, this hypothesis is supported by our data. We have access to data on all firms, unionized and non-unionized, in Singapore. The firms are classified into three categories: those with 10–49 workers (small establishments), those with 50–99 workers (medium establishments) and those with more than 99 workers (large establishments). The data base enables us to examine whether the percentage of establishments which are unionized is smallest for establishments with 10–49 workers, and largest for firms with more than 99 workers.

Table 5.7 presents the breakdown of establishments in the Singapore manufacturing sector by size and unionization as at 31 May 1985. There were 2,611 small establishments in the manufacturing sector, accounting for 73 per cent of all industrial establishments in Singapore. There were 442 medium establishments and 513 large establishments, each contributing 12 per cent and 14 per cent respectively to the total number of industrial establishments in Singapore. Thus, the Singapore manufacturing sector is heavily dominated by small establishments. Indeed, small and medium establishments combined account for 86 per cent of all industrial establishments. This special feature in the manufacturing sector has thus adversely affected the effort of unions in their membership drive.

As Table 5.7 clearly shows, the percentage of unionization among small establishments was only 2.9 per cent. The percentage of unionization among medium and large establishments was 18.3 per cent and 50.9 per cent respectively. This shows that the degree of success in a membership drive depends to a great extent on the size of the company.

In Singapore, the manufacturing sector is sub-classified into 34 industries. We will examine the relationship between unionization and firm size for those industries which have more than 100 industrial establishments. Table 5.8 presents this relationship for the food manufacturing industry, the textile, apparel and footwear industry, the sawn-timber and wood products (except furniture) industry, the furniture and fixtures (except primarily of metal) industry, the printing and publishing industry, the plastic products industry, the fabricated metal products industry, the machinery industry, the electrical machinery, apparatus and appliances industry, the electronic products and components industry, the transport equipment industry, and the other manufacturing industries group.

Without exception, the rate of unionization in small establishments in each industry was the lowest compared to that in medium and large companies in the same industry. In particular, for the sawn-timber and wood products (except furniture) industry and the furniture and fixtures (except primarily of metal) industry, none of the workers in the small establishments were unionized.

The percentage of unionization in medium establishments was much higher than in small establishments. With the exception of the apparel industry, the percentage of unionization in medium establishments ranged from 9 per cent to as high as 34 per cent. As expected, the percentage of unionization in large establishments was the highest. It ranged from 32 per cent in the apparel industry to 71 per cent in the electrical machinery, apparatus and appliances industry.

The difference in the percentage of unionization across industries, to a large extent, can be attributed to the effective organization of the unions. But firm size is a common variable affecting all unions in their membership drives.

We have thus theoretically and empirically shown that, despite the effective organization of the unions, the rate of organization is lower for smaller firms. But we do not know the exact causality between unionization and firm size. Do smaller firms discourage unions from conducting a membership drive in these firms or is the rate of success very low in smaller firms?

According to some industrial relations officers, the reasons for the low rate of unionization in smaller firms are that employers in small firms are more likely to resist the formation of a union in the company, their employees are less eager to form a union and union officials find it hard to form a union in small firms due to a lack of economies of scale in union activities. Basically, a union, due to budget constraints, is understaffed. An industrial relations officer is responsible for covering 5–15 unionized companies. Besides servicing these unionized companies in such areas as collective bargaining and the settling of industrial disputes, each of them is also expected to reach out to workers in non-unionized firms and persuade them to form a union in their place of work, which is a very time-consuming activity. Most non-unionized firms usually do not allow unionists to go to their plants to talk to the workers. Thus, unionists have to persuade workers outside the factory during a change of shift. Only when unionists have managed to get at least 51 per cent of the workers in a particular factory to support the intention of forming a union, are they then permitted to approach the management for necessary action.

With limited time and manpower, unions naturally will concentrate on organizing workers to form unions in bigger firms, where the rate of success is higher, the cost of servicing is lower, and the yield in terms of membership is higher. We expect that unionists will concentrate on smaller firms only when the rate of unionization among large firms is sufficiently high. This hypothesis is not refuted by the data. Table 5.8 shows that the rate of unionization is the highest for small establishments of the food manufacturing industry (7 per cent), the machinery industry (2 per cent), and the electrical machinery, apparatus and appliances industry (8 per cent), which also have the highest rates of unionization among their large establishments, 65 per cent, 65 per cent and 71 per cent respectively.

Conclusion

Using the analytical framework presented in Chapter 3, we have found that small firms have been more labour intensive than large firms.

Small firms have also been less export oriented as they generally produce for the domestic market. Small firms, however, have produced more industrial linkages proportionately for they often play the role of subcontractors.

Many small firms are organized as sole proprietorships, partnerships, and private limited companies. But there has been a clear trend in favour of private limited companies instead of sole proprietorships and partnerships among small firms, reflecting the entrepreneur's preference for ability to raise funds over control. Many small firms are also locally owned.

Having discussed the concept, the economic contribution, and also the changing structure of small firms in Chapters 3, 4, and 5, we might be left with the impression that small firms are generally not as efficient as large firms. We might be tempted to draw the conclusion that the optimal size of the firm should be large. Conceptually, of course, optimal firm size should be defined in terms of the lowest average cost per unit of output. However, empirically, optimal firm size may be defined in terms of value-added per worker, output per worker, value-added per unit of labour cost, linkage effect, and export intensity, depending on the researcher's perception of what the optimum is.

Table 5.9 presents the performance indicators of establishments by number of workers for 1983. In terms of value-added per worker, output per worker, and value-added per unit of labour cost, the optimal firm size was '300–499 workers' because establishments in this category had the highest ratios. On the basis of the linkage effect, defined as the ratio of work given out to output, the optimal firm size was '10–19 workers'. Using export intensity as the criterion, the optimal firm size was '500 and over workers'. Thus, there is no single optimal firm size that will meet all the criteria.

We should therefore not be too concerned with firm size. As the economy progresses, the degree of complementarity between various firm sizes will increase. Each has an important role to play in the industrialization process.

1. One may wish to argue that low wages may reflect the low quality of the worker. However, conceptually, a low quality worker will also reduce value-added and therefore will not necessarily affect value-added per labour cost.

2. Singapore, Department of Statistics, *Report on the Census of Industrial Production*, 1983.

3. For a detailed discussion on the influence of these variables on union membership, see G. S. Bain and P. Elias, 'Trade Union Membership in Great Britain: An Individual-Level Analysis', *British Journal of Industrial Relations*, Vol. 1, March 1985.

4. Unfortunately I do not have the necessary data to compute the adjusted union density which takes into account firm size. The adjusted union density can only be estimated when we have access to data on the number of workers and the number of unionized members, if applicable, of all the firms in Singapore.

TABLE 5.1

Capital Expenditure and Labour Remuneration of Manufacturing
Establishments, 1968–1983

	Year			Average Annual Increase (%)
	1968	1973	1983	
Capital expenditure *per establishment ($)*				
Small	18,200	130,461	134,902	44.2
Medium	76,806	165,831	536,942	19.5
Large	386,652	2,089,063	17,740,010	68.9
Capital expenditure *per worker ($)*				
Small	859	6,155	6,747	44.5
Medium	1,133	2,401	7,792	19.2
Large	1,483	4,706	8,094	19.1
Worker's remuneration *per establishment*				
Small	48,018	72,147	219,327	13.8
Medium	179,806	291,132	1,047,544	17.4
Large	861,606	2,019,717	5,051,489	17.1

Source: Singapore, Department of Statistics, *Report on the Census of Industrial Production*,
various years.
Note: Data on tiny establishments are not available.

TABLE 5.2

Labour Productivity and Labour Remuneration of Manufacturing
Establishments, 1963–1983

	Year			Average Annual
	1963	1973	1983	Increase (%)
Value-added per worker ($)				
Tiny	3,240	5,215	14,572	10.9
Small	4,184	9,984	25,049	13.2
Medium	8,408	11,644	34,185	10.6
Large	9,002	13,540	39,771	11.1
Value-added per $1,000				
labour cost				
Tiny	2,503	3,218	3,078	1.1
Small	2,126	2,933	2,284	0.7
Medium	3,097	2,762	2,249	−1.3
Large	2,663	2,976	2,899	0.4
Remuneration per worker ($)				
Tiny	1,295	1,621	4,735	9.9
Small	1,968	3,404	10,969	13.4
Medium	2,715	4,215	15,201	14.4
Large	3,380	4,550	13,717	10.7

Source: See Table 5.1.

Note: Value-added per $1,000 labour cost = $\dfrac{\text{Total Value-added}}{\left(\dfrac{\text{Total Worker's Remuneration}}{\$1,000}\right)}$

TABLE 5.3

Sales and Exports of Manufacturing Establishments, 1973–1983

	Year		
	1973	*1978*	*1983*
Total sales ($'000)			
Small	1,040,602	2,217,778	4,300,971
Medium	738,212	1,344,754	3,377,230
Large	6,182,479	15,993,973	29,732,918
Direct exports ($'000)			
Small	223,240	726,048	1,277,627
Medium	223,380	440,586	1,256,821
Large	3,823,156	11,466,100	20,106,323
Direct exports			
Total sales (%)			
Small	21.5	32.7	29.7
Medium	30.3	32.8	37.2
Large	61.8	71.7	67.6

Source: See Table 5.1.
Note: Data on tiny establishments are not available.

TABLE 5.4

Output and Work Given Out by
Manufacturing Establishments, 1968–1983

	Year		
	1968	*1973*	*1983*
Total output ($'000)			
Small	484,953	1,053,046	4,313,819
Medium	694,078	752,047	3,389,551
Large	996,637	6,132,981	29,518,149
Work given out ($'000)			
Small	7,384	18,944	285,240
Medium	3,957	17,145	164,391
Large	7,638	94,631	547,254
Work given out			
Total output (%)			
Small	1.5	1.8	6.6
Medium	0.6	2.3	4.8
Large	0.8	1.5	1.9

Source: See Table 5.1.
Note: Data on tiny establishments are not available.

TABLE 5.5

Establishments by Legal Organization and Industry, 1968 and 1983

Industry Group	Total 1968 No.	Total 1968 %	Total 1983 No.	Total 1983 %	Sole Proprietorship 1968 No.	1968 %	1983 No.	1983 %	Partnership 1968 No.	1968 %	1983 No.	1983 %	Private Limited Companies 1968 No.	1968 %	1983 No.	1983 %	Public Limited Companies 1968 No.	1968 %	1983 No.	1983 %
Food manufacturing	239	100	311	100	50	20.9	48	15.4	88	36.8	76	24.4	91	38.1	172	55.3	10	4.2	14	4.5
Textiles, apparel, footwear	213	100	566	100	95	44.6	123	21.7	75	35.2	132	23.3	42	19.7	308	54.4	1	0.5	2	0.4
Wood products (except furniture)	152	100	110	100	24	15.8	11	10.0	81	52.3	26	23.6	44	28.9	70	63.6	3	2.0	3	2.7
Furniture & fixtures	51	100	127	100	28	54.9	27	21.3	11	21.6	40	31.5	12	23.5	59	46.5	—	—	1	0.8
Paper & paper products	54	100	88	100	17	31.5	7	8.0	22	40.7	13	14.8	15	27.8	68	77.3	—	—	—	—
Printing & publishing	153	100	321	100	46	30.1	38	11.8	60	39.2	75	23.4	45	29.4	202	62.9	1	0.7	4	1.2
Chemicals & chemical products	87	100	135	100	7	8.1	4	3.0	13	14.9	5	3.7	64	73.6	122	90.4	3	3.4	4	3.0
Petroleum & petroleum products	9	100	11	100	—	—	—	—	—	—	—	—	8	88.9	10	90.9	1	11.1	1	9.1
Rubber products	28	100	36	100	3	10.7	1	2.8	11	39.3	4	11.1	14	50.0	31	86.1	—	—	—	—
Plastic products			215	100			17	7.9			18	8.4			177	82.3			3	1.4
Non-metallic products	47	100	100	100	7	14.9	6	6.0	13	27.7	7	7.0	25	53.2	77	77.0	2	4.3	6	6.0
Basic metal	25	100	33	100	5	20.0	1	3.0	9	36.0	7	21.2	8	32.0	24	72.7	3	12.0	1	3.0
Fabricated metal products	138	100	426	100	45	32.6	55	12.9	39	28.3	66	15.5	50	36.2	290	68.1	4	2.9	12	2.8
Machinery	104	100	341	100	38	36.5	30	8.8	38	36.5	66	19.4	23	22.1	232	68.0	5	4.8	4	1.2
Electrical/Electronics products	41	100	315	100	5	12.2	7	2.2	7	17.1	14	4.4	26	63.4	285	90.5	3	7.3	3	1.0
Transport equipment	98	100	291	100	29	29.6	27	9.3	26	26.5	51	17.5	38	38.8	208	71.5	5	5.1	5	1.8
Instrumentation equipment			46	100			1	2.2			2	4.3			43	93.5			—	—
Other manufacturing	147	100	144	100	39	26.5	13	9.0	45	30.6	27	18.8	63	42.9	104	72.2	—	—	—	—
All industry groups*	1,586	100	3,616	100	438	27.6	416	11.5	538	33.9	629	17.4	568	35.8	2,482	68.6	41	2.6	63	1.7

Source: Singapore, Department of Statistics, Report on the Census of Industrial Production, 1968 and 1983.

Note: There are five categories of legal organization, i.e. sole proprietorship, partnership, private limited companies, public limited companies, and 'others'. The number of establishments for 'others' can be derived from the above table.

* Excludes rubber processing and granite quarrying.

TABLE 5.6

Establishments by Capital Structure and Industry, 1968 and 1983

Industry Group	Total				Wholly Local				More than Half Local				Less than Half Local				Wholly Foreign			
	1968		1983		1968		1983		1968		1983		1968		1983		1968		1983	
	No.	%	No.	%	No.	%	No.	%	No.	%	No.	%	No.	%	No.	%	No.	%	No.	%
Food manufacturing	239	100	311	100	204	85.4	230	74.0	16	6.7	40	12.9	14	5.9	23	7.4	5	2.1	18	5.8
Textiles, apparel, footwear	213	100	566	100	176	82.6	431	76.1	13	6.1	86	15.2	17	8.0	26	4.6	7	3.3	23	4.1
Wood products	152	100	110	100	128	84.2	83	75.5	16	10.5	12	10.9	4	2.6	5	4.5	4	2.6	10	9.1
Furniture & fixtures	51	100	127	100	46	90.2	105	82.7	1	2.0	15	11.8	1	2.0	4	3.1	3	5.9	3	2.4
Paper & paper products	54	100	88	100	43	79.6	64	72.7	3	5.6	10	11.4	4	7.4	7	8.0	4	7.4	7	8.0
Printing & publishing	153	100	321	100	138	90.2	270	84.1	11	7.2	26	8.1	1	0.7	12	3.7	3	2.0	13	4.0
Chemicals & chemical products	87	100	135	100	41	47.1	53	39.3	17	19.5	17	12.6	11	12.6	17	12.6	18	20.7	48	35.6
Petroleum & petroleum products	9	100	11	100	3	33.3	2	18.2	—		1	9.1	—		1	9.1	6	66.7	7	63.6
Rubber products	28	100	36	100	24	85.7	25	69.4	2	7.1	4	11.1	—		1	2.8	2	7.1	6	16.7
Plastic products	—		215	100	—		156	72.6	—		30	14.0	—		15	7.0	—		14	6.5
Non-metallic products	47	100	100	100	35	74.5	58	58.0	6	12.8	19	19.0	3	6.4	8	8.0	3	6.4	15	15.0
Basic metal	25	100	33	100	21	84.0	16	48.5	2	8.0	3	9.1	1	4.0	4	12.1	1	4.0	10	30.3
Fabricated metal products	138	100	426	100	113	81.9	302	70.9	7	5.1	43	10.1	7	5.1	25	5.9	11	8.0	56	13.1
Machinery	104	100	341	100	90	86.5	211	61.9	6	5.8	28	8.2	1	1.0	32	9.4	7	6.7	70	20.5
Electrical/Electronics products	41	100	315	100	19	46.3	94	29.8	5	12.2	36	11.4	10	24.4	37	11.7	7	17.1	148	47.0
Transport equipment	98	100	291	100	84	85.7	221	75.9	5	5.1	27	9.3	3	3.1	12	4.1	6	6.1	31	10.7
Instrumentation equipment	36	100	46	100	6	16.7	9	19.6	7	19.4	7	15.2	10	27.8	3	6.5	13	36.1	27	58.7
Other manufacturing	147	100	144	100	111	75.5	99	68.8	14	9.5	22	15.3	13	8.8	10	6.9	9	6.1	13	9.0
All industry groups*	1,586	100	3,616	100	1,276	80.5	2,429	67.2	124	7.8	426	11.8	90	5.7	242	6.7	96	6.1	519	14.4

Source: See Table 5.5.

* Excludes rubber processing and granite quarrying.

TABLE 5.7

Number of Establishments by Firm Size and Unionization in the
Manufacturing Sector, 1985

Firm Size (Number of Workers)	Number of Establishments		Number of Unionized Establishments	
	Number	Percentage	Number	Percentage
10–49	2,611	73.2	75	2.9
50–99	442	12.4	81	18.3
100 & above	513	14.4	261	50.9
Total	3,566	100.0	417	11.7

Source: An unpublished document, National Trades Union Congress, Singapore, 1985.
Note: Data on tiny establishments are not available.

TABLE 5.8

Number of Establishments By Firm Size and Unionization
in Selected Industries, 1985

Industry Groups	Firm Size (Number of Workers)	Number of Establishments		Number of Unionized Establishments	
		Number	Percentage	Number	Percentage
Food Manu-facturing	10–49	230	83.3	16	7.0
	50–99	23	8.3	8	34.8
	100 & above	23	8.3	15	65.2
	Total	276	100.0	39	14.1
Textiles, apparel, & footwear	10–49	294	73.7	1	0.3
	50–99	40	10.0	1	2.5
	100 & above	65	16.3	21	32.3
	Total	399	100.0	23	5.8
Sawn-timber & wood products except furniture	10–49	107	78.7	—	0
	50–99	17	12.5	4	23.5
	100 & above	12	8.8	7	58.3
	Total	136	100.0	11	8.1
Furniture and fixtures except primarily of metal	10–49	94	75.2	—	0
	50–99	19	15.2	3	15.8
	100 & above	12	9.6	5	41.7
	Total	125	100.0	8	6.4

(continued)

TABLE 5.8 (continued)

Industry Groups	Firm Size (Number of Workers)	Number of Establishments		Number of Unionized Establishments	
		Number	Percentage	Number	Percentage
Printing and publishing	10–49	265	86.3	3	1.1
	50–99	24	7.8	2	8.3
	100 & above	18	5.9	10	55.6
	Total	307	100.0	15	4.9
Plastic products	10–49	166	76.9	3	1.8
	50–99	30	13.9	5	16.7
	100 & above	20	9.3	7	35.0
	Total	216	100.0	15	6.9
Fabricated metal products	10–49	306	77.1	4	1.3
	50–99	48	12.1	10	20.8
	100 & above	43	10.8	23	53.5
	Total	397	100.0	37	9.3
Machinery except electrical and electronic	10–49	268	79.8	6	2.2
	50–99	28	8.3	3	10.7
	100 & above	40	11.9	26	65.0
	Total	336	100.0	35	10.4
Electrical machinery, apparatus and appliances	10–49	61	53.5	5	8.2
	50–99	22	19.3	2	9.1
	100 & above	31	27.2	22	71.0
	Total	114	100.0	29	25.4
Electronic products and components	10–49	53	28.8	1	1.9
	50–99	37	20.1	4	10.8
	100 & above	94	51.1	44	46.8
	Total	184	100.0	49	26.6
Transport equipment	10–49	212	73.1	3	1.4
	50–99	34	11.7	8	23.5
	100 & above	44	15.2	21	47.7
	Total	290	100.0	32	11.0
Other manufacturing	10–49	122	81.9	4	3.3
	50–99	9	6.0	1	11.1
	100 & above	18	12.1	6	33.3
	Total	149	100.0	11	7.4

Source: See Table 5.7.
Notes: See Table 5.7.

TABLE 5.9
Various Indicators of Firms by Number of Workers, 1983

Number of Workers	Value-added per Worker	Output per Worker	Value-added per Labour Cost	Ratio of Work Given Out to Output	Direct Export / Total Sales
10–19	22,541	67,127	2.33	8.5	17.8
20–29	25,000	72,968	2.33	7.8	24.2
30–39	25,478	88,046	2.21	4.0	24.9
40–49	30,008	119,984	2.24	5.4	52.5
50–69	31,020	88,281	2.29	4.6	31.8
70–99	37,266	115,032	2.21	5.0	41.2
100–149	32,763	105,742	2.58	2.0	43.2
150–199	44,301	114,189	3.08	2.2	63.4
200–299	34,820	88,661	2.48	5.4	52.8
300–499	47,752	325,980	3.52	0.1	61.9
500 and over	39,905	156,054	2.89	1.8	75.6
Total	36,230	137,295	2.71	2.7	60.5

Source: Singapore, Department of Statistics, *Report on the Census of Industrial Production*, 1983.
Note: Excludes rubber processing and granite quarrying.

6

REGRESSION ANALYSES OF THE CONCENTRATION OF SMALL FIRMS BY INDUSTRY

An analysis of the concentration of small firms across industries will shed light on why small firms flourish in certain industries and not others. Although the theoretical framework in Chapter 3 accounts for the existence of small firms, it does not explicitly explain the number of small firms in a given circumstance.

The theoretical discussion in Chapter 3 suggests that small firms are more labour intensive. Chapters 5 and 6 discuss the hypothesis that small firms are not only more labour intensive but also less export oriented. An industry which has a higher concentration of small firms will thus be more labour intensive and less export oriented than the average industry. It is therefore not enough to use labour intensity and export orientation to explain concentration of small firms across industries as they amount to the same thing. We must try to analyse the variation of concentration of small firms across industries based on explicit theoretical ground.

The Demand for Subcontracting Small Firms: Some Observations

As has been discussed in Chapter 3, small firms face output, capital, and entrepreneurial constraints. But capital and entrepreneurial constraints in themselves cannot be important factors in explaining variations in the concentration of small firms across industries as they are not industry-specific variables. An output constraint, on the other hand, is an important factor as it is an industry-specific variable. The reason is that an output constraint is, to a large extent, related to the degree of competition in an industry. If an industry is highly competitive, then one will expect that it is relatively easy for new firms to enter that industry. With the market to be shared by more firms, an output constraint is more likely to be operative. Thus, if an industry is highly competitive there will be more small firms operating in that industry.

Moreover, when the demand for a firm's output is uncertain, the firm will find it advantageous to subcontract any excessive order rather than to expand the existing production resources to cope with the excessive order. This is especially true when an increase in demand is perceived to be temporary.

Thus, firms which are not prepared to commit themselves to excessive investment in capital and labour inputs tend to subcontract to small firms. There is consequently a persistent demand for the services and products of small firms in an industry which faces cyclical changes or unpredictable changes in product demand. Output fluctuations therefore can be an important factor accounting for the variation of concentration of small firms across industries.

Minato found that the Japanese industry has a greater number of small firms than the American industry.[1] In 1981, there were 713,000 firms in the Japanese manufacturing sector with 10,568,000 workers, producing US$275 billion worth of value-added. In comparison, he noted that the number of manufacturing firms in the US was 352,000, employing 21,917,000 workers, and producing US$581 billion worth of value-added.

As the above figures clearly indicate, the Japanese manufacturing sector and their work-force are half those of the US while the number of companies is double. This implies that proportionately there are more small firms in the Japanese manufacturing sector than the American manufacturing sector. In fact, Minato found that the average number of employees per firm is 15 in Japan and 60 in the US.

Why are there so many more small firms in Japan than in the US? Minato attributed it to the Japanese subcontracting system but he did not explain why the subcontracting system is popular in Japan and not in the US. Although cultural factors are important, there must be economic reasons that make the subcontracting system popular in Japan.

In Japan, big firms pride themselves in providing lifetime employment for their employees. Once a worker is recruited by a firm, the stability of his job is ensured. This implies that workers are a fixed factor of production to the big Japanese companies. They will therefore be very cautious in expanding their work-force. If the demand for the product fluctuates, they will have to find ways to keep their employees on the payroll. Thus, if the demand for the product is uncertain, the big Japanese firms will find it advantageous not to expand the work-force and production facilities but to subcontract to smaller firms. Consequently, the demand for subcontracting is very strong in Japan.

The employment situation is quite different in the US. There is no lifetime employment in the US. American firms lay off workers when they are short of work. Thus, workers in the US can be considered as a variable factor of production. American firms are more likely to expand the work-force than their Japanese counterparts when the demand for the product rises.

Another important factor accounting for the relatively larger proportion of small firms in Japan than in the US lies in the variation in the demand for the products faced by firms in the two countries. Most American firms cater to domestic demand, which is more predictable, whereas Japanese firms sell more to the international market, which is more unpredictable.

Thus, two factors, namely, output fluctuation and the lifetime employment system, could substantially account for the proportionately larger number of small firms in Japan than in the US.

A survey on the demand for subcontracting in Singapore was carried out in December 1985. In total, 52 large firms (with 100 and more workers) were approached. Table 6.1 shows the industry coverage of the 52 firms surveyed. As Table 6.2 shows, 18 out of the 52 firms indicated that they subcontracted to small firms to produce finished goods, while 47 of the firms subcontracted to small firms to produce unfinished goods.

On the kind of assistance given to subcontracting firms, technical guidance is very common (36 firms acknowledged), followed by management guidance (28 firms), and the supply of raw material (15 firms) (see Table 6.3). The large firms surveyed reported that they experienced a few problems with the subcontracting firms (see Table 6.4). The most common problem is the quality of the products produced by subcontracting firms (32 firms acknowledged), followed by the delivery of the products (28 firms). Twenty firms indicated that there is a shortage of subcontracting firms in Singapore.

Table 6.5 shows that 36 large firms subcontracted to small firms due to full capacity. As many as 32 firms indicated that they subcontracted because they did not want to expand their work-force unnecessarily to avoid retrenchment during periods of recession. As Table 6.6 shows, 28 firms indicated that their demand for subcontracting was stable while 16 firms reported that their demand for subcontracting was not stable.

The results of the survey imply that if large firms need to rely on small firms for subcontracting, they will have to create a consistent demand for the goods and services of small firms. If the demand is not stable, small firms will not flourish. Two conclusions can be noted: firstly, small firms are useful to large firms for subcontracting; secondly, it is in the interest of large firms to keep subcontracting firms in business by giving them regular orders, especially during periods of recession.

An Inter-industry Regression Analysis of the Concentration of Small Firms

The discussion in the above section implies that if large firms consistently use small firms as a buffer to cushion the effects of the cyclical changes in demand for output, there will be a persistent demand for the services of small firms. Consequently, small firms will tend to flourish in those industries whose output demand is cyclical in nature. However, if output fluctuations are too extreme, small firms will suffer more than large firms.

Thus, an industry will have proportionately more small firms if the demand for the industry's output is unstable. However, if the demand for the industry's output is extremely unstable, then this industry will have proportionately fewer small firms. The extent to which the demand for an industry's output is considered unstable or extremely unstable is an empirical question which we shall deal with in this section.

Apart from subcontracting from large firms, small firms do compete with large firms in the finished product market. If small firms account for more than, say, 85 per cent of the total number of establishments in an industry, many small firms must compete with large firms in the product market of this industry. In this case, one would expect that output fluctuations will hurt small firms (as well as large firms).

In the regression analysis it is therefore necessary to measure the degree of output fluctuation at the industrial level. The instability or variation in the demand for the industry's output can be measured by the following method:[2]

$$I = \sum_{t=1}^{n} \left(\left| G_t - G_{t-1} \right| \right)^J \tag{6.1}$$

where I = output fluctuation index

G_t = growth rate of output in the tth period

n = the n periods under consideration

$| |$ = absolute value of $G_t - G_{t-1}$

J = 2 if G_t and G_{t-1} have opposite signs

and J = 1 if G_t and G_{t-1} have the same signs

A good way to measure output fluctuations must take both the magnitude and direction of change in output into account. This is what the I index measures. The I index does not simply add up to the difference in the growth rates of two consecutive periods. It gives more weight when there is a change in the sign of the growth rate of output by squaring the absolute difference between G_t and G_{t-1}.

Besides output fluctuations, another important factor affecting the concentration of small firms across industries is the degree of competition at the industrial level. The degree of competition is positively related to the degree of ease of entry. If there are substantial barriers to entry into an industry, the degree of competition in that industry will not be high. According to the economic theory of the firm, the degree of competition and degree of ease of entry will affect the rate of return on capital. If an industry is more competitive than the average industry, its rate of return on capital ought to be lower than the average rate of return on capital in the economy. In other words, a competitive industry will have a lower rate of return on capital while a monopolized industry will enjoy a higher rate of return on capital. It also implies that if the rate of return on capital is high in an industry, there will be relatively few small firms in that industry due to the small degree of competition and substantial barriers to entry, and vice versa.

We propose to examine empirically the concentration of small firms across industries using the following equation:[3]

$$P_{si} = a_0 + a_1 R_i + a_2 I_i \qquad (6.2)$$

where P_{si} = percentage of small firms in the ith industry

R_i = rate of return on capital in the ith industry, defined as

$$\frac{\text{value-added} - \text{wage bill}}{\text{capital assets}}$$

I_i = output fluctuation index in the ith industry

and a_i's are the respective coefficients

When there is a substantial degree of output fluctuation, a_2 is expected to be positive, implying that the larger the output fluctuation the higher the percentage of small firms. But where output fluctuations are extremely unstable, small firms as subcontractors will suffer more than large firms, implying that a_2 should be negative.

In an industry where small firms account for some 85 per cent or more of the total number of firms, many small firms directly compete with large firms in the finished product market. Thus, output fluctuations will hurt small firms directly, implying that a_2 should also be negative.

In our study, small firms consist of tiny establishments (5–9 workers), small establishments (10–49 workers), and medium establishments (50–99 workers). Data on tiny establishments are not available annually and therefore are not included in the regression analysis. Furthermore, for certain industries, data on small firms are not available in the late 1960s. For consistency, the inter-industry regression analysis in this section and the time series one in the next section are carried out for the period 1970–84.

The percentage of small establishments in the total number of establishments (P_{s1}), that of medium establishments (P_{s2}), the rate of return on capital (R), and the rate of growth of industry's output (G) for each industry from 1970–84 are plotted in Figure 6.1. Generally, one can see that P_{s1} and P_{s2} are rather stable within each industry, indicating that the percentage of small and medium establishments combined ($P_{s1} + P_{s2}$, not shown in Figure 6.1) is also stable. Of course, they are substantial differences between P_{s1}, P_{s2}, and $P_{s1} + P_{s2}$ across industries as well as within each industry. By comparison, R and G fluctuated more than P_{s1}, P_{s2}, and $P_{s1} + P_{s2}$. This is to be expected as R and G are the rates of change while P_{s1}, P_{s2}, and $P_{s1} + P_{s2}$ are the levels.

Two interesting features should be noted here. Firstly, P_{s1} lies above R for the food, textiles, wood and cork, and rubber products industries, while R lies above P_{s1} in the beverage, tobacco products, chemicals and chemical products, petroleum and petroleum products, and non-metallic mineral products industries. For the remaining industries, P_{s1} and R overlap many times during the period under consideration. Secondly, P_{s2} is consistently below R for all industries. This shows that one has to consider P_{s1} and P_{s2} separately in the regression analysis of concentration of small firms across industries as well as within each industry.

The average value of P_{s1} $(\overline{P_{s1}})$, that of P_{s2} $(\overline{P_{s2}})$, that of $P_{s1} + P_{s2}$ $(\overline{P_{s1} + P_{s2}})$, that of R $(\overline{R})$, and the output fluctuation index for 1970–84 (I) are given in Table 6.7. The ranking of industries in terms of $\overline{P_{s1}}$, $\overline{P_{s2}}$, $\overline{P_{s1} + P_{s2}}$, $\overline{R}$ and I are also presented in the table. In terms of $\overline{P_{s1}}$, the printing and publishing industry ranks first with 86 per cent, followed by the leather products industry with 83 per cent. On the basis of $\overline{P_{s2}}$, the non-metallic products industry ranks first with 24 per cent, followed by the paper and paper products industry with 21 per cent. In terms of $\overline{P_{s1} + P_{s2}}$, the leather and leather products industry ranks first with 96 per cent, followed by the printing and publishing industry (94 per cent), rubber products industry (91 per cent), food industry (91 per cent) and furniture and fixtures industry (90 per cent).

The earlier discussion in the above section implies that $\overline{P_{s1} + P_{s2}}$ should be related to $\overline{R}$. The respective rankings of $\overline{R}$ of the leather and leather products, printing and publishing, rubber products, food, furniture and fixtures industries are sixth, fifth, fourteenth, fifteenth and eleventh. The results do not exactly support the hypothesis of a negative relationship between the ranking of $\overline{P_{s1} + P_{s2}}$ and that of $\overline{R}$.

Besides $\overline{R}$, I may be relevant in explaining $\overline{P_{s1} + P_{s2}}$. The respective rankings of I of the leather and leather products, printing and publishing, rubber, food, and furniture and fixtures industries are eighth, sixteenth, nineteenth, tenth, and twelfth. Again, the results do not indicate a positive relationship between the ranking of $\overline{P_{s1} + P_{s2}}$ and that of I.

A systematic way of examining the relationship involving $\overline{R}$ and I can be done by regression analysis. We thus estimated the following equations across industries based on the statistics in Table 6.7.

$$\overline{P_{s1i}} = \underset{(8.82)}{86.91} - \underset{(1.17)}{10.92}\ \overline{R}_i - \underset{(2.54)^*}{4.79}\ I_i \tag{6.3}$$

$$R^2 = 0.34$$
$$D.W. = 1.95$$
$$d = -0.13$$
$$(0.58)$$

$$\overline{P_{s2i}} = \underset{(4.97)}{13.52} - \underset{(0.93)}{2.55}\ \overline{R}_i - \underset{(0.46)}{0.23}\ I_i \tag{6.4}$$

$$R^2 = 0.16$$
$$D.W. = 1.94$$

$$\overline{P_{s1i} + P_{s2i}} = \underset{(11.96)}{101.42} - \underset{(1.03)}{8.19}\ \overline{R}_i - \underset{(3.41)^*}{5.51}\ I_i \tag{6.5}$$

$$R^2 = 0.47$$
$$D.W. = 1.98$$

where i = 1, 2, ... 20 industries
    $D.W.$ = Durbin Watson statistics
    d = Auto-correlation coefficients
    *   indicates that the coefficient is significant at 95 per cent level of significance
    and   values in brackets indicate t statistics.

The three regressions perform reasonably well in terms of R^2 and $D.W.$ statistics. $\overline{R}$ is consistently insignificant in the three regressions. With respect to I, it is significant and negative in equations (6.3) and (6.5), implying that output fluctuations have hurt rather than benefited small establishments and, therefore, small firms. This shows that small firms were dominated by small establishments and not by medium establishments.

Equations (6.3), (6.4) and (6.5) indicate that the percentage of small firms is dependent upon $\overline{R}$ and I across industries. For instance, an industry with a high value of $\overline{R}$ will imply substantial barriers to entry and consequently few new small firms will enter this industry. Thus, it indicates that a high value of $\overline{R}$ will be associated with minimum changes in the number of small firms. We should therefore examine the changes in the number of small firms yearly in the inter-industry regression analysis.

Hence, another three equations with the average values of yearly differentials in $\overline{P_{s1}}$, $\overline{P_{s2}}$ and $\overline{P_{s1} + P_{s2}}$ as dependent variables are estimated:

$$\overline{P_{ds1i}} = \underset{(3.79)^*}{1.74} - \underset{(1.68)^*}{0.76 \ \overline{R_i}} - \underset{(3.69)^*}{0.32 \ I_i} \tag{6.6}$$

$$R^2 = 0.47$$
$$D.W. = 1.99$$

$$\overline{P_{ds2i}} = \underset{(0.08)}{-0.03} - \underset{(2.43)^*}{0.93 \ \overline{R_i}} - \underset{(1.81)^*}{0.12 \ I_i} \tag{6.7}$$

$$R^2 = 0.38$$
$$D.W. = 2.18$$

$$\overline{P_{ds1i} + P_{ds2i}} = \underset{(16.24)^*}{7.64} - \underset{(3.85)^*}{1.66 \ \overline{R_i}} - \underset{(3.44)^*}{0.31 \ I_i} \tag{6.8}$$

$$R^2 = 0.64$$
$$D.W. = 1.95$$

Where $\overline{P_{ds1}} = \dfrac{\sum\limits_{t=1}^{n} (\overline{P_{s1_t} - P_{s1_{t-1}}})}{n - 1}$, same for $\overline{P_{ds2}}$ and $\overline{P_{ds1} + P_{ds2}}$.

Equations (6.6), (6.7) and (6.8) perform much better than equations (6.3), (6.4) and (6.5) in terms of R^2. R is now consistently significant and negative in the three equations implying that when $\bar{R}$ is high, fewer new small firms are attracted into the industries, and vice versa.

With respect to I, it is found to be negative and significant in equations (6.6) to (6.8), implying that output fluctuations did not benefit small establishments, medium establishments and, therefore, small firms. The greater the degree of output fluctuation, the smaller the differentials in the number of small establishments, medium establishments and, therefore, small firms.

The inter-industry study indicates that both rate of return and output fluctuations are important determinants of concentration of small firms across industries. The rate of return has a significant and negative relationship with the average annual changes in the number of small establishments ($\overline{P_{ds1}}$), medium establishments ($\overline{P_{ds2}}$), and small firms ($P_{ds1} + P_{ds2}$). Output fluctuations also have a negative and significant relationship with the average annual changes in the number of small establishments, medium establishments, and small firms.

A Time Series Regression Analysis of the Concentration of Small Firms by Industry

As industries are quite heterogeneous in terms of market structure and production technology, a time series regression analysis of small firms for each industry is conducted to complement the inter-industry regression analysis of small firms. The same equation is therefore estimated but with some modifications for each industry for the period 1970–84:

$$P_t = a_0 + a_1 R_t + a_2 I_t \qquad (6.9)$$

where P_t = percentage of small firms in the total number of establishments in an industry in the tth period

R_t = rate of return on capital in the tth period

I_t = output fluctuation index in the tth period[4]

$$= (|G_t - G_{t-1}|)^J + (|G_{t-1} - G_{t-2}|)^J + (|G_{t-2} - G_{t-3}|)^J$$

and a_i's are the respective coefficients.

It is possible that P_t may respond to I with a time-lag. Thus, equation (6.9) is also estimated with I_{t-1} instead of I_t. The final regressions, which are selected on the basis of R^2 and $D.W.$ statistics, are reported in Table 6.8. The coefficients of the explanatory variables, R_i and I_i, are assessed at 95 per cent level of significance.

The Food Industry

The food industry is heavily dominated by small establishments (80 per cent). Medium establishments account for 11 per cent. Thus, in total, 91 per cent of the firms are small firms. Table 6.8 shows that R is consistently not a significant variable in all the three equations. I, however, is only significant with a negative coefficient in the $P_{s1} + P_{s2}$ equation. The negative coefficient implies that output fluctuations have caused small firms to decline. The degree of output fluctuations cannot be considered to be extremely unstable as the industry only ranks tenth in terms of the output fluctuations index (Table 6.7). It is therefore argued that, as more than 90 per cent of the firms in this industry are small firms, output fluctuations have affected small firms directly as small firms compete with large firms in the finished product market. Consequently $P_{s1} + P_{s2}$ declined as I increased, and vice versa. It can therefore be interpreted that output fluctuations have hurt small firms.

The Beverage Industry

Small establishments account for 49 per cent and medium establishments for 18 per cent of the total number of establishments in this industry. It ranks only eighteenth in terms of $P_{s1} + P_{s2}$ across industries as shown in Table 6.7.

Table 6.8 shows that both R and I are not significant in the three equations. The regression results indicate that the concentration of small firms in this industry cannot be explained by R and I.

The Cigarettes and Other Tobacco Products Industry

The cigarettes and other tobacco products industry ranks sixteenth in terms of $P_{s1} + P_{s2}$ across industries. Small establishments account for 50 per cent and medium establishments for 18 per cent of the total number of establishments in this industry.

R is not found to be a significant factor in the three equations. $I(-1)$, however, is found to be highly significant with a positive sign in the $P_{s1} + P_{s2}$ equation. Output fluctuations are therefore positively related to the percentage of small firms in this industry. The result implies that small firms have benefited from output fluctuations.

The Textile and Textile Manufactures Industry

Contrary to common belief, the textile industry only ranks seventeenth in terms of $P_{s1} + P_{s2}$ across industries. In this industry, 52 per cent of firms are small establishments and 15 per cent are medium establishments.

R is again not found to be significant in all the three equations. I, however, is significant with a negative sign in the P_{s2} equation. It implies that output fluctuations have hurt the medium establishments. It is difficult to explain the negative relationship between I and P_{s2} as output fluctuation cannot be considered very extreme in this industry (ranking thirteenth in terms of $P_{s1} + P_{s2}$ across industries). We cannot understand why medium establishments are not able to use small establishments as a buffer against output fluctuations.

The Apparel and Footwear Industry

In this industry, 75 per cent of firms are small establishments and 11 per cent medium establishments, making a total of 86 per cent of small firms here.

I is not found to be significant in the three equations. R is almost a significant variable with a negative coefficient in the $P_{s1} + P_{s2}$ equation, implying that the higher the rate of return on capital, the smaller the percentage of small firms, and vice versa.

The Wood and Cork Industry

Small establishments account for 76 per cent and medium establishments for 14 per cent of the total number of establishments in this industry. The industry ranks ninth in terms of $P_{s1} + P_{s2}$ across industries.

R is not significant here. $I(-1)$ is only significant with a positive coefficient in the P_{s1} equation. It implies that the greater the degree of output fluctuations, the higher the percentage of small establishments. Small establishments have thus benefited from output fluctuations.

The Furniture and Fixtures Industry

This industry ranks fifth in terms of $P_{s1} + P_{s2}$ across industries. Small establishments account for 79 per cent and medium establishments for 12 per cent of the total number of establishments here.

R is not significant. $I(-1)$ is significant with a negative coefficient in the $P_{s1} + P_{s2}$ equation. The negative coefficient implies that output fluctuations have hurt small firms, which is not surprising as small firms account for 91 per cent of the total number of establishments in the furniture and fixtures industry.

The Paper and Paper Products Industry

Small establishments account for 68 per cent and medium establishments for 21 per cent of the total number of establishments in this industry. This industry has the second largest number of medium establishments in the manufacturing sector.

R is not significant. $I(-1)$ is significant with a negative coefficient in the P_{s2} equation. The negative coefficient of $I(-1)$ implies that output fluctuations have hurt medium establishments directly. We again cannot understand why medium establishments are not able to use small establishments as a buffer against unstable demand.

The Printing and Publishing Industry

This industry has the largest percentage of small establishments (86 per cent), although medium establishments account for only 8 per cent of the total number of establishments.

R is significant in all three equations. It has a positive coefficient in the P_{s1} equation and negative coefficients in the P_{s2} and $P_{s1} + P_{s2}$ equations. It remains a puzzle as to why the rate of return on capital is not negatively related to the percentage of small establishments in this industry, which has 86 per cent of its establishments in small establishments.

I is also significant in all three equations. The coefficient of I is positive in the P_{s1} equation but negative in the P_{s2} and $P_{s1} + P_{s2}$ equations. The results show that small establishments have benefited from output fluctuations but output fluctuations have hurt medium establishments.

The Leather and Leather Products Industry

This industry has the largest percentage of small firms (97 per cent) in the manufacturing sector. Small establishments account for 84 per cent and medium establishments for 13 per cent of the total number of establishments.

R is not significant. The coefficient of I is positive and almost significant in the P_{s1} equation, implying that small establishments have benefited from output fluctuations.

The Rubber and Rubber Products Industry

Small establishments account for 76 per cent and medium establishments for 16 per cent of the total number of establishments in this industry which ranks third in terms of $P_{s1} + P_{s2}$ across industries.

R is significant with a negative coefficient in the $P_{s1} + P_{s2}$ equation. It implies that the higher the rate of return, the lower the percentage of small firms.

$I(-1)$ is significant in the three equations. Its coefficient is positive in the P_{s1} equation and negative in the P_{s2} and $P_{s1} + P_{s2}$ equations. The regression results imply that output fluctuations have benefited small establishments but hurt medium establishments and small firms.

The Chemicals and Chemical Products Industry

This industry ranks eighth in terms of $P_{s1} + P_{s2}$ across industries. Small establishments comprise 72 per cent of the firms while 18 per cent are medium establishments.

R is not significant. $I(-1)$ is significant with a negative coefficient in the P_{s2} equation. Output fluctuations have hurt medium establishments.

The Petroleum and Petroleum Products Industry

This industry, as expected, has the smallest percentage of small firms (40 per cent). It ranks twentieth in terms of P_{s1} and fourteenth in terms of P_{s2}.

R and I are not significant. It should be noted that the coefficient of I in the P_{s1} is negative and almost significant. Since this industry ranks first in terms of the output fluctuation index, output fluctuations have hurt small establishments, as implied by the negative coefficient.

The Non-metallic Mineral Products Industry

Small firms account for 85 per cent of the total number of establishments in this industry, implying that many small firms must compete with large firms in the product market. It ranks fifteenth in terms of P_{s1} and first in terms of P_{s2}.

R is not significant. I is significant with a negative coefficient in the $P_{s1} + P_{s2}$ equation. The results imply that output fluctuations have affected small firms directly in the sense that the percentage of small firms increases as output fluctuation becomes smaller. Output fluctuations have therefore hurt small firms.

The Basic Metal Industry

Small establishments account for 66 per cent and medium establishments for 17 per cent of the total number of establishments in this industry. It ranks fourteenth in terms of $P_{s1} + P_{s2}$.

R and I are not significant in the three equations.

The Fabricated Metal Products Industry

It ranks sixth in terms of $P_{s1} + P_{s2}$ across industries. Small establishments account for 75 per cent and medium establishments for 15 per cent of the total number of establishments here.

R is significant with a positive coefficient in the P_{s2} equation. It is difficult to explain the positive coefficient except to take note that R^2 of this equation is low compared to those of the other two equations.

I has a significant and negative coefficient in the P_{s1} and $P_{s1} + P_{s2}$ equations. The results imply that output fluctuations have hurt small establishments and, therefore, small firms which dominate this industry.

The Machinery (Except Electrical and Electronics) Industry

Small establishments account for 79 per cent and medium establishments for 11 per cent of the total number of establishments in this industry. It ranks seventh in terms of $P_{s1} + P_{s2}$ across industries.

R is not significant. I is significant with a positive coefficient in the P_{s2} equation. It implies that output fluctuations have benefited medium establishments in this industry.

The Electrical Machinery, Apparatus, Appliances and Supplies Industry

This industry ranks nineteenth in terms of $P_{s1} + P_{s2}$ across industries. About 40 per cent of the firms are small establishments and 17 per cent are medium establishments.

R is not significant. I is significant with a negative coefficient in the $P_{s1} + P_{s2}$ equations. Output fluctuations in this industry have been greater as it ranks third in terms of the output fluctuation index. It can therefore be concluded that extreme output fluctuations have hurt small firms in this industry.

The Transport Equipment Industry

Small establishments account for 65 per cent and medium establishments for 14 per cent of the total number of establishments in this industry. It ranks fifteenth in terms of $P_{s1} + P_{s2}$ across industries.

R is not significant. $I(-1)$ is significant with a negative coefficient in the P_{s1} equation and a positive coefficient in the P_{s2} equation. The results indicate that output fluctuations have hurt small establishments and benefited medium establishments. This industry ranks ninth in terms of the output fluctuation index. Thus, the output fluctuations in this industry have been quite great. Medium establishments, which may subcontract to small establishments, therefore can benefit from output fluctuations, but not the small establishments, which have no buffer to rely on.

The Other Manufacturing Industries

This industry ranks eleventh in terms of $P_{s1} + P_{s2}$ across industries. Small establishments and medium establishments account for 74 per cent and 15 per cent respectively of the total number of establishments in the industry.

$I(-1)$ is not significant. R has a significant and negative coefficient in both the P_{s2} and $P_{s1} + P_{s2}$ equations. The results imply that the higher the rate of return, the lower the percentage of medium establishments and, therefore, small firms, and vice versa.

We have estimated a total of 30 equations. Among the 30 equations, R is significant in 7 equations and I is significant in 19 equations. Considering that the hypotheses concerning R and I are tested at the two-digit level of industrial classification, the results have been quite satisfactory. Generally, output fluctuations have been an important factor in determining the percentage of small firms at the industrial level.

There remains a puzzle as to why medium establishments cannot benefit from output fluctuations in six industries which have negative and significant coefficients of I in the respective P_{s2} equations. Why are medium establishments not able to use small establishments as a buffer against unstable demand by means of subcontracting? One possible explanation could be that small establishments in these six industries do not want to accept subcontracting from medium establishments as the latter's demand for the former's services may be highly unreliable.

Conclusion

In this chapter we argue that small firms flourish because of output fluctuations and also low entry barriers. Output fluctuations are measured by I and entry barriers are represented by the rate of return on capital (R). Thus, we expect the percentage of small establishments (P_{s1}), of medium establishments (P_{s2}), and of small firms ($P_{s1} + P_{s2}$) in a given industry to be positively related to I and negatively related to R.

However, it is argued that if output fluctuations are very extreme, they eventually will hurt small firms. This implies that P_s is negatively related to I under extreme output fluctuations. P_s can also be negatively related to I in those industries where small firms account for more than some 85 per cent of the total number of establishments, implying that output fluctuations have directly affected small firms as many small firms compete with large firms in the finished product market.

The inter-industry regression analysis shows that both the rate of return and output fluctuations are important determinants of the concentration of small firms across industries.

Generally, the time series regression analysis of small firms by industries shows that output fluctuations have been an important factor in the determination of small firms across industries. The rate of return on capital (R), has not been found to be a significant factor in the small firms equations.

The main reason why there is no overwhelming evidence in support of our hypotheses concerning output fluctuations and the rate of return on capital is that the two-digit level of classifying industries is too aggregative for the analysis. For instance, products under the food industry can vary greatly, ranging from ice-cream through jam to bread. Firms in the food industry may not compete in the same product market. Thus, ideally, one should estimate equation (6.9) at the five-digit level of industrial classification, using categories such as ice-cream, jam and bread. Only at this level of disaggregation can our hypotheses on output fluctuations and the rate of return on capital be fully examined. However, the necessary data at that level of disaggregation are not available for analysis.

Nevertheless, this chapter has provided some strong evidence that output fluctuation is an important determinant of concentration of small firms at the industrial level. The analyses show that small firms are determined, to a large extent, by the cyclical nature of the industries concerned. Furthermore, the studies also imply that, if we succeed in implementing a flexible wage system in Singapore, there will be, *ceteris paribus*, fewer small firms as wages will become more flexible than before.

1. Tetsuo Minato, 'The Japanese System of Subcontracting', *Sumitomo Corporation News*, Vol. 48, January 1985.

2. The more conventional method is the standard deviation of the growth rate of output (SD) and the mean (G). As indicated in note 3, this method is not empirically useful.

3. We also estimated the following equation:

$$P_{si} = a_0 + a_1 R_i + a_2 SD_i + a_3 G;$$

but the empirical results have been poor.

4. See equation (6.1) for the definition of J.

TABLE 6.1
Number of Large Firms Surveyed by Industry in 1985

Type of Industry	Number of Large Firms
Textiles	7
Apparel	3
Footwear	4
Wood & cork products	3
Furniture & fixtures	3
Paper & paper products	4
Plastic products	2
Glass & glass products	6
Industrial chemicals	5
Fabricated metal	4
Machinery	3
Electrical & electronic products	8
Total	52

Source: Data extrapolated from a survey conducted of 52 large firms in December 1985.

TABLE 6.2
Subcontracting to Small Firms in 1983

Response	Number of Large Firms that Acknowledged	
	Finished Products	Unfinished Products
Yes	18	47
No	34	5
Total	52	52

Source: See Table 6.1.

TABLE 6.3
Kind of Assistance Given to Subcontracting Small Firms in 1983

Assistance	Number of Large Firms that Acknowledged*
Supply of raw material	15
Technical guidance	36
Management guidance	28
Supply of equipment	10
Financial assistance	7

Source: See Table 6.1.
* Firms were instructed to choose no more than two responses.

TABLE 6.4
Difficulties in Dealing with Subcontracting Small Firms in 1983

Difficulties	Number of Large Firms that Acknowledged*
Delivery	28
Quality	32
Price	10
Shortage of subcontracting firms	20
Unstable management of subcontracting firms	8

Source: See Table 6.1.
* Firms were instructed to choose no more than two responses.

TABLE 6.5
Reasons for Subcontracting to Small Firms in 1983

Reasons	Number of Large Firms that Acknowledged*
Beyond capacity	36
Cost saving	15
Government guidance	10
Maintain stable work-force	32
Avoid excessive investment in plant and equipment	21

Source: See Table 6.1.
* Firms were instructed to choose no more than two responses.

TABLE 6.6
Regularity in Subcontracting Demand in 1983

Response	Number of Large Firms that Acknowledged
Regular	28
Not regular	16
No answer	8
	52

Source: See Table 6.1.

TABLE 6.7
Ranking of Small Firms by Industry, 1970–1984

Industry Group	$\overline{P}_{s1}$	Rank	$\overline{P}_{s2}$	Rank	$\overline{P}_{s1} + \overline{P}_{s2}$	Rank	$\overline{R}$	Rank	I	Rank
Food	80.5	3	10.9	18	91.4	4	0.6	15	1.9	10
Beverages	48.6	18	17.7	5	66.2	18	0.9	8	1.3	18
Cigarettes & other tobacco products	49.6	17	18.5	3	68.1	16	1.6	1	0.8	20
Textiles & textile manufactures	51.6	16	15.2	9	66.8	17	0.3	20	1.8	13
Apparel & footwear	74.7	9	10.8	19	85.4	12	0.7	10	2.2	7
Wood & cork products	75.6	7	13.8	12	89.4	9	0.5	19	3.2	4
Furniture & fixtures	78.6	5	12.1	16	90.7	5	0.7	11	1.8	12
Paper & paper products	67.8	12	21.1	2	88.9	10	0.6	13	1.4	17
Printing & publishing	86.0	1	8.1	20	94.2	2	0.9	5	1.6	16
Leather & leather products	83.7	2	12.8	15	96.5	1	0.9	6	2.0	8
Rubber & rubber products	76.0	6	15.8	8	91.8	3	0.6	14	1.1	19
Chemical & chemical products	71.7	11	17.9	4	89.6	8	1.0	3	3.0	5
Petroleum & petroleum products	26.8	20	12.8	14	39.6	20	0.5	18	8.6	1
Non-metallic products	61.2	15	24.2	1	85.4	13	0.8	9	1.8	11
Basic metals	65.5	13	16.6	7	82.1	14	0.9	7	2.5	6
Fabricated metals	75.3	8	14.8	10	90.1	6	0.7	12	1.6	15
Machinery	78.7	4	11.1	17	89.9	7	1.0	4	4.4	2
Electrical & electronic products	39.9	19	17.4	6	57.3	19	1.6	2	3.5	3
Transport equipment	65.0	14	13.6	13	78.6	15	0.6	17	1.9	9
Other manufacturing	74.2	10	14.6	11	88.8	11	0.6	16	1.7	14

Source: Singapore, Department of Statistics, *Report on the Census of Industrial Production,* various years.

Notes:

$\overline{P}_{s1}$ = annual average percentage of small establishments in the total number of establishment for each industry for 1970–84.

$\overline{P}_{s2}$ = annual average percentage of medium establishments in the total number of establishment for each industry for

$\overline{P}_{s1} + \overline{P}_{s2}$ = annual average percentage of small and medium establishments in the total number of establishment for each industry for 1970–84.

$\overline{R}$ = annual average of rate of return on capital for 1970–84 for each industry.

I = the output-fluctuation index calculated based on output growth for 1970–84.

TABLE 6.8

Time Series Regression Results by Industry, 1970–1984

$(P_s = a_0 + a_1R + a_2F$ where F is either I or $I(-1))$

Industry Group	P_s	a_0	a_1	a_2	R^2	D.W.	d
Food	P_{s1}	84.65	−6.25	−1.03	0.97	2.10	0.59
		(25.92)*	(1.22)	(0.31)			(2.83)
	P_{s2}	10.74	1.12	−2.23	0.13	2.22	0.30
		(4.09)*	(0.26)	(0.84)			(1.15)
	$P_{s1} + P_{s2}$	94.53	−3.64	−3.72	0.96	2.14	0.23
		(47.99)*	(1.13)	(1.89)*			(0.87)
Beverages	P_{s1}	64.46	−14.27	−17.67	0.31	0.63	
		(8.91)*	(1.50)	(0.52)			
	P_{s2}	10.72	6.92	4.28	0.23	1.47	
		(2.78)*	(1.36)	(0.23)			
	$P_{s1} + P_{s2}$	75.18	−7.35	−13.40	0.22	0.55	
		(14.58)*	(1.08)	(0.55)			
Cigarettes and other tobacco products	P_{s1}	33.08	6.53	58.41	0.23	2.22	0.53
		(2.56)*	(0.92)	(1.67)			(2.26)
	P_{s2}	25.19	−3.36	−20.56	0.10	2.14	0.58
		(1.40)	(0.35)	(0.42)			(2.43)
	$P_{s1} + P_{s2}$	55.06	5.23	40.64	0.63	1.48	0.36
		(7.38)*	(1.23)	(2.03)*			(1.14)
Textiles and textile manufactures	P_{s1}	58.76	−10.74	1.66	0.15	1.15	0.96
		(3.56)*	(0.82)	(0.52)			(18.57)
	P_{s2}	14.79	5.76	−3.70	0.20	1.86	0.28
		(4.27)*	(0.69)	(1.95)*			(1.07)
	$P_{s1} + P_{s2}$	74.45	−3.76	−2.87	−0.05	0.95	0.96
		(4.57)*	(0.31)	(0.97)			(20.71)
Apparel and footwear	P_{s1}	79.11	−5.38	−1.47	0.20	1.36	
		(29.60)*	(1.48)	(0.46)			
	P_{s2}	9.95	0.16	2.31	0.12	1.68	
		(6.14)*	(0.07)	(1.19)			
	$P_{s1} + P_{s2}$	89.07	−5.22	0.84	0.20	1.31	
		(40.45)*	(1.74)	(0.32)			
Wood and cork	P_{s1}	75.04	−1.01	2.27	0.29	1.52	
		(53.43)*	(0.43)	(2.09)*			
	P_{s2}	14.31	−0.07	−0.97	0.03	0.89	
		(6.95)*	(0.02)	(0.61)			
	$P_{s1} + P_{s2}$	89.34	−1.07	1.30	0.07	0.80	
		(43.76)*	(0.32)	(0.82)			

(continued)

TABLE 6.8 (*continued*)

Industry Group	P_s	a_0	a_1	a_2	R^2	D.W.	d
Furniture and fixtures	P_{s1}	73.66 (26.55)*	4.27 (0.93)	5.73 (1.14)	0.34	0.89	
	P_{s2}	18.17 (5.23)*	−3.72 (0.64)	−1.63 (1.68)	0.40	0.70	
	$P_{s1} + P_{s2}$	91.83 (68.37)*	0.55 (0.25)	−4.91 (2.01)*	0.33	1.14	
Paper and paper products	P_{s1}	68.75 (22.38)*	−3.70 (0.86)	8.29 (1.27)	0.93	1.96	0.65 (3.25)
	P_{s2}	22.54 (5.45)*	5.47 (1.08)	−22.23 (2.89)*	0.62	2.02	0.77 (4.57)
	$P_{s1} + P_{s2}$	88.12 (30.20)*	3.18 (0.69)	−5.26 (0.70)	0.87	1.84	0.26 (0.93)
Printing and publishing	P_{s1}	81.67 (55.47)*	3.90 (2.58)*	3.25 (1.86)*	0.46	1.48	
	P_{s2}	14.36 (9.33)*	−5.34 (3.38)*	−5.63 (3.08)*	0.64	1.59	
	$P_{s1} + P_{s2}$	96.03 (142.00)*	−1.44 (2.07)*	−2.38 (2.96)*	0.53	1.39	
Leather and leather products	P_{s1}	80.02 (16.07)*	2.15 (0.71)	7.85 (1.66)	0.80	2.01	0.81 (4.90)
	P_{s2}	12.42 (2.97)*	1.17 (0.30)	−2.18 (0.37)	0.22	1.86	0.52 (2.04)
	$P_{s1} + P_{s2}$	94.31 (62.66)*	1.67 (1.18)	2.72 (1.30)	0.97	1.45	0.53 (2.22)
Rubber and rubber products	P_{s1}	79.73 (14.92)*	−10.82 (1.21)	15.06 (2.41)*	0.86	1.65	0.50 (2.10)
	P_{s2}	21.25 (3.85)*	−3.17 (0.34)	−18.88 (2.84)*	0.50	1.78	0.28 (0.99)
	$P_{s1} + P_{s2}$	101.63 (35.58)*	−14.25 (2.98)*	−6.20 (1.85)*	0.79	1.86	−0.12 (0.41)
Chemicals and chemical products	P_{s1}	70.39 (16.46)*	−2.64 (0.85)	10.83 (1.64)	0.25	0.53	
	P_{s2}	17.58 (5.55)*	3.54 (1.54)	−8.90 (1.82)*	0.36	1.10	
	$P_{s1} + P_{s2}$	87.98 (50.00)*	0.91 (0.71)	1.93 (0.71)	0.07	0.81	
Petroleum and petroleum products	P_{s1}	23.71 (3.89)*	10.13 (0.95)	−1.52 (1.69)	0.50	1.69	0.53 (2.22)
	P_{s2}	11.32 (1.17)	2.83 (0.21)	1.70 (1.41)	0.15	2.02	0.78 (4.76)
	$P_{s1} + P_{s2}$	37.99 (5.92)*	10.51 (1.20)	−0.13 (0.17)	0.60	1.85	0.78 (4.65)

(*continued*)

TABLE 6.8 (continued)

Industry Group	P_s	a_0	a_1	a_2	R^2	D.W.	d
Non-metallic mineral products	P_{s1}	63.92 (11.29)*	−1.60 (0.27)	−7.27 (0.68)	0.62	1.58	0.46 (1.85)
	P_{s2}	24.13 (6.06)*	1.44 (0.34)	−3.83 (0.51)	0.46	1.80	0.46 (1.91)
	$P_{s1} + P_{s2}$	87.66 (28.07)*	0.09 (0.03)	−11.21 (2.20)*	0.95	1.21	0.68 (3.33)
Basic metal	P_{s1}	68.62 (13.47)*	−4.41 (0.82)	2.70 (0.36)	0.21	1.90	0.15 (0.53)
	P_{s2}	16.76 (2.35)*	2.63 (0.35)	−7.51 (0.72)	0.05	1.99	0.14 (0.50)
	$P_{s1} + P_{s2}$	85.33 (14.59)*	−1.28 (0.22)	−6.17 (0.76)	0.09	1.96	0.03 (0.12)
Fabricated metal products	P_{s1}	83.43 (12.46)*	−7.63 (0.84)	−14.96 (2.15)*	0.67	1.99	0.29 (1.00)
	P_{s2}	6.86 (2.25)*	10.80 (2.53)*	3.77 (1.29)	0.33	1.97	−0.16 (0.57)
	$P_{s1} + P_{s2}$	86.56 (16.92)*	9.87 (1.38)	−13.23 (2.77)*	0.94	1.74	−0.35 (1.23)
Machinery except electrical and electronics	P_{s1}	77.64 (25.46)*	2.06 (0.70)	−1.47 (1.03)	0.11	0.60	
	P_{s2}	11.31 (10.40)*	−0.99 (0.95)	1.28 (2.52)*	0.37	1.84	
	$P_{s1} + P_{s2}$	88.96 (27.40)*	1.07 (0.34)	−0.19 (0.12)	0.01	0.25	
Electrical machinery, apparatus, appliances and supplies	P_{s1}	42.10 (10.22)*	0.76 (0.25)	−5.74 (1.29)	0.16	0.56	
	P_{s2}	17.89 (6.13)*	1.51 (0.71)	4.92 (1.68)	0.19	1.19	
	$P_{s1} + P_{s2}$	60.00 (11.66)*	2.28 (0.61)	−10.66 (2.07)*	0.28	0.83	
Transport equipment	P_{s1}	73.75 (8.98)*	−4.27 (0.37)	−19.06 (3.03)*	0.46	0.72	
	P_{s2}	9.82 (2.72)*	0.25 (0.05)	11.28 (4.08)*	0.62	1.10	
	$P_{s1} + P_{s2}$	83.57 (13.36)*	−4.02 (0.45)	−7.78 (1.62)	0.18	0.51	
Other manufacturing	P_{s1}	76.71 (31.35)*	−3.50 (1.05)	−1.72 (0.54)	0.09	1.18	
	P_{s2}	16.00 (12.06)*	−3.26 (1.80)*	2.38 (1.38)	0.40	1.37	
	$P_{s1} + P_{s2}$	92.70 (46.93)*	−6.76 (2.51)*	0.66 (0.26)	0.40	1.07	

Source: Singapore, Department of Statistics, *Report on the Census of Industrial Production*, various years.

Notes:

P_{s1}	=	Percentage of small establishments in the total number of establishments.
P_{s2}	=	Percentage of medium establishments in the total number of establishments.
$P_{s1} + P_{s2}$	=	Percentage of small firms in the total number of establishments.
R	=	Rate of return on capital.
I	=	Output fluctuation index.
R^2	=	Coefficient of determination.
$D.W.$	=	Durbin Watson statistics.
*	=	Indicates that the coefficient is significant at 10 per cent level of significance. Values is brackets represent t statistics for the respective coefficient.
d	=	Represents auto-correlation coefficient. d is the result of correcting auto-correlation. Some regressions do not have 'd' statistics either because the $D.W.$ statistics are acceptable or an attempt to correct auto-correlation did not improve the $D.W.$ statistics.

FIGURE 6.1

Some Indicators of Small Firms in Manufacturing by Industry, 1970–1984

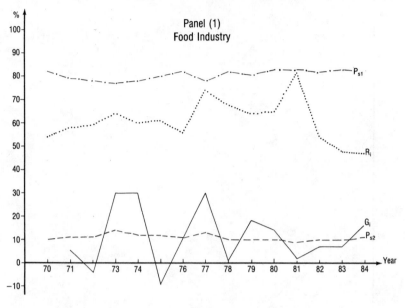

Panel (1)
Food Industry

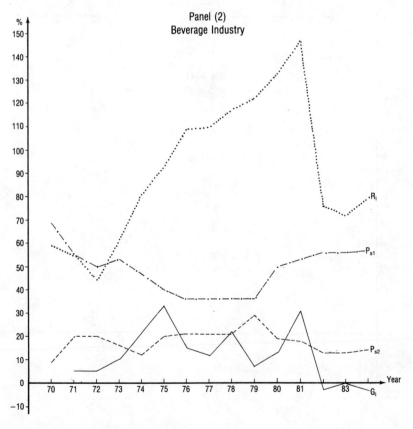

Panel (2)
Beverage Industry

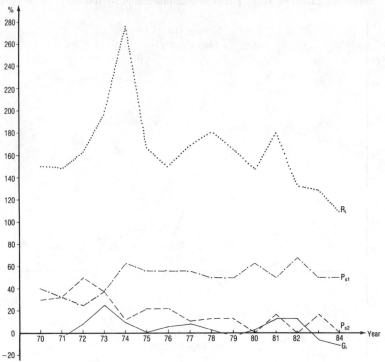

Panel (3)
Cigarettes and Other Tobacco Products Industry

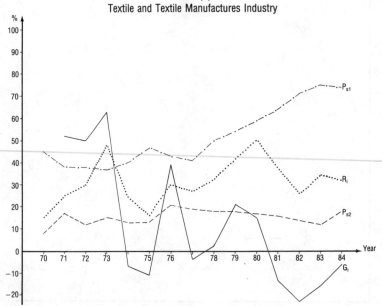

Panel (4)
Textile and Textile Manufactures Industry

Panel (5)
Apparel and Footwear Industry

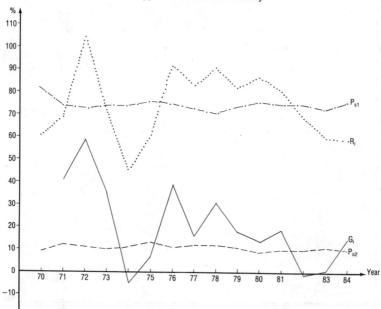

Panel (6)
Wood and Cork Products Industry

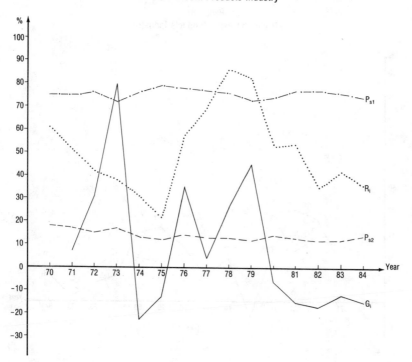

Panel (7)
Furniture and Fixtures Industry

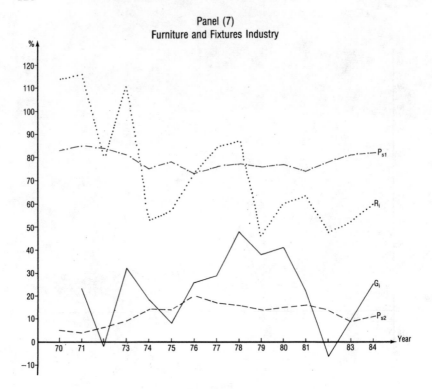

Panel (8)
Paper and Paper Products Industry

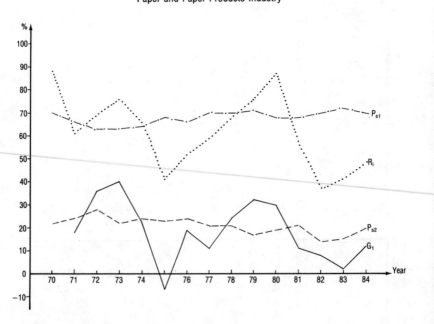

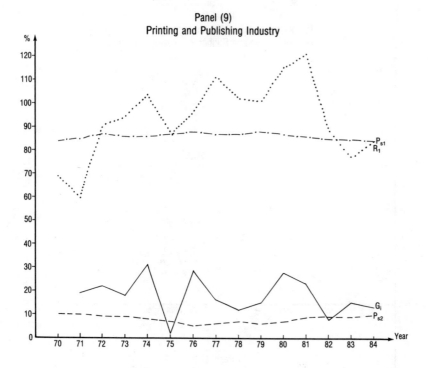

Panel (9)
Printing and Publishing Industry

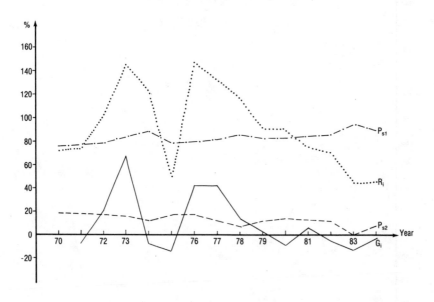

Panel (10)
Leather and Leather Products Industry

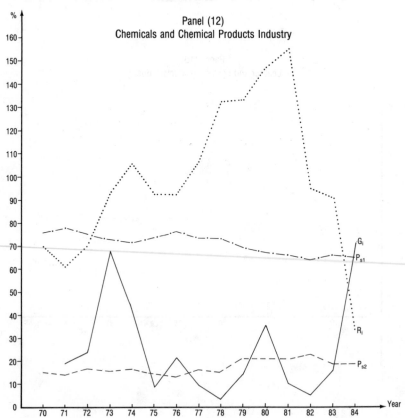

Panel (11)
Rubber and Rubber Products Industry Except
Footwear, Toys and Rubber Processing Industry

Panel (12)
Chemicals and Chemical Products Industry

Panel (13)
Petroleum and Petroleum Products Industry

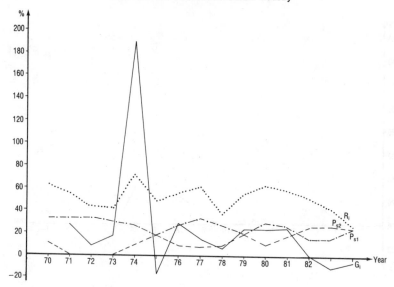

Panel (14)
Non-metallic Mineral Products Industry

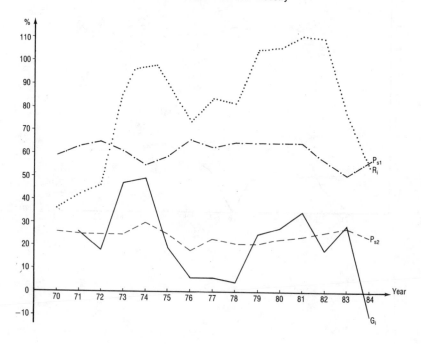

Panel (15)
Basic Metal Industry

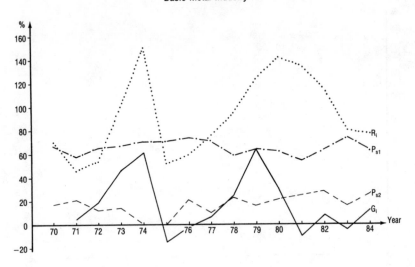

Panel (16)
Fabricated Metal Products Industry

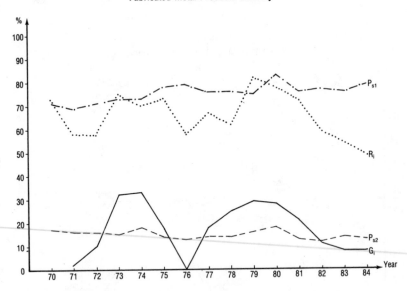

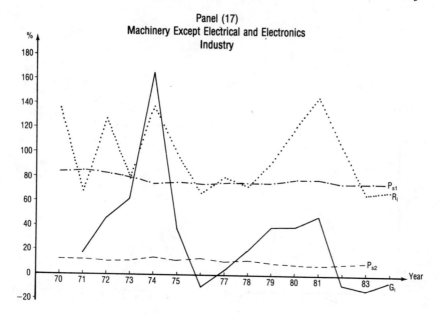

Panel (17)
Machinery Except Electrical and Electronics
Industry

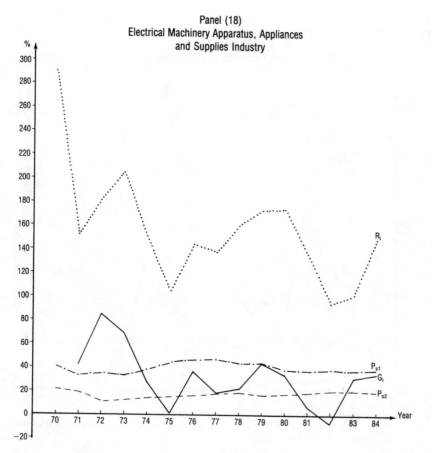

Panel (18)
Electrical Machinery Apparatus, Appliances
and Supplies Industry

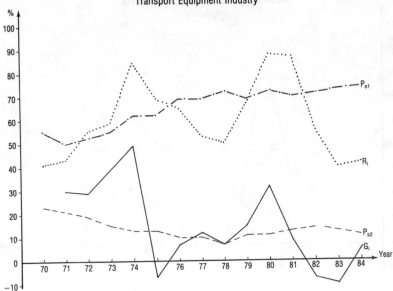

Panel (19)
Transport Equipment Industry

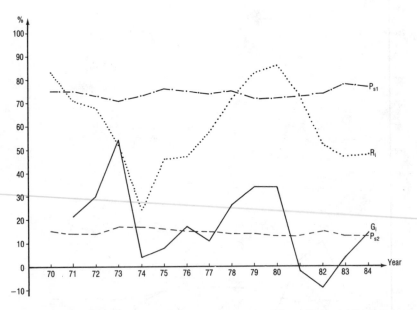

Panel (20)
Other Manufacturing Industries

Source: Singapore, Department of Statistics, *Report on the Census of Industrial Production*, various years.

Note: P_{s1} = Percentage of small establishments in the total number of establishments.

$\quad$ P_{s2} = Percentage of medium establishments in the total number of establishments.

$\quad$ R $\quad$ = Rate of return on capital.

$\quad$ G $\quad$ = Growth rate of industrial output.

7

THE PROBLEMS AND
GROWTH POTENTIAL OF
SMALL AND MEDIUM
ESTABLISHMENTS

THE problems encountered by small and medium establishments (SMEs) in Singapore are diverse. They range from problems inherent in their basic production structure to extraneous problems such as the shortage of labour. The extent to which these problems are alleviated determines their potential for future growth.

This chapter reports research findings on SMEs in the manufacturing sector. The data come from a 1985 field survey of SMEs in both labour-intensive and capital-intensive industries. The survey was carried out during October–December 1985 and was supported by a grant from the Institute of Developing Economies of Japan. An attempt will be made to compare the SMEs in labour-intensive and capital-intensive industries. In interpreting these findings, however, it should be borne in mind that the survey sample may not be a representative sample of the whole spectrum of SMEs in manufacturing.

The Structure of SMEs

The survey conducted in 1985 involved a total of 146 SMEs from labour-intensive and capital-intensive industries in the manufacturing sector of Singapore. The labour-intensive industries were the textiles industry, the apparel industry, the footwear industry, the wood and cork products industry, the furniture and fixtures industry, the paper and paper products industry, the plastic products industry, and the glass and glass products industry. The capital-intensive industries included the industrial chemicals industry, the fabricated metal industry, the machinery industry, the electrical and electronic products industry, the professional and scientific equipment industry, and other manufacturing industries.

Altogether, 45 medium establishments from the labour-intensive industries, 49 small establishments from the labour-intensive industries, and 52 small establishments from the capital-intensive industries participated in the survey. Table 7.1 presents the number of sample establishments according to size and industry type.

General Aspects of SMEs

The form of business organization preferred by the SMEs interviewed was the limited company rather than the sole proprietorship or partnership. Table 7.2 gives the legal organization of the surveyed sample. Of those surveyed, 55.6 per cent of the medium establishments, 44.9 per cent of the small labour-intensive establishments, and 48.1 per cent of the small capital-intensive establishments were limited companies, while 33.3 per cent of the medium establishments, 34.7 per cent of the small labour-intensive establishments, and 36.5 per cent of the small capital-intensive establishments were partnerships and only 11.1 per cent of the medium establishments, 20.4 per cent of the small labour-intensive establishments, and 15.4 per cent of the small capital-intensive establishments were sole proprietorships. Therefore, about half of the SMEs interviewed were limited companies, about one-third were partnerships, and about one-sixth were sole proprietorships. Furthermore, among the labour-intensive establishments in the survey sample, proportionately more of the medium establishments formed limited companies than the small establishments, and proportionately more of the small establishments formed partnerships and sole proprietorships than the medium establishments. When the small establishments are compared according to industry type, the survey shows that proportionately more of those in the capital-intensive industries were limited companies and partnerships, while proportionately more of those in the labour-intensive industries were organized as sole proprietorships. This shows that while the SMEs interviewed prefer to form limited companies, which have easier access to foreign capital, technology, and markets but have lesser flexibility in management and operation, the medium establishments and the small capital-intensive establishments compared to the small labour-intensive establishments, prefer fund-raising to control.

Table 7.3 is a summary of the total production of the sample SMEs for 1983. Among those in the labour-intensive industries, a larger proportion of the small establishments (20.4 per cent) than the medium establishments (4.4 per cent) produced less than $200,000 in 1983, while among the small establishments, a larger proportion of those from the labour-intensive industries (20.4 per cent) than those from the capital-intensive industries (15.4 per cent) had a total production of below $200,000 for the same year. As for those that produced $3 million and above in 1983, the proportion of the medium labour-intensive establishments (26.7 per cent) was more than ten times that of the small labour-intensive establishments (2.0 per cent). Similarly, when the small establishments are compared by industry type, those that produced $3 million and above in the capital-intensive industries (21.1 per cent) were ten times more than those in the labour-intensive industries. Therefore, the total production in 1983 among the SMEs surveyed was lower for the small establishments, particularly the small labour-intensive establishments. In general, however, about half of the SMEs interviewed produced between $200,000 and $3 million in 1983, accounting for 53.3 per cent of the medium establishments, 55.1 per cent of the small labour-intensive establishments, and 50 per cent of the small capital-intensive establishments.

In the survey, the SMEs interviewed were asked whether they engaged in subcontracting in 1983. The results are presented in Table 7.4. Results show that 46.7 per cent of the medium establishments, 42.9 per cent of the small labour-intensive establishments, and 25.0 per cent of the small capital-intensive establishments were subcontractors in 1983, indicating that small and medium establishments were active in subcontracting.

With regard to the size of capital, Tables 7.5 and 7.6 show that 26.5 per cent of the small labour-intensive establishments, 21.2 per cent of the small capital-intensive establishments, and only 8.9 per cent of the medium establishments surveyed had a registered capital of less than $100,000. Those with a registered capital of $3 million and above in the sample accounted for 20.0 per cent of the medium establishments, 15.4 per cent of the small capital-intensive establishments, and only 6.1 per cent of the small labour-intensive establishments. Forty per cent of the medium establishments in the survey had between $1–3 million of registered capital, while 38.8 per cent of the small labour-intensive establishments and 42.3 per cent of the small capital-intensive establishments had a registered capital of $100,000–$1 million.

A similar conclusion can be drawn by comparing the paid-up capital of the sample establishments. Those with paid-up capital of less than $100,000 accounted for 32.7 per cent of the small labour-intensive establishments, 23.1 per cent of the small capital-intensive establishments, and only 13.3 per cent of the medium establishments. On the other hand, those with paid-up capital of $3 million and above accounted for 20.0 per cent of the medium establishments, 15.4 per cent of the small capital-intensive establishments, and 10.2 per cent of the small labour-intensive establishments. One out of every three medium establishments in the survey had a paid-up capital of between $1–3 million, while 22.5 per cent of the small labour-intensive establishments and 13.5 per cent of the small capital-intensive establishments surveyed had $1–3 million of paid-up capital. The foregoing suggests that the size of an establishment may, in fact, be defined by the amount of capital, either registered or paid-up. Indeed, in countries like Taiwan, SMEs are defined in terms of the amount of capital (see Chapter 8).

The Background of the Entrepreneur

The background of the entrepreneur is an important element for the emergence of an enterprise. Tables 7.7–7.14 provide an insight into the background of the entrepreneurs in the SMEs surveyed.

Table 7.7 indicates that 68.9 per cent of the medium establishments, 53.1 per cent of the small labour-intensive establishments, and 67.9 per cent of the small capital-intensive establishments interviewed had entrepreneurs with ages between 30 and 49 years. In other words, the majority of the sample entrepreneurs were between 30 and 49 years old. As for the entrepreneurs aged 50–60 years, a larger percentage belonged to the small establishments in the labour-intensive industries (22.5 per cent) followed by the small capital-intensive establishments (13.2 per cent), and the medium establishments (11.1 per cent). Those aged 20–29 years constituted a very small percentage of the entrepreneurs surveyed. Only 2.2 per cent of the medium establishments, 6.1 per cent of the small labour-intensive establishments, and 5.7 per cent of the small capital-intensive establishments interviewed had entrepreneurs aged 20–29 years.

Regarding the entrepreneurs' places of birth, Table 7.8 shows that 70–80 per cent of the entrepreneurs interviewed were either born in Singapore or Malaysia. Of those interviewed, 58.0 per cent of the entrepreneurs from medium establishments, 47.2 per cent of those from small labour-intensive establishments, and 61.8 per cent from small capital-intensive establishments quoted Singapore as their place of birth, while 14.0 per cent of those from medium establishments, 28.3 per cent of those from small labour-intensive establishments, and 16.4 per cent of those from small capital-intensive establishments said that they were born in Malaysia. Thus, among the entrepreneurs in the labour-intensive industries surveyed, a larger proportion of the locally born were from the medium establishments, while among the entrepreneurs in the small establishments surveyed, a larger proportion of those born in Singapore were found in the capital-intensive industries.

Another aspect of the entrepreneurs' background is their academic qualifications. In the survey, 34.8 per cent of the medium establishments, 39.6 per cent of the small capital-intensive establishments, and only 14.0 per cent of the small labour-intensive establishments had entrepreneurs with tertiary education (see Table 7.9). Thus, among the labour-intensive establishments, more medium establishments than small establishments had entrepreneurs with tertiary education, while among the small establishments, more of the capital-intensive establishments than the labour-intensive establishments had tertiary-educated entrepreneurs. As for the entrepreneurs with secondary education, more of them were attached to the small labour-intensive establishments (34.0 per cent) than the medium labour-intensive establishments (26.1 per cent), although the small labour-intensive establishments have an almost equal percentage with the small capital-intensive establishments (30.2 per cent). Establishments with entrepreneurs with only primary education in the survey accounted for about the same percentage of small and medium establishments in the labour-intensive establishments (16.0 per cent and 15.2 per cent respectively) but represented a higher percentage of the small labour-intensive establishments than the small capital-intensive establishments (9.4 per cent). Establishments with entrepreneurs who had no education constituted only a small section of the medium establishments (6.5 per cent) and the small capital-intensive establishments (5.7 per cent) but a larger ratio of the small labour-intensive establishments (18.0 per cent).

In summary, more of the entrepreneurs of the medium capital-intensive establishments surveyed had attained tertiary education than those from the small labour-intensive establishments, while the latter also had the largest proportion of uneducated entrepreneurs.

What were the occupations of the entrepreneurs' parents? The survey reveals that nearly half of the entrepreneurs' parents were engaged in a different occupation, implying that the majority of the entrepreneurs interviewed did not inherit their businesses from their parents. These comprised 44.4 per cent of the medium establishments, 42.9 per cent of the small labour-intensive establishments, and 46.2 per cent of the small capital intensive establishments in the sample (see Table 7.10). A higher percentage of the entrepreneurs' parents in the small capital-intensive establishments (17.3 per cent) than the small labour-intensive establishments (11.8 per cent) and the medium establishments (14.0 per cent) were traders. The percentage of the entrepreneurs' parents who were wage earners are 23.1, 21.6 and 12.0 for the small capital-intensive establishments, small labour-intensive establishments, and medium establishments, respectively (see Table 7.11).

What then motivated the entrepreneurs in the sample SMEs to set up their present businesses? Table 7.12 shows that the majority of the entrepreneurs founded their businesses on perceiving their growth potential. This accounted for a larger proportion of the small capital-intensive establishments (66.7 per cent), followed by the small labour-intensive establishments (60.8 per cent), and the medium labour-intensive establishments (51.9 per cent). Almost a sixth of the entrepreneurs interviewed said that they received advice from their friends and parents. These represented a slightly larger percentage of those from the small labour-intensive establishments (15.7 per cent) than the small capital-intensive establishments (13.0 per cent), and the medium establishments (13.0 per cent).

The previous occupations of the entrepreneurs interviewed were seldom in a different line. They were mostly from the same or related occupations. As Table 7.13 shows, about an equal proportion of the entrepreneurs of the small labour-intensive and capital-intensive establishments (42.0 per cent and 40.4 per cent respectively) were formerly from the same line of business, although among the labour-intensive industries, a larger percentage of the entrepreneurs from the small establishments (42.0 per cent) than the medium establishments (23.9 per cent) were previously in the same occupation. Those who were in a related occupation constituted a larger percentage in the medium establishments (41.3 per cent) than in the small capital-intensive establishments (34.6 per cent) and the small labour-intensive establishments (32.0 per cent).

As for their source of technological know-how, Table 7.14 shows that about half of the entrepreneurs interviewed acquired their technological know-how from previous jobs. One in four in the medium establishments obtained their technological know-how through schools

(34.8 per cent had tertiary education) compared to 14.8 per cent in the small labour-intensive establishments (only 14.0 per cent had tertiary education), and 21.3 per cent in the small capital-intensive establishments (39.6 per cent had tertiary education). Nearly a fifth of the entrepreneurs surveyed obtained their technological know-how from their parents and relatives.

With regard to their management and administration skills, almost half of the entrepreneurs interviewed from the medium establishments, in contrast to 35.3 per cent of those from the small labour-intensive establishments and 21.8 per cent of the small capital-intensive establishments, said that they acquired these skills from former jobs. Those who learnt their management and administration skills through school accounted for a larger percentage of the medium establishments (31.6 per cent) than the small labour-intensive establishments (23.5 per cent), and the small capital-intensive establishments (20.6 per cent). Only about a tenth of those from the medium establishments, compared to nearly a quarter of those from the small establishments, learnt their management and administrative skills from their parents and relatives. From the foregoing, we gather that among the SMEs interviewed, the entrepreneurs' former jobs played an important role in the formation of the enterprise. However, the entrepreneurs from the small capital-intensive establishments seemed to benefit less in terms of management and administration skills from previous jobs compared to the medium establishments and small labour-intensive establishments.

Characteristics of the Work-force

The work-force in the SMEs surveyed can be analysed in terms of their average years of employment, educational attainment, and percentage of unionization.

Table 7.15 illustrates the average years of employment of the work-force surveyed. The length of employment of the majority of the workers in the survey sample was less than 5 years. A greater proportion of the work-force in the medium establishments (63.8 per cent) than in the small capital-intensive establishments (60.0 per cent) and in the small labour-intensive establishments (56.6 per cent) had been in employment for an average of 4 years or less. About 30 per cent of the sample SMEs had workers employed for an average of between 5 and 9 years. Establishments with workers in employment for an average of 10 years or more constituted the smallest percentage of the SMEs surveyed. These accounted for 4.3 per cent, 5.7 per cent, and 9.1 per cent for medium establishments, small labour-intensive establishments and capital-intensive establishments respectively.

In terms of educational level, as many as two out of every three of the medium establishments surveyed had 10–49 per cent of their workers with no education, i.e who were low-skilled (see Table 7.16). Nearly half of the small labour-intensive establishments (44.9 per cent) had this many workers with no education while they accounted for 32.7

per cent of the small capital-intensive establishments. On the other hand, 11.1 per cent of the medium establishments, 24.5 per cent of the small labour-intensive establishments, and 32.7 per cent of the small capital-intensive establishments had none of their employees with no education. Therefore, among the sample SMEs in the labour-intensive industries, the medium establishments had more uneducated, low-skilled employees than the small establishments. When the small establishments are compared according to industry type, the labour-intensive establishments seemed to fare worse than the capital-intensive establishments. Hence, the SMEs, particularly those in the labour-intensive industries, could do well to upgrade the educational (and skill) level of their work-force, and look seriously toward programmes such as the Continuing Education and Training (CET) programme and the Basic Education for Skills Training (BEST) programme.

As for the employees with primary education, Table 7.17 shows that 42.2 per cent of the medium establishments, 40.8 per cent of the small labour intensive establishments, and 19.2 per cent of the small capital-intensive establishments had 30–49 per cent of workers with primary education. More than one in four of the sample SMEs had between 50–74 per cent of their workers with primary education. This conforms with the generally low educational attainment of the work-force surveyed.

Slightly more of the small labour-intensive establishments (40.8 per cent) than the medium labour-intensive establishments (35.6 per cent) had 30–49 per cent of the work-force with secondary education, while more of the small labour-intensive establishments than the small capital-intensive establishments (15.4 per cent) had this many workers with secondary education. About one in five of the SMEs in the labour-intensive industries surveyed had 10–29 per cent of the work-force with secondary education, compared to one in three of the small capital-intensive establishments (see Table 7.18).

With regard to workers with tertiary education, Table 7.19 reveals that about one in five of the SMEs surveyed did not have any workers with tertiary education. However, 44.4 per cent of the medium labour-intensive establishments and 42.9 per cent of the small labour-intensive establishments interviewed said that they had 1–9 per cent of employees with tertiary education, while more of the small labour-intensive establishments (42.9 per cent) than the small capital-intensive establishments (34.6 per cent) had this many workers with tertiary education. About one in four of the SMEs in the labour-intensive industries had 10–29 per cent of the work-force with tertiary education, while almost 40 per cent of the small capital-intensive establishments had this many employees with tertiary education.

It can be concluded that among the establishments surveyed small labour-intensive establishments had more less educated workers than the medium labour-intensive establishments and small capital-intensive establishments.

The importance of unionization in the SMEs surveyed is illustrated in

Tables 7.20 and 7.21. Labour unions were absent in the majority of the SMEs interviewed, with 83.7 per cent of the small labour-intensive establishments, 66.7 per cent of the medium labour-intensive establishments, and 78.8 per cent of the small capital-intensive establishments having no unions. Only 15 medium establishments, 6 small labour-intensive establishments, and 11 small capital-intensive establishments had labour unions. Among the establishments with labour unions, one in three of the medium establishments had 1–49 per cent of their employees as union members, one in three of the small labour-intensive establishments had 50–74 per cent of their employees belonging to unions and slightly more than one in three of the small capital-intensive establishments had between 1–49 per cent of their work-force belonging to unions. Thus, among the labour-intensive establishments interviewed, the small labour-intensive establishments had a larger proportion of workers who were union members than the medium establishments, and among the small establishments surveyed, a greater proportion of the work-force in the labour-intensive industries opted to be union members than those in the capital-intensive industries.

Problems Faced by SMEs

SMEs typically operate under three types of constraint, namely entrepreneurial constraints, output constraints, and capital constraints. These constraints dictate the problems encountered by SMEs that are inherent in the businesses. In addition, SMEs also face certain extraneous problems, such as the business environment in which they operate.

Table 7.22 shows that in the area of modernization of business administration, 80–100 per cent of the SMEs surveyed had production plans, quality control systems, and regular inventory checks, and use the double-entry method of accounting. However, proportionately fewer small labour-intensive establishments than medium establishments implemented these forms of business management. There were also proportionately fewer small capital-intensive establishments with quality control systems than small labour-intensive establishments. There is, therefore, further scope for improvement among the small establishments in business administration.

As is implied in the theoretical discussion in Chapter 3, the entrepreneur of the small firm is expected to be a one man manager because there is no division of labour. The entrepreneur has to devote time to accounting, production, marketing, quality control, etc. Table 7.23 shows that 30.8 per cent of medium labour-intensive establishments, 36.8 per cent of small labour-intensive establishments, and 31.9 per cent of small capital-intensive establishments indicated that production was their most important business function. Marketing was considered the most important business function by 29.2 per cent of medium establishments, 21.7 per cent of small labour-intensive establishments, and 22.2 per cent of small capital-intensive establishments.

Very few establishments considered fund raising or wage negotiation as the most important business function.

With regard to the operating fund, Table 7.24 shows that the major source of capital for the SMEs interviewed was their own internal funds. More of the small capital-intensive establishments (57.7 per cent) than the small labour-intensive establishments (49 per cent) and the medium establishments (24.4 per cent) had to rely completely on their own funds for business. Table 7.25 shows that the greatest obstacle to the procurement of funds by the SMEs surveyed was the high interest rate.[1] More of the medium establishments (43.8 per cent) than the small labour-intensive establishments (35.9 per cent), and the small capital-intensive establishments (30.4 per cent) faced this difficulty. About a quarter of the SMEs experienced shortage of mortgage, while more of the small capital-intensive establishments (26.8 per cent) than the small labour-intensive establishments (20.8 per cent) and the medium establishments (16.7 per cent) said that the loans extended to them are too small.

The problems faced by the SMEs in the survey discussed above are inherent to their businesses. In addition, SMEs also encountered some extraneous problems, one of the most serious being the shortage of skilled labour. Table 7.26 indicates that the medium establishments (44.3 per cent) and the small capital-intensive establishments (33.3 per cent) experienced this problem to a greater extent than the small labour-intensive establishments (25.3 per cent).

The second most common problem faced by the SMEs surveyed with respect to their work-force is the turnover rate. As shown in Table 7.26, 30.4 per cent of the medium establishments, 26.5 per cent of the small labour intensive establishments, and 33.3 per cent of the small capital-intensive establishments complained of a high turnover rate among their workers. This is consistent with the earlier findings that the average length of employment of the work-force in 29.8 per cent of the medium establishments, 24.5 per cent of the small labour-intensive establishments, and 30.9 per cent of the small capital-intensive establishments in the survey was less than 3 years (see Table 7.15).

The SMEs interviewed also face demands for wage increments by their work-force. As Table 7.26 shows, a larger proportion of the small labour-intensive establishments (24.1 per cent) than the small capital-intensive establishments (18.5 per cent), and the medium establishments (13.9 per cent) encountered this problem. One possible explanation may be the absence of unionization in a larger proportion of the small labour-intensive establishments than in the medium establishments and the small capital-intensive establishments[2] (see the sub-section 'Characteristics of the Work-force' above).

With regard to wages, Table 7.27 indicates that 44.3 per cent of the medium establishments, 32.6 per cent of the small labour-intensive establishments, and 34.6 per cent of the capital-intensive establishments felt that the wages were 'too high'. Those that thought their wages were 'just right' constituted 49.0 per cent of the medium establishments, 28.6 per cent of the small labour-intensive establishments, and 42.3 per cent of the small capital-intensive establishments. None of the medium establishments and the small capital-intensive establishments, compared to only 2.0 per cent of the small labour-intensive establishments, said that their wages were 'on the low side'.

When asked to compare their wages with those in the other Asian NICs, the majority of the SMEs that responded said that their wages were 'just right' compared to those in Hong Kong, with the feeling being stronger among the small labour-intensive establishments (20.4 per cent) than the medium establishments (17.8 per cent) and the small capital-intensive establishments (19.2 per cent) (see Table 7.28). However, when the SMEs compared their wages with those in South Korea and Taiwan, they generally felt that their wages were 'too high'. As Table 7.29 shows, about 15.0 per cent of the SMEs from the labour-intensive industries surveyed said that their wages were 'too high' compared to wages in South Korea, while 9.6 per cent of the small capital-intensive establishments agreed. Table 7.30 shows that about 22.0 per cent of the SMEs in the labour-intensive industries and 15.4 per cent of the small capital-intensive establishments felt that their wages were 'too high' compared to wages in Taiwan.

In order to understand why 'too high' wages are experienced by the majority of the sample SMEs, it will be helpful if we look at the way in which wages were determined in the SMEs surveyed. Table 7.31 gives a summary of the important factors in wage determination. The most important factor for the SMEs interviewed was the wage level of firms in the same industry. This accounts for about 40 per cent of the respondents. The second most important factor in the determination of wages in the SMEs surveyed was the National Wages Council (NWC) wage guidelines. About an equal proportion of the SMEs in the medium and small labour-intensive industries (26.3 per cent and 25.0 per cent respectively) relied on the NWC wage guidelines when determining their wages, while 21.8 per cent of the small capital-intensive establishments followed the NWC wage guidelines. Between 10 and 15 per cent of the SMEs surveyed said that they followed the wage levels of firms in a different industry. The proportion is larger for the small capital-intensive establishments (14.6 per cent) than the small labour-intensive establishments (13.0 per cent) and the medium establishments (9.5 per cent). Consequently, between 50 and 55 per cent of the SMEs interviewed were dependent on the wage level of firms in the same or a different industry. This is a natural consequence of the tight labour market of Singapore, which may explain why 30–45 per cent of the SMEs interviewed experienced wages that were 'too high'. Nearly one out of every five of the SMEs surveyed also considered productivity in wage determination.

As for the influence of the government on wage increases, 42.2 per cent of the medium establishments, 32.7 per cent of the small capital-intensive establishments, and 26.5 per cent of the small labour-intensive establishments said that the effect was 'moderate'. Almost an equal proportion of the small labour-intensive and capital-intensive establishments (40.8 per cent and 42.3 per cent respectively) and a smaller proportion of the medium establishments (35.6 per cent) felt that the effect was 'slight'. Thus, the majority of the SMEs interviewed felt that the influence of the government on wage increases was 'moderate' or 'slight' (see Table 7.32).

In addition, the SMEs interviewed also provided non-remunerative incentives for their workers. The results are presented in Table 7.33. The most common form of non-remunerative incentive among the respondent was medical or dental care. About 13.3 per cent of the medium establishments, 16.3 per cent of the small labour-intensive establishments, and 17.3 per cent of the capital-intensive establishments provided medical or dental care. About 12.2 per cent of the small labour-intensive establishments compared to none of the medium establishments and 3.8 per cent of the small capital-intensive establishments offered food and board as fringe benefits.

With regard to the entrepreneurs' relationships with the staff, Table 7.34 shows that all of the SMEs surveyed did not encounter any problems. A larger proportion of the small labour-intensive establishments surveyed (24.0 per cent) than the medium establishments (20.0 per cent), and the small capital-intensive establishments (22.6 per cent) had 'excellent' relations with their staff. More of the medium establishments (66.7 per cent) than the small labour-intensive establishments (56.0 per cent) assessed their present relations with their staff as 'well'. The proportion of the small capital-intensive establishments that assessed relations with staff as 'well' was almost equal to that of the small labour-intensive establishments.

The method most often used by the majority of the SMEs to maintain good relations with their staff was frequent dialogue. Among the labour-intensive establishments, the medium establishments (69.6 per cent) tended to engage more in frequent dialogue than the small labour-intensive establishments (60.3 per cent), and the small capital-intensive establishments (60.0 per cent) (see Table 7.35). About a fifth of the small and medium labour-intensive establishments also resorted to wage increases to maintain good staff relations, compared to 13.9 per cent of the small capital-intensive establishments. A smaller proportion of SMEs surveyed provided good facilities for recreation and other activities. Table 7.35 indicates that 7.1 per cent of the medium establishments, 10.3 per cent of the small labour-intensive establishments, and 15.4 per cent of the small capital-intensive establishments used such methods to maintain good relations with their staff. Thus, the small size of the SMEs is an advantage because it enables greater ease of maintaining good staff relations through frequent dialogue, a less costly measure than providing wage increments or good facilities.

The Impact of Recession on Workers in SMEs

This section looks at the impact of the recession in 1985 on the work-force of the SMEs surveyed. In the preceding sections we analysed the structure of the SMEs and the problems that they encountered. These would determine the behaviour of the SMEs during the recession and consequently the impact of the recession on the work-force.

In 1985, the Singapore economy shrank for the first time in two decades, recording −1.8 per cent real GDP growth. Over 35,000 workers from the manufacturing sector were laid off.[3] Table 7.36 illustrates the countermeasures for cost increase among the SMEs surveyed. A quarter of the medium establishments, 21.7 per cent of the small labour-intensive establishments, and 26.7 per cent of the small capital-intensive establishments in the survey laid off workers to cut down the increase in costs. However, 53.6 per cent of the medium establishments, 53.3 per cent of the small labour-intensive establishments, and 55.0 per cent of the small capital-intensive establishments resorted to mechanization. About 5 per cent of the small and medium labour-intensive establishments saved energy, and about 9 per cent of the SMEs in the labour-intensive industries managed to reduce the price of their raw materials, compared to 5 per cent of the small capital-intensive establishments.

Table 7.37 outlines the training period of the sample SMEs. Some 40 per cent of the small labour-intensive and capital-intensive establishments and 33.3 per cent of the medium establishments had a training period of 1 month. On the other hand, 40.0 per cent of the medium establishments, 34.0 per cent of the small labour-intensive establishments, and 30.8 per cent of the small capital-intensive establishments trained their workers for 2–3 months.

Table 7.38 gives the class of workers who were retrenched. From the survey, 22.2 per cent of the medium establishments, 18.4 per cent of the small labour-intensive establishments, and 23.0 per cent of the small capital-intensive establishments laid off production operators. This is in accordance with Walter Y. Oi's Short-run Theory of Employment, which is based on the concept of labour as a quasi-fixed factor.[4] From the firm's viewpoint, labour is a quasi-fixed factor whose total employment cost is partly variable and partly fixed. The variable portion is largely made up of the variable wage bill while the fixed employment costs represent an investment by the firm in its labour force and are composed of hiring and training costs. The costs of hiring and training production workers in manufacturing tend to be lower than those for non-production workers. Consequently, firms often prefer to retrench production workers during a recession.

In order to keep their workers busy during the recession, 8.9 per cent of the medium establishments, 8.2 per cent the small labour-intensive establishments, and 9.6 per cent of the small capital-intensive establishments interviewed said that they adjusted the working hours. Only 8.2 per cent of the small labour-intensive establishments assigned their workers to other work, such as painting and fixing doors, compared to none in the other establishments. About 4 per cent of the SMEs surveyed assigned their workers to maintenance of equipment (see Table 7.39).

The Growth Potential of SMEs

In order to assess the growth potential of the SMEs in the sample, we will examine the extent to which the problems discussed in the above section can be overcome by the joint efforts of the entrepreneurs and the government.

First, let us review the efforts made by the entrepreneurs interviewed to improve their managerial and technical performances. Table 7.22 shows that in terms of modernization of business administration, over 80 per cent of the entrepreneurs surveyed indicated that they had a systematic management policy with respect to production planning.

What are the most common methods by which the SMEs interviewed upgrade their technology? Table 7.40 shows that the majority of the SMEs chose to introduce new machines. Proportionately more of the small labour-intensive establishments (55.9 per cent) than the medium establishments (34.9 per cent) and the small capital-intensive establishments (39.7 per cent) improved their technology by introducing new machines. One in four of the medium establishments provided technical training in contrast to 15.3 per cent of the small labour-intensive establishments and 15.9 per cent of the small capital-intensive establishments. About one out of every ten of the small labour-intensive and capital-intensive establishments introduced new technology to their establishments, while 17.5 per cent medium establishments used this method.

An important factor that contributes greatly to the growth of an enterprise is the utilization of associations. The survey shows that 28.9 per cent of the medium establishments, 30.6 per cent of the small labour-intensive establishments, and 30.8 per cent of the small capital-intensive establishments were members of the Singapore Manufacturers' Association (see Table 7.41). The Trade Development Board was considered to be useful by 20 per cent of the medium establishments, 14.3 per cent of the small labour-intensive establishments, and 13.5 per cent of the small capital-intensive establishments.

The benefits of belonging to an association were, in order of importance, the provision of information, sales expansion, fund raising, and the procurement of raw materials. Table 7.42 shows that 37.8 per cent of the medium establishments, 26.5 per cent of the small labour-intensive establishments, and 30.8 per cent of the capital labour-intensive establishments obtained useful information from the associations. About 16–18 per cent of the three categories of SMEs used the associations to secure sales. On the other hand, 4.4 per cent of the medium establishments, 8.2 per cent of the small labour-intensive establishments, and 3.8 per cent of the small capital-intensive establishments relied on the associations for fund raising. The proportions of surveyed firms which used the associations to produce raw materials are only 2.2 per cent, 4.1 per cent, and 3.8 per cent for the medium establishments, the small labour-intensive establishments, and the small capital-intensive establishments respectively.

The heavy reliance of the SMEs surveyed on the trade associations for essential business activities, such as obtaining information, marketing, fund raising, and the procurement of raw materials, suggests the need for the associations to increase measures to help SMEs in these areas. Indeed, the Singapore Manufacturers' Association launched a Workshop Consultancy Programme in February 1986 to improve the competitiveness of SMEs by providing them with advice on finance, marketing, production, and management, as well as ideas on how to solve work-related problems through workshops, lectures, and training sessions.[5]

It is interesting to observe the relations of the SMEs with the community. Table 7.43 indicates that 22.2 per cent of the medium establishments, 20.4 per cent of the small labour-intensive establishments, and 23.1 per cent of the small capital-intensive establishments contributed to community service in one way or another. The proportion of the surveyed firms which participated in public service are 6.7 per cent, 4.1 per cent, and 1.9 per cent for the medium, the small labour-intensive and the small capital-intensive establishments respectively.

Another factor that is of importance to the growth of an enterprise is an awareness of the entrepreneurs with respect to their current operating status and future prospects. Regarding current business activities, those who answered 'fair' represent the majority at between 60 and 65 per cent, while 30–35 per cent cited 'excellent' business activities. None of the medium establishments and small capital-intensive establishments had 'unsatisfactory' current business activities, while 2.0 per cent of the small labour-intensive establishments expressed dissatisfaction. From this we gather that over 90 per cent of the SMEs surveyed are satisfied with their current status, although slightly more of the small labour-intensive establishments are dissatisfied (see Table 7.44).

As for the future prospects of their businesses, the entrepreneurs were generally optimistic about the future prospects of their businesses and they believed that they would be able to weather the current economic recession. Table 7.45 shows that 66.7 per cent of the medium establishments, 59.2 per cent of the small labour-intensive establishments, and 69.3 per cent of the capital-intensive establishments regarded their future as 'excellent' and 'well'.

What plans do these establishments have for the future? Table 7.46 shows that the majority of the sample SMEs intended to continue with their businesses. A larger percentage of the small labour-intensive establishments (68.6 per cent) than the medium establishments (53.3 per cent) and the small capital-intensive establishments (51.7 per cent) expected to continue as they were. Conversely, proportionately more of the medium establishments (44.4 per cent) and the small capital-intensive establishments (43.1 per cent) compared to the small labour-intensive establishments (23.5 per cent) had plans to expand and diversify. None of the small capital-intensive establishments and the medium establishments intended to discontinue their businesses, in contrast with 2.0 per cent of the small labour-intensive establishments interviewed. Only about 2 per cent of the SMEs surveyed intended to convert to other businesses.

It is enlightening to note the sources of advice of the entrepreneurs for this will determine the way in which their businesses are conducted and ultimately the scope for growth of the SMEs. As Table 7.47 shows, the main source of advice for the entrepreneurs was one of the directors in their own companies. This, however, accounts for proportionately fewer small labour-intensive establishments (34.7 per cent) than medium establishments (46.0 per cent) and small capital-intensive establishments (48.5 per cent). A simple explanation is the smaller incidence of limited companies among the small labour-intensive establishments interviewed.[6] A larger proportion of the entrepreneurs of small labour-intensive establishments (22.2 per cent) sought the advice of parents and relatives than those of the medium establishments (9.5 per cent) and the small capital-intensive establishments (13.2 per cent). Less than a fifth of the entrepreneurs also sought the advice of fellow traders, while a large proportion of those of small labour-intensive establishments (13.9 per cent) than those of the medium establishments (4.8 per cent) and the small capital-intensive establishments (10.3 per cent) consulted their friends. In addition, 12.7 per cent of the entrepreneurs in the medium establishments also consulted their parent companies compared to 1.4 per cent and 1.5 per cent of the small labour-intensive and capital-intensive establishments respectively.

As many as 45.1 per cent of the small labour-intensive establishments, 30.8 per cent of the small capital-intensive establishments, and 20.0 per cent of the medium establishments in the survey said that they were not aware of government policies on small industries (see Table 7.48). About 10 per cent of the small labour-intensive establishments and 28.9 per cent of the medium establishments surveyed were 'very much' aware of government policies. With regard to 'a little' awareness, the corresponding figures are 46.7 per cent, 39.2 per cent, and 53.9 per cent for the medium establishments, the small labour-intensive establishments, and the small capital-intensive establishments respectively.

Table 7.49 gives a detailed statement of the actual and expected benefits of the sample SMEs from the government policies. For the medium establishments interviewed, 'information' and 'SDF' surpassed their expectations, although they expected more help from the government in the form of 'subsidy', 'tax holiday', 'availability of loans', 'technical training and development', 'sale of products' and 'provision of foreign workers'. For the small labour-intensive firms, the benefits obtained from the government in the form of 'information' and 'purchase of government properties' exceeded their expectations, while

the benefits from 'subsidy', 'tax holiday', procurement of raw materials', 'availability of loans', 'technical training and development', 'sale
of products', 'SDF', and 'provision of foreign workers' were below
their expectations. As for the small capital-intensive establishments, the
items that exceeded their expectations were 'information', 'purchase of
government properties', 'SDF' and 'sale of products'; and the items that
fell short of their expectations were 'subsidy', 'tax holiday', 'procurement of raw materials', 'availability of loans', 'technical training and
development' and particularly 'provision of foreign workers'. Therefore, 'provision of foreign workers' was the prime expected benefit of
the SMEs surveyed, which is not surprising if we recall that the most
common problem faced by the enterprises is the acquisition of skilled
workers in the tight labour market of Singapore.

Conclusion

The survey on SMEs shows that those interviewed preferred to form
limited companies instead of sole proprietorships and partnerships,
indicating their greater inclination for 'ability to raise funds' over
'control'. Compared to the medium establishments and the small
capital-intensive establishments, however, the small labour-intensive
establishments surveyed showed greater preference for 'control'.

The SMEs surveyed were also afflicted by low output value, about
half of them producing $200,000–$3 million in 1983. As expected, the
small labour-intensive establishments had the lowest production for
1983 compared with the medium and the small capital-intensive establishments.

A substantial percentage of SMEs in the labour-intensive industries
(43–47 per cent) engaged in subcontracting compared to only 25 per
cent of the small capital-intensive establishments, which have greater
difficulty in expanding output by subcontracting.

We have also shown that the problems encountered by the SMEs
surveyed are diverse, ranging from internal problems, such as difficulties
in procuring funds, to extraneous problems, such as the shortage of
skilled manpower and 'high' wages.

Almost half of the entrepreneurs surveyed acquired their technological know-how and management and administration skills from their
previous jobs. This suggests that some of the problems encountered by
the sample SMEs can be better served by means of self-help rather than
from official sources. For instance, the SMEs surveyed should look
seriously into upgrading their work-force through on-the-job-training
or by sending them for programmes such as the BEST programme.
The indications are that official help in the training of the work-force is
already available but the SMEs interviewed were either largely apathetic
or ignorant of the programmes.

As for the efforts on the part of the government to help overcome the
problems faced by the SMEs, the majority interviewed said that they
were not aware of government policies on small firms but they expected

the government to provide more help in several areas, foremost of which is the procurement of foreign labour. The government has launched several programmes to foster the growth of SMEs since the survey, and these will be discussed in Chapter 9. It will be interesting to observe the adoption rate of the programmes by the SMEs. The enthusiasm of the government to help SMEs will certainly help alleviate the difficulties faced by the SMEs, thereby enhancing their potential for future growth.

1. For example, the banks' prime lending rate was 10.33 per cent at the end of September 1984 and 7.20 per cent at the end of December 1985. SMEs normally pay 0.5 per cent above prime if they offer the full value of their facilities as collateral, and 2.00–2.75 per cent above prime if it is a first legal mortgage of a residential property. A new business with no track record and no tangible security to offer faces even more difficulties in getting loans (see *The Business Times*, 6 May 1985 and 21 March 1986).

2. In many countries unionization leads to greater wage demands but in Singapore, unions refrain from asking excessive wage demand.

3. Singapore, Ministry of Trade and Industry, Report of the Economic Committee, *The Singapore Economy: New Directions*, February 1986, pp. 38–9.

4. Walter Y. Oi, 'Labour as a Quasi-Fixed Factor', *Journal of Policy Economy*, Vol. 70, December 1962.

5. *The Business Times*, 3 January 1986. (See Chapter 9 on the role of the government in assisting small firms.)

6. See the sub-section 'General Aspects of SMEs' in this chapter.

TABLE 7.1

Number of Establishments Surveyed by Size and Industry Type

Type of Industry	Number of Establishments		
	M_L	S_L	S_K
Textiles	10	12	
Wearing apparel	6	4	
Footwear	5	6	
Wood & cork products	5	7	
Furniture & fixtures	4	6	
Paper & paper products	8	3	
Plastic products	4	7	
Glass & glass products	3	4	
Industrial chemicals			4
Fabricated metal			12
Machinery			10
Electrical & electronic products			10
Professional & scientific equipment			4
Other manufacturing			12
Total	45	49	52

Source: Author's own data, based on a survey conducted of 45 medium establishments and 101 small establishments in December 1985.

Notes: M_L denotes medium labour-intensive establishments (50–99 workers).

S_L denotes small labour-intensive establishments (10–49 workers).

S_K denotes small capital-intensive establishments (10–49 workers).

TABLE 7.2

The Form of Business Enterprise

Type of Establishment	Percentage of Establishments		
	M_L	S_L	S_K
Limited company	55.6	44.9	48.1
Partnership	33.3	34.7	36.5
Sole proprietorship	11.1	20.4	15.4

Source: See Table 7.1.

Notes: See Table 7.1.

TABLE 7.3
Total Production for 1983

Amount of Production	Percentage of Establishments		
	M_L	S_L	S_K
Below $200,000	4.4	20.4	15.4
$200,000 to less than $1 million	13.3	26.5	28.8
$1 million to less than $3 million	40.0	28.6	21.2
$3 million to less than $10 million	26.7	2.0	17.3
$10 million & above	0.0	0.0	3.8
No answer	15.6	22.5	13.5

Source: See Table 7.1.
Notes: See Table 7.1.

TABLE 7.4
Subcontracting in 1983

Subcontracted	Percentage of Establishments		
	M_L	S_L	S_K
Yes	46.7	42.9	25.0
No	46.7	51.0	67.3
No answer	6.7	6.1	7.7

Source: See Table 7.1.
Notes: See Table 7.1.

TABLE 7.5
Registered Capital

Amount of Registered Capital	Percentage of Establishments		
	M_L	S_L	S_K
Below $100,000	8.9	26.5	21.2
$100,000 to less than $1 million	31.1	38.8	42.3
$1 million to less than $3 million	40.0	28.6	21.1
$3 million & above	20.0	6.1	15.4

Source: See Table 7.1.
Notes: See Table 7.1.

TABLE 7.6
Paid-up Capital

Amount of Paid-up Capital	Percentage of Establishments		
	M_L	S_L	S_K
Below $100,000	13.3	32.7	23.1
$100,000 to less than $1 million	33.3	34.7	48.1
$1 million to less than $3 million	33.3	22.5	13.5
$3 million & above	20.0	10.2	15.4

Source: See Table 7.1.
Notes: See Table 7.1.

TABLE 7.7
Entrepreneur's Age

Age Group	Percentage of Establishments		
	M_L	S_L	S_K
20–29	2.2	6.1	5.7
30–39	37.8	18.4	45.3
40–49	31.1	34.7	22.6
50–60	11.1	22.5	13.2
No answer	17.8	18.3	13.2

Source: See Table 7.1.
Notes: See Table 7.1.

TABLE 7.8
Entrepreneur's Birthplace

Country	Percentage of Establishments		
	M_L	S_L	S_K
Singapore	58.0	47.2	61.8
Malaysia	14.0	28.3	16.4
Other	12.0	9.4	9.1
No answer	16.0	15.1	12.7

Source: See Table 7.1.
Notes: See Table 7.1.

TABLE 7.9
Entrepreneur's Academic Career

Level of Education	Percentage of Establishments		
	M_L	S_L	S_K
No education	6.5	18.0	5.7
Primary education	15.2	16.0	9.4
Secondary education	26.1	34.0	30.2
Tertiary education	34.8	14.0	39.6
No answer	17.4	18.0	15.1

Source: See Table 7.1.
Notes: See Table 7.1.

TABLE 7.10
Entrepreneur's Parent's Occupation

Relation to Entrepreneur's Occupation	Percentage of Establishments		
	M_L	S_L	S_K
Same	28.9	26.5	21.2
Different	44.4	42.9	46.2
No answer	26.7	30.6	32.6

Source: See Table 7.1.
Notes: See Table 7.1.

TABLE 7.11
Entrepreneur's Parent's Other Occupation

Occupation	Percentage of Establishments		
	M_L	S_L	S_K
Academicians	0.0	0.0	7.7
Traders	14.0	11.8	17.3
Wage earners	12.0	21.6	23.1
Other	14.0	15.7	15.4
No answer	60.0	51.0	36.5

Source: See Table 7.1.
Notes: See Table 7.1.

TABLE 7.12

Entrepreneur's Strongest Motivation in Business

Motivation	Percentage of Establishments		
	M_L	S_L	S_K
Interest in business potential	51.9	60.8	66.7
Advice from friends & parents	13.0	15.7	13.0
Advice from EDB/Government	9.3	2.0	0.0
Advice from bankers	0.0	0.0	0.0
Others	9.3	3.9	3.7
No answer	16.5	17.6	16.6

Source: See Table 7.1.
Notes: See Table 7.1.

TABLE 7.13

Entrepreneur's Former Occupation

Relation to Present Occupation	Percentage of Establishments		
	M_L	S_L	S_K
Same	23.9	42.0	40.4
Related	41.3	32.0	34.6
Different	15.2	4.0	11.5
No answer	19.6	22.0	13.5

Source: See Table 7.1.
Notes: See Table 7.1.

TABLE 7.14

Entrepreneur's Technology Know-how and Management
and Administration Skills

Source of Skills/Know-how	Percentage of Establishments					
	Technology Know-how			Management and Administration Skills		
	M_L	S_L	S_K	M_L	S_L	S_K
Through school	25.4	14.8	21.3	31.6	23.5	20.6
Through former job	50.7	50.8	48.0	47.4	35.3	21.8
Through parents & relatives	18.3	19.7	16.0	12.3	23.5	21.8
Others	2.8	8.2	8.0	5.3	11.8	7.3
No answer	2.8	6.5	6.7	3.4	5.9	28.5

Source: See Table 7.1.
Notes: See Table 7.1.

TABLE 7.15
Average Years of Employment

Number of Years	Percentage of Establishments		
	M_L	S_L	S_K
Less than 3 years	29.8	24.5	30.9
3–4 years	34.0	32.1	29.1
5–9 years	29.8	30.2	27.3
10 years & above	4.3	5.7	9.1
No answer	2.1	7.6	3.6

Source: See Table 7.1.
Notes: See Table 7.1.

TABLE 7.16
Employees with No Education

Percentage of Employees	Percentage of Establishments		
	M_L	S_L	S_K
0	11.1	24.5	32.7
1–9	8.9	8.2	7.7
10–29	40.0	16.3	23.1
30–49	26.7	28.6	9.6
50–74	4.4	8.2	9.6
75–100	2.2	8.2	9.6
No answer	6.7	6.1	7.7

Source: See Table 7.1.
Notes: See Table 7.1.

TABLE 7.17
Employees with Primary Education

Percentage of Employees	Percentage of Establishments		
	M_L	S_L	S_K
0	2.2	2.0	5.8
1–9	4.4	2.0	7.7
10–29	17.8	20.4	19.2
30–49	42.2	40.8	19.2
50–74	26.7	28.6	28.9
75–100	0.0	0.0	13.5
No answer	6.7	6.1	5.8

Source: See Table 7.1.
Notes: See Table 7.1.

TABLE 7.18

Employees with Secondary Education

Percentage of Employees	Percentage of Establishments		
	M_L	S_L	S_K
0	0.0	2.0	5.8
1–9	11.1	2.0	11.5
10–29	22.2	20.4	32.7
30–49	35.6	40.8	15.4
50–74	17.8	28.6	11.5
75–100	6.7	0.0	17.3
No answer	6.7	6.1	5.8

Source: See Table 7.1.
Notes: See Table 7.1.

TABLE 7.19

Employees with Higher Education

Percentage of Employees	Percentage of Establishments		
	M_L	S_L	S_K
0	17.8	20.4	21.2
1–9	44.4	42.9	34.6
10–29	28.9	24.5	38.5
30–49	0.0	0.0	0.0
50–74	2.2	4.1	0.0
75–100	0.0	0.0	0.0
No answer	6.7	8.2	5.8

Source: See Table 7.1.
Notes: See Table 7.1.

TABLE 7.20

Presence of Labour Unions

Unions	Percentage of Establishments		
	M_L	S_L	S_K
Present	33.3	12.2	21.2
Absent	66.7	83.7	78.8
No answer	0.0	4.1	0.0

Source: See Table 7.1.
Notes: See Table 7.1.

TABLE 7.21

Percentage of Employees who are Union Members
in Unionized Establishments

Percentage	Percentage of Establishments		
	M_L	S_L	S_K
0	6.7	16.7	27.3
1–49	33.3	0.0	36.4
50–74	20.0	33.3	27.3
75–100	6.7	16.7	9.1
No answer	33.3	33.3	0.0

Source: See Table 7.1.
Note: The number of unionized establishments for medium establishments (M_L), small labour-intensive establishments (S_L) and small capital-intensive establishments (S_K) is 15, 6 and 11 respectively.

TABLE 7.22

Management Policies

Policy	Percentage of Establishments		
	M_L	S_L	S_K
Have production plan	100	83.7	82.7
Have quality control system	97.8	85.7	78.9
Have inventory checks			
Regularly	95.6	83.7	82.7
Irregularly	4.4	10.2	11.5
Accounting method			
Double-entry	91.1	89.8	92.5
Cash basis	2.2	2.0	7.6

Source: See Table 7.1.
Notes: See Table 7.1.

TABLE 7.23
Most Important Business Function

Function	Percentage of Establishments		
	M_L	S_L	S_K
Accounting	12.3	14.5	12.5
Production	30.8	36.8	31.9
Marketing	29.2	21.7	22.2
Fund raising	4.6	1.5	0.0
Quality control	3.1	13.0	8.3
Inventory control	3.1	2.9	2.8
Technical development	13.9	4.4	16.7
Wage negotiations	3.1	1.5	0.0
Others	0.0	0.0	1.4
No answer	0.0	3.7	4.2

Source: See Table 7.1.
Notes: See Table 7.1.

TABLE 7.24
Percentage of Own Funds

Percentage	Percentage of Establishments		
	M_L	S_L	S_K
0	0.0	0.0	0.0
1–49	15.6	6.1	3.9
50–74	35.6	26.5	17.3
75–99	17.8	4.1	11.5
100	24.4	49.0	57.7
No answer	6.7	14.3	9.6

Source: See Table 7.1.
Notes: See Table 7.1.

TABLE 7.25
The Most Serious Difficulty in Procurement of Funds

Difficulties	Percentage of Establishments		
	M_L	S_L	S_K
Tight monetary policy	2.1	9.4	12.5
High interest rate	43.8	35.9	30.4
Shortage of mortgage	29.2	24.5	26.8
Loan too small	16.7	20.8	26.8
Other difficulties	8.3	9.4	3.6

Source: See Table 7.1.
Notes: See Table 7.1.

TABLE 7.26

The Most Common Problem with Workers Faced by Management

Problems	Percentage of Establishments		
	M_L	S_L	S_K
Difficulties in acquiring skilled workers	44.3	25.3	33.3
Job hopping	30.4	26.5	33.3
Seasonal quitting	5.1	8.4	2.5
Demand for wage increase	13.9	24.1	18.5
Frequent absence	5.1	10.8	6.2
Outrageous behaviour	0.0	0.0	2.5
Others	0.0	3.6	2.5
No answer	1.3	1.2	1.2

Source: See Table 7.1.
Notes: See Table 7.1.

TABLE 7.27

Comparison of Wages with Home Country

Rating by/Opinion of Firm	Percentage of Establishments		
	M_L	S_L	S_K
Too high	44.3	32.6	34.6
Just right	49.0	28.6	42.3
On the low side	0.0	2.0	0.0
No answer	6.7	36.7	23.1

Source: See Table 7.1.
Notes: See Table 7.1.

TABLE 7.28

Comparison of Wages with Hong Kong

Rating by/Opinion of Firm	Percentage of Establishments		
	M_L	S_L	S_K
Too high	8.9	6.1	5.8
Just right	17.8	20.4	19.2
On the low side	6.7	4.1	0.0
No answer	66.7	69.4	75.0

Source: See Table 7.1.
Notes: See Table 7.1.

TABLE 7.29

Comparison of Wages with South Korea

Rating by/Opinion of Firm	Percentage of Establishments		
	M_L	S_L	S_K
Too high	15.6	14.3	9.6
Just right	8.9	10.2	7.7
On the low side	6.7	4.1	3.8
No answer	68.9	71.4	78.8

Source: See Table 7.1.
Notes: See Table 7.1.

TABLE 7.30

Comparison of Wages with Taiwan

Rating by/Opinion of Firm	Percentage of Establishments		
	M_L	S_L	S_K
Too high	22.2	22.4	15.4
Just right	8.9	8.2	5.8
On the low side	2.2	0.0	1.9
No answer	66.7	69.4	76.9

Source: See Table 7.1.
Notes: See Table 7.1.

TABLE 7.31

The Most Important Factor in Wage Determination

Factor	Percentage of Establishments		
	M_L	S_L	S_K
Wage level of firms in same industry	43.2	38.9	40.9
Wage level of firms in different industry	9.5	13.0	14.6
Union	4.2	0.9	3.6
NWC wage guidelines	26.3	25.0	21.8
Productivity	16.8	15.7	16.4
Wage in sister plant	0.0	1.9	0.0
No answer	0.0	4.6	2.7

Source: See Table 7.1.
Notes: See Table 7.1.

TABLE 7.32
Influence of Government on Wage Increases

Rating by/Opinion of Firm	Percentage of Establishments		
	M_L	S_L	S_K
Serious	8.9	6.1	5.8
Moderate	42.2	26.5	32.7
Slight	35.6	40.8	42.3
None	6.7	18.4	7.7
No answer	6.7	8.2	11.5

Source: See Table 7.1.
Notes: See Table 7.1.

TABLE 7.33
The Most Important Non-remunerative Incentive

Type of Incentive	Percentage of Establishments		
	M_L	S_L	S_K
Medical/Dental care	13.3	16.3	17.3
Provide food & board	0.0	12.2	3.8
Housing	2.2	0.0	1.9
Education	0.0	0.0	1.9
Recreation club	0.0	2.0	0.0
Others	26.7	24.5	15.4
No answer	57.8	44.9	59.6

Source: See Table 7.1.
Notes: See Table 7.1.

TABLE 7.34
Assessment of Present Relations with Staff

Assessment of Firm	Percentage of Establishments		
	M_L	S_L	S_K
Excellent	20.0	24.0	22.6
Well	66.7	56.0	54.7
Fair	13.3	14.0	17.0
Not good	0.0	0.0	0.0
No answer	0.0	6.0	5.7

Source: See Table 7.1.
Notes: See Table 7.1.

TABLE 7.35

The Most Important Measure of Maintaining
Good Relations with Staff

Measures Taken	Percentage of Establishments		
	M_L	S_L	S_K
Frequent dialogue	69.6	60.3	60.0
Good facilities	7.1	10.3	15.4
Wage increases	21.4	19.0	13.9
Others	0.0	5.2	6.2
No answer	1.9	5.2	4.5

Source: See Table 7.1.
Notes: See Table 7.1.

TABLE 7.36

The Most Important Countermeasure for Cost Increase

Measures Used/Taken	Percentage of Establishments		
	M_L	S_L	S_K
Reduce number of workers	25.0	21.7	26.7
Mechanization	53.6	53.3	55.0
Energy saving	5.4	5.0	1.7
Reduce price of raw materials	8.9	8.3	5.0
Others	5.4	6.7	3.3
No answer	1.7	5.0	8.3

Source: See Table 7.1.
Notes: See Table 7.1.

TABLE 7.37

Length of Training

Length of Time	Percentage of Establishments		
	M_L	S_L	S_K
1 month	33.3	40.0	40.4
2–3 months	40.0	34.0	30.8
4–5 months	15.6	6.0	5.8
6–9 months	11.1	12.0	13.5
No answer	0.0	8.0	9.5

Source: See Table 7.1.
Notes: See Table 7.1.

TABLE 7.38

The Most Frequent Class of Employee Affected by Retrenchment

Class	Percentage of Establishments		
	M_L	S_L	S_K
Non-production worker	0.0	0.0	0.0
Without experience	0.0	2.0	2.0
Production operator	22.2	18.4	23.0
No education	2.2	8.2	0.0
Lazy	2.2	2.0	2.0
Not applicable/affected	0.0	14.3	11.5
No answer	73.3	55.1	61.5

Source: See Table 7.1.

Notes: Strictly speaking, these classes are not mutually exclusive (i.e. you can have a production operator who is also inexperienced and lazy). But the entrepreneur was asked to pick only one single class for retrenchment. See also Table 7.1.

TABLE 7.39

The Most Important Way to Keep Workers Busy

Methods Adopted	Percentage of Establishments		
	M_L	S_L	S_K
Adjust working hours	8.9	8.2	9.6
Assign to other work	0.0	8.2	0.0
Assign to maintenance	4.4	4.1	3.8
Look for other sources	2.2	0.0	0.0
Other steps	22.2	24.4	28.8
No answer	62.2	55.1	57.8

Source: See Table 7.1.
Notes: See Table 7.1.

TABLE 7.40

The Most Common Way of Improving Technology

Methods Adopted	Percentage of Establishments		
	M_L	S_L	S_K
Introduction of new machines	34.9	55.9	39.7
Technical training	25.4	15.3	15.9
Introduction of new technology	17.5	11.9	9.5
Hire technicians	4.8	3.4	6.4
In the management field	4.8	0.0	1.6
Others	0.0	0.0	0.0
No answer	12.6	13.5	26.9

Source: See Table 7.1.
Notes: See Table 7.1.

TABLE 7.41

The Association which Firms Most Utilized

Name of Association	Percentage of Establishments		
	M_L	S_L	S_K
Chamber of Commerce and Industry	8.8	18.4	7.7
Manufacturers' Association	28.9	30.6	30.8
Trade Development Board	20.0	14.3	13.5
Traders' Association	2.2	4.1	1.9
Others	2.2	2.0	1.9
No answer	37.8	30.6	44.2

Source: See Table 7.1.
Notes: See Table 7.1.

TABLE 7.42

The Most Important Area of Utilization of Associations

Areas of Utilization	Percentage of Establishments		
	M_L	S_L	S_K
Procurement of raw materials	2.2	4.1	3.8
Sales	17.8	18.4	15.4
Fund raising	4.4	8.2	3.8
Information	37.8	26.5	30.8
Others	4.4	8.2	5.8
No answer	33.3	34.7	40.4

Source: See Table 7.1.
Notes: See Table 7.1.

TABLE 7.43

The Most Important Area of Relations with the Community

Type/Area of Interaction	Percentage of Establishments		
	M_L	S_L	S_K
Contribution to community service	22.2	20.4	23.1
Participation in public service	6.7	4.1	1.9
Membership of co-operatives	4.4	2.0	7.7
Other associations	2.2	0.0	7.7
Others	8.9	12.2	5.8
No answer	55.6	61.1	53.9

Source: See Table 7.1.
Notes: See Table 7.1.

TABLE 7.44

Entrepreneur's Evaluation of Present Business Activities

Rating/Assessment	Percentage of Establishments		
	M_L	S_L	S_K
Excellent	35.6	30.6	32.7
Fair	64.4	61.2	63.5
Unsatisfactory	0.0	2.0	0.0
No answer	0.0	6.1	3.8

Source: See Table 7.1.
Notes: See Table 7.1.

TABLE 7.45

Entrepreneur's Evaluation of Future Business Activities

Rating/Assessment	Percentage of Establishments		
	M_L	S_L	S_K
Excellent	17.8	16.3	23.1
Well	48.9	42.9	46.2
Fair	31.1	30.6	23.1
Poor	2.2	6.1	1.9
No answer	0.0	4.1	5.7

Source: See Table 7.1.
Notes: See Table 7.1.

TABLE 7.46

Entrepreneur's Plans for Business in Future

Plans	Percentage of Establishments		
	M_L	S_L	S_K
Continue	53.3	68.6	51.7
Expansion & diversification	44.4	23.5	43.1
Conversion to other business	2.2	2.0	1.7
Discontinue	0.0	2.0	0.0
No answer	0.0	3.9	3.5

Source: See Table 7.1.
Notes: See Table 7.1.

TABLE 7.47

Party that Entrepreneur Consulted Most Frequently

	Percentage of Establishments		
Party Consulted	M_L	S_L	S_K
Parents & relatives	9.5	22.2	13.2
Friends	4.8	13.9	10.3
A director in own company	46.0	34.7	48.5
Fellow traders	17.5	16.7	14.7
Bankers	3.2	2.8	1.5
Parent company	12.7	1.4	1.5
Associations & co-operatives	3.2	1.4	4.4
Others	1.6	0.0	0.0
No answers	1.5	6.9	5.9

Source: See Table 7.1.
Notes: See Table 7.1.

TABLE 7.48

Entrepreneur's Awareness of Government Policies on Small Firms

	Percentage of Establishments		
Level of Awareness	M_L	S_L	S_K
Very much	28.9	9.8	9.6
A little	46.7	39.2	53.9
None	20.0	45.1	30.8
No answer	4.4	5.9	5.7

Source: See Table 7.1.
Notes: See Table 7.1.

TABLE 7.49

Actual and Expected Benefits from Government Policies

| | Percentage of Establishments | | | | | |
| | M_L | | S_L | | S_K | |
Type of Benefit	A	E	A	E	A	E
General subsidy	3.1	8.8	0.0	9.4	3.3	8.2
Tax holiday	7.8	8.8	1.6	10.6	1.6	8.2
Procurement of raw materials	0.0	0.0	4.9	7.1	1.6	6.1
Availability of loans	7.8	8.8	3.3	10.6	6.6	10.2
Purchase of government properties	0.0	0.0	3.3	1.2	1.6	0.0
Technical training & development	15.6	17.5	6.6	7.1	8.2	15.3
Information	7.8	6.3	8.2	2.4	8.2	6.1
Sale of products	1.6	5.0	0.0	7.1	6.6	5.1
Skill Development Fund's subsidy	21.9	15.0	9.8	10.6	16.4	12.2
Provision of foreign workers	4.7	28.8	13.1	28.2	6.6	19.4
Others	0.0	0.0	3.3	3.5	0.0	1.0

Source: See Table 7.1.

Notes: A represents actual benefit.

E represents expected benefit.

See also Table 7.1.

8

SMALL FIRMS:
A COMPARATIVE ANALYSIS

IN the preceding chapters we dealt exclusively with small firms in the manufacturing sector of Singapore. In this chapter we attempt a comparative analysis of small firms in Taiwan, Thailand, Japan, and Singapore. Such a comparative analysis is useful for shedding light on the relationship between small firms and the stages of economic development. This is so because Taiwan is comparable to Singapore as another Asian NIC, Thailand is comparable as an industrially less developed country and Japan as an industrially developed country.

Small Firms in Taiwan

Over the past forty years, Taiwan has developed very rapidly in terms of some common economic indicators. On the basis of global comparisons, the real GDP growth of Taiwan was among the highest in the world in the 1960s (8.8 per cent) and the 1970s (10.1 per cent) (see Table 1.2). The Taiwanese unemployment rate over the years has declined and her population growth rate has also decelerated.

One of the most important reasons accounting for the high economic growth rate in Taiwan is the remarkable performance of her manufacturing sector. The contribution of the manufacturing sector towards gross domestic product rose from 24 per cent in the 1961–4 period to 40 per cent in 1983. With respect to the total employment, the contribution of the manufacturing sector increased from 15 per cent to 32 per cent over the same time period.

The economic contribution of small firms in Taiwan is examined according to the following criteria: the number of establishments, employment, output and value-added. An examination of the structure of the small firms in Taiwan will also be given here.

Small Firms

Small firms in Taiwan comprise, in accordance with Singapore, tiny establishments, small establishments, and medium establishments. The data on Taiwanese industries are obtained from the Taiwan *Industrial and Commercial Census Report*, which is published every five years, i.e. 1971, 1976, and 1981.

TINY ESTABLISHMENTS

In Taiwan, tiny establishments are those that employ fewer than 10 workers. Table 8.1 shows the number, employment, output, and value-added of tiny establishments in the manufacturing sector for the years 1971, 1976, and 1981. First, we will look at the trend in the number of tiny establishments. In 1971, there were 19,317 tiny establishments. The number increased more than twofold to 47,358 in 1976. By 1981, there were 64,318 tiny establishments, representing more than a 200 per cent increase over the 1971 figure. However, as can be seen from Table 8.1, the rate of increase of the absolute number of tiny establishments declined over the decade. On the other hand, the relative contribution of tiny establishments in the total number of establishments increased, from 59.1 per cent in 1971 to 68.1 per cent in 1976 and 70.3 per cent in 1981.

A similar trend is observed in the employment figures of tiny establishments. In 1971, there were 113,614 workers employed by tiny establishments. This rose to 192,848 workers in 1976 and to 237,500 in 1981. Over the decade 1971–81, the absolute contribution of tiny establishments in employment rose by over 100 per cent while the rate of absolute increase decelerated. In relative terms, tiny establishments steadily gained importance. Of the total number of workers employed in manufacturing in 1971, 9.5 per cent were in tiny establishments. The figure rose to 10.1 per cent in 1976 and further to 10.8 per cent in 1981.

With regard to output, tiny establishments produced a total of NT$19,238 million in 1971 and this rose to NT$54,361 million in 1976.[1] Moreover, the output of tiny establishments surged upwards in 1981 by 462 per cent over 1971, registering NT$108,084 million. On the other hand, tiny establishments slipped in relative importance in output. In 1971, tiny establishments contributed 7.9 per cent of total manufacturing output but this fell to 6.6 per cent in 1976 and to 5.3 per cent in 1981.

The labour intensity of tiny establishments can be examined by comparing their relative contributions in employment and output. For all three years under study, the relative contributions of tiny establishments in employment surpassed their relative contributions in output (9.5 per cent vs. 7.9 per cent in 1971, 10.1 per cent vs. 6.6 per cent in 1976 and 10.8 per cent vs. 5.3 per cent in 1981). This shows that tiny establishments are more labour intensive and have a lower ratio of labour productivity than the average establishment. Moreover, the gap in labour productivity between tiny establishments and the average establishment, measured by the absolute difference between the two relative contributions, widened between 1971 and 1981.

As for the value-added of tiny establishments, Table 8.1 shows that the value-added of tiny establishments increased, rising from NT$2,497 million in 1971 to NT$10,656 million in 1976 and NT$34,085 million in 1981. However, the relative contribution of tiny establishments in value-added shows some fluctuations, rising in the period 1971–6 from

6.0 per cent to 7.7 per cent and falling in the period 1976–81 from 7.7 per cent to 6.4 per cent.

A similar comparison of the relative contributions of tiny establishments in employment and value-added reveals that tiny establishments were more labour intensive than the average establishment (9.5 per cent vs. 6.0 per cent in 1971, 10.1 per cent vs. 7.7 per cent in 1976, and 10.8 per cent vs. 6.4 per cent in 1981), implying that tiny establishments employed more labour per dollar's worth of value-added.

When the relative contributions of tiny establishments in output and value-added are compared, the results show that tiny establishments generated less value-added per dollar of output in 1971 (7.9 per cent vs. 6.0 per cent) but generated more value-added per dollar of output in 1976 (6.6 per cent vs. 7.7 per cent) and in 1981 (5.3 per cent vs. 6.4 per cent). Therefore, tiny establishments were less value-added oriented in 1971 but more value-added oriented thereafter.

The relative contributions of tiny establishments in the number of establishments, employment, output, and value-added are also given in Table 8.1. The relative contributions of tiny establishments in the number of establishments and employment rose but the relative contribution in output fell in the period 1971–81. The relative contribution in value-added rose in the period 1971–6 but fell between 1976 and 1981.

SMALL ESTABLISHMENTS

Small establishments in Taiwan are defined as firms which employ 10–49 workers. The economic contribution of small establishments in terms of the number of establishments, employment, output and value-added is given in Table 8.2. With respect to the number of establishments, there were 9,822 small establishments in 1971. The number increased to 15,875 in 1976 and to 19,702 in 1981. Over the decade, the number of small establishments rose by 101 per cent. On the other hand, the relative contribution of small establishments diminished. In 1971, small establishments accounted for 30.0 per cent of the total number of industrial establishments. The figure dropped to 22.8 per cent in 1976 and further to 21.5 per cent in 1981.

The rate of increase in the number of workers employed by small establishments in the period 1971–81 followed a similar pace as the rate of increase in the number of establishments. Over the decade, the employment of small establishments rose by 104 per cent, from 203,862 workers in 1971, to 332,827 workers in 1976, and to 416,467 workers in 1981. The relative contribution indicated a rising trend, from 17.0 per cent of total employment in 1971, to 17.4 per cent in 1976 and to 19.0 per cent in 1981.

Regarding output, the trend was rather unusual. In 1971, small establishments produced NT$28,870 million and the output rose to NT$97,803 million in 1976. In 1981, the output was NT$243,445 million. The relative contribution of small establishments in output was, however, 11.9 per cent of total output in 1971, 1976, and 1981.

Once again, we can study the labour intensity of small establishments by comparing the relative contributions in employment and output. The results are obvious: small establishments, like tiny establishments, were more labour intensive than the average establishment, which is consistent with our theoretical discussion in Chapter 3. Moreover, the gap in labour productivity between small establishments and the average establishment widened in the period 1971–6 but stabilized in the period 1976–81.

With respect to value-added, small establishments contributed NT$4,076 million worth of value-added in 1971. This went up to NT$17,400 million in 1976 and even further to NT$60,446 million in 1981. In terms of relative contribution, small establishments were responsible for 9.8 per cent of value-added in manufacturing. The figure rose to 12.5 per cent in 1976 but fell to 11.3 per cent in 1981.

When the relative contributions of small establishments in employment and value-added are compared, we find that small establishments, like tiny establishments, were more labour-intensive than the average establishment for all three years. However, unlike tiny establishments, which were less value-added oriented in 1971 but more value-added oriented in 1976 and 1981, small establishments were less value-added oriented in 1971 (11.9 per cent vs. 9.8 per cent), became more value-added oriented in 1976 (11.9 per cent vs. 12.5 per cent) but reverted to being less value-added oriented in 1981 (11.9 per cent vs. 11.3 per cent).

Table 8.2 also shows the four relative contributions of small establishments. While the relative contributions in employment and value-added followed the same trend as that of tiny establishments, the relative contributions of small establishments in the number of establishments and output were quite different from that of tiny establishments. Instead, the relative contribution of small establishments in the number of establishments fell while their relative contribution in output remained remarkably stable throughout the period 1971–81.

MEDIUM ESTABLISHMENTS

Medium establishments, like those in Singapore, are classified as firms which employ 50–99 workers. The statistics of medium establishments in Taiwan's manufacturing sector are tabulated in Table 8.3.

In 1971, there were 1,600 medium establishments. Over the five-year period from 1971 to 1976, the number of medium establishments expanded to 2,988 units. By 1981, medium establishments grew to 3,758 units, representing an increase of over 100 per cent for the decade. From Table 8.3 it is clear that the relative contribution of medium establishments in the total number of establishments fell in the period 1971–6 and levelled off between 1976 and 1981. Indeed, over the latter half of the decade under study, the percentage contribution of medium establishments to the total number of manufacturing establishments slipped by only 0.2 per cent, from 4.3 per cent to 4.1 per cent.

Medium establishments employed 110,785 workers in 1971. They expanded their employment in 1976 and 1981 to 209,702 workers and 261,075 workers respectively. Thus, over the ten-year period from 1971 to 1981, the work-force of medium establishments had a 2.4-fold increase in strength. Unlike tiny and small establishments, the relative contribution of medium establishments in employment rose in the period 1971–81, from 9.2 per cent in 1971 to 11.0 per cent in 1976 and 11.9 per cent in 1981.

The output of medium establishments grew steadily over the decade. In 1971, medium establishments produced NT$16,849 million and in 1976, NT$71,685 million. By 1981, the output was NT$195,349 million. In terms of the relative contribution in output, Table 8.3 shows that the relative contribution increased from 6.9 per cent in 1971 to 9.6 per cent in 1981.

In our foregoing discussion, we found that tiny and small establishments were more labour intensive than the average establishment. The same holds true for medium establishments. For all three years under study, medium establishments accounted for a larger proportion of the total manufacturing employment than of the total manufacturing output. However, unlike tiny establishments, whose gap in labour productivity with the average establishment had widened in the period 1971–81, and small establishments, whose gap in labour productivity with the average establishment had widened from 1971 to 1976 but stabilized between 1976 and 1981, the gap in labour productivity of medium establishments with the average establishment had remained the same in the period 1971–81.

The value-added of medium establishments were NT$2,359 million, NT$11,141 million, and NT$43,084 million in 1971, 1976, and 1981 respectively. Over the ten-year period, the value-added of medium establishments increased 18.3-fold. Its relative contribution in value-added increased from 5.7 per cent to 8.0 per cent in the period 1971–6 but reached a plateau from 1976 to 1981 (see Table 8.3).

The relative contributions of medium establishments in employment for 1971, 1976, and 1981 were greater than their relative contributions in value-added. Therefore, medium establishments were more labour intensive than the average establishment in the period 1971–81. The relative contribution of medium establishments in output was higher than their relative contribution in value-added for 1971, 1976, and 1981. Therefore, medium establishments were less value-added oriented in the period 1971–81. The preceding discussion shows that tiny, small, and medium establishments were more service oriented than the average establishment. As such, they employed more labour per unit of output and value-added. The difference in labour productivity between tiny and small establishments with the average establishment widened over 1971–81. For medium establishments, the gap in labour productivity was smaller for the period 1971–6 but remained stable between 1976 and 1981. Tiny establishments were less value-added oriented in 1971 but became more value-added oriented in 1976 and 1981. Small establishments were less value-added oriented in 1971 and 1981. Medium establishments were consistently less value-added oriented in the period 1971–81.

What has been the aggregate effect of the economic contributions of tiny, small, and medium establishments? The statistics of the relative contributions of small firms in the number of establishments, employment, output, and value-added are presented in Table 8.4. Clearly, the relative contributions of the small firms in the number of establishments and employment rose between 1971 and 1981. Their relative contribution in output rose from 1971 to 1976 but fell from 1976 to 1981. Similarly, their relative contribution in value-added rose in the period 1971–6 but fell in the period 1976–81.

For all three years, 1971, 1976, and 1981, the relative contribution of small firms in employment surpassed their relative contribution in output, implying that small firms were more labour intensive than the average establishment from 1971 to 1981 (see Table 8.4). Moreover, the relative contribution in employment exceeded the relative contribution in value-added, which means that small firms had not only employed more labour per unit of output, they had also employed more labour per unit of value-added. This is what we would expect from the individual contributions of tiny, small and medium establishments.

Furthermore, small firms were less value-added oriented than the average establishment in 1971 and 1981 but were more value-added oriented in 1976. This is because the relative contribution in output surpassed that in value-added in 1971 and 1981 but fell behind in 1976.

Medium Firms

Apart from small firms, it is also interesting to briefly look at medium firms in Taiwan. Medium firms comprise those which employ 100–499 workers. Table 8.5 reports the number of establishments, employment, output, and value-added of medium firms. In the period 1971–81, the number of medium firms increased by 98.7 per cent from 1,628 units in 1971 to 2,851 units in 1976 and 3,235 units in 1981. The rate of growth of the number of medium firms in the period 1971–81 was therefore slower than that of small firms. The relative contribution of medium firms in the total number of establishments, however, declined over the same period, from 5.0 per cent in 1971 to 4.1 per cent in 1976 and 3.5 per cent in 1981.

The work-force of the medium firms also expanded, from 339,389 workers in 1971 to 576,084 workers in 1976 and 632,700 workers in 1981. Over the decade, the work-force grew by 86.4 per cent, which is slower than the rate of growth of the work-force in small firms. The relative contribution of the medium firms rose initially from 28.2 per cent in 1971 to 30.2 per cent in 1976 but fell to 28.8 per cent in 1981.

In terms of output, the medium firms produced NT$63,121 million in 1971, NT$239,107 million in 1976, and NT$537,169 million in 1981. Over the ten-year period, output multiplied 8.5-fold. Compared to the small firms, the output of the medium firms increased at a faster rate.

The relative contribution of medium firms in output rose from 26.0 per cent in 1971 to 29.2 per cent in 1976 but fell to 26.3 per cent in 1981.

The Structure of Small Firms in Taiwan

The structure of small firms in Taiwan is examined with respect to assets, market orientation, and legal organization.

ASSETS

To observe the changing capital intensity of the manufacturing establishments according to firm size, we will limit our analysis to 1976 and 1981 as the data are only available for these two years. Tables 8.6 and 8.7 give the distribution of capital per establishment by firm size for the years 1976 and 1981 respectively.

With respect to tiny establishments, those with below NT$1 million in assets accounted for 72.2 per cent of the tiny establishments in 1976 but the proportion decreased to 34.7 per cent in 1981. Instead, the tiny establishments sector became dominated by firms which had NT$1–10 million in assets in 1981, accounting for 63.6 per cent of the tiny establishments, in contrast with 27.4 per cent in 1976. The number of tiny establishments with assets valued at NT$10–50 million also increased from 0.3 per cent in 1976 to 1.6 per cent in 1981, but there was only a negligible increase in the number of tiny establishments with NT$50–500 million in assets from 1976 to 1981 and none of the tiny establishments had above NT$500 million in assets in 1981. Therefore, while the capital-intensity of the tiny establishments increased over the five-year period from 1976 to 1981, the asset value per establishment continued to be concentrated at the lower end of the scale.

The small establishments also become more capital intensive. While approximately the same proportion of small establishments had NT$1–10 million in assets in 1976 (71.0 per cent) and 1981 (69.4 per cent), the proportion with below NT$1 million in assets shrank from 18.8 per cent in 1976 to 5.0 per cent in 1981 while the proportion with NT$10–50 million in assets rose from 9.4 per cent in 1976 to 22.9 per cent in 1981. The number of small establishments with NT$50–500 million in assets also expanded, from 0.8 per cent in 1976 to 2.7 per cent in 1981.

The medium establishments too invested more capital in their operations. In 1976, 49.0 per cent of the medium establishments had NT$1–10 million in assets, 41.2 per cent had NT$10–50 million in assets and 7.8 per cent had NT$50–500 million in assets. The respective proportions in 1981 were 28.4 per cent, 50.1 per cent and 20.9 per cent. The few medium establishments that had less than NT$1 million in assets in 1976 (1.9 per cent) declined even further to 0.6 per cent in 1981.

A comparison of Tables 8.6 and 8.7 shows that the percentage of medium firms with below NT$1 million, NT$1–10 million, and NT$10–50 million in assets decreased (0.7 per cent to 0.09 per cent,

19.9 per cent to 11.7 per cent, 43.4 per cent to 34.3 per cent respectively) from 1976 to 1981, while those with NT$50–500 million increased from 33.6 per cent in 1976 to 53.9 per cent in 1981.

From the preceding discussion, we can say that the amount of assets per establishment is least for the majority of the tiny establishments, followed by the small establishments and the medium establishments, and that most of the small and medium firms have become more capital intensive in the period 1976–81.

MARKET ORIENTATION

Unfortunately, data on market orientation and the legal organization of firms are not available in terms of the number of employees. We can only analyse these features of firms by assets. Thus, in Tables 8.8 and 8.9, small and medium firms are those which have assets of less than NT$10 million. As can be seen from Tables 8.6 and 8.7, the definition of small and medium firms by assets is not quite the same as the definition of small and medium firms by number of employees. We have to bear this in mind in the analysis with respect to market orientation and legal organization.

Table 8.8 presents the exports of small and medium firms in the manufacturing sector of Taiwan for the period 1981–4. In 1981, small and medium firms together contributed 71.8 per cent to total exports. In 1982, the share of exports by small and medium firms rose slightly to 73.5 per cent. However, the share of exports fell after 1982, with small and medium firms being responsible for 66.9 per cent of the total exports in 1983 and 62.5 per cent in 1984.

It is clear, therefore, that small and medium firms in the Taiwanese manufacturing sector were highly export oriented. Their relative contributions to exports for the years 1981–4 were very high. However, we also find that the relative importance of small and medium firms in exports declined between 1982 and 1984.

It should be highlighted that most of the small and medium firms did not export their products under their own brand names. Rather, the bulk of the exports of small and medium firms came under borrowed (foreign) brand names, i.e. they produced for foreign companies. This implies that Taiwanese small and medium firms are cost effective but they have no control over markets.

LEGAL ORGANIZATION

The distribution of small and medium firms by legal organization is given in Table 8.9. In 1984, sole proprietorship accounted for 59.7 per cent of the small and medium firms in Taiwan while 38.9 per cent were registered companies. Only 1.3 per cent of the small and medium firms were organized as partnerships. The substantial proportion of small and medium firms organized as registered companies in 1984 thus indicates that two out of every five small and medium firms in Taiwan preferred ease in raising funds for business expansion over flexibility in management and operation.

Small Firms in Thailand

The economic development of Thailand has also been impressive. During the period 1976–81, the average annual growth rate of the Thai GDP in constant prices was 7 per cent. The manufacturing sector was the leading sector, exhibiting an average annual GDP growth rate of 8.4 per cent during the same period. For the agricultural sector, the corresponding figure was 2.9 per cent. Not surprisingly, the share of the agricultural sector in the total GDP decreased from 30 per cent in 1976 to 24 per cent in 1981 while that of the manufacturing sector was around 21 per cent in the period 1979–81.

Within the manufacturing sector, the following industries were the high growth industries in terms of high average annual GDP growth rate: the chemicals and chemical products industry (16 per cent), the apparel industry (12.5 per cent), the engineering industry (11.8 per cent), and the textiles industry (10.2 per cent). On the other hand, the average annual GDP growth rate was −1.1 per cent for the petroleum refining and petroleum products industry and 3.6 per cent for the food industry. During this high growth period in which the manufacturing sector was performing remarkably well, small firms were expected to play an important role in the Thai industrialization process.

Small firms in Thailand are also classified under the same three categories: tiny establishments with 5–9 workers, small establishments with 10–49 workers, and medium establishments with 50–99 workers. Medium firms in Thailand are those establishments with 100–199 workers while those with 200 workers and more are classified as large firms.

Table 8.10 shows that there were a total of 36,333 industrial firms in 1978, of which 51 per cent were tiny establishments, 39 per cent small establishments, and 5 per cent medium establishments. Thus, small firms accounted for 95 per cent of all industrial firms in Thailand.[2]

Small firms also contributed significantly to the employment in Thailand. Tiny establishments, small establishments, and medium establishments accounted for 10 per cent, 24 per cent, and 11 per cent of the total labour force in 1978 respectively (see Table 8.10). Thus, 45 per cent of employment was associated with small firms, indicating the significance of small firms in providing employment opportunities in a labour surplus economy such as Thailand. The contribution of small establishments to total output and total value-added were 17 per cent and 15 per cent respectively in 1978. The contribution of small firms to Thai output and value-added is estimated to be around 25 per cent.[3]

Thus, small firms played an indispensable role in the Thai economy, contributing 95 per cent of all establishments, 45 per cent in terms of employment, and 25 per cent of total output and value-added.

Based on a field survey, Tambunlertchai and Loohawenchit studied a profile of small firms (tiny, small, and medium establishments) as well as medium and large firms.[4] Their results are summarized as follows:

1. There is a positive relationship between firm size and initial capital outlay per factory. The initial capital per factory was only 799,000 bahts for tiny establishments, compared to 1.578 million bahts for small establishments, 4.702 million bahts for medium establishments, and 8.174 million bahts for medium firms.

2. The production per factory for tiny establishments, small establishments, medium establishments, and medium firms were 583,000 bahts, 2.309 million bahts, 10.672 million bahts, and 21.063 million bahts respectively.

3. The value-added per factory for tiny establishments was 153,300 bahts which is insignificant compared to 655,700 bahts for small establishments, 3.173 million bahts for medium establishments and 6.929 million bahts for medium firms.

4. Fixed assets per worker did not increase as firm size increased. The fixed assets per worker for tiny establishments was 85,600 bahts, which is larger than that of small establishments (67,700 bahts) and medium establishments (77,600 bahts). The fixed assets per worker for medium firms was 87,600 bahts, marginally greater than that of tiny establishments.

5. The production per worker for tiny establishments, small establishments, and medium establishments were 85,500 bahts, 101,900 bahts, and 157,900 bahts respectively. The production per worker for medium firms was only 157,800 bahts, which is about the same as that of medium establishments.

6. There is a positive relationship between value-added per worker and firm size. The value-added per worker for tiny establishments, small establishments, medium establishments, and medium firms were 22,500 bahts, 29,200 bahts, 46,600 bahts, and 51,900 bahts respectively.

7. The composition of goods produced varies as firm size varies. For tiny establishments, 71 per cent of the products were consumer goods, 16.3 per cent intermediate goods, and 12.7 per cent capital goods. For small establishments, the proportions were 56.9 per cent for consumer goods, 21.3 per cent intermediate goods, and 21.8 per cent capital goods.

Quite surprising, medium establishments and medium firms tend to concentrate less on capital goods. For medium establishments, 46.7 per cent of output were consumer goods, 42.5 per cent intermediate goods, and only 10.8 per cent capital goods. For medium firms, 39.1 per cent of output were consumer goods, 47.0 per cent intermediate goods, and 13.9 per cent capital goods.

8. The composition of fixed assets varies as firm size changes. Bigger firms allocate a smaller percentage of fixed assets on buildings and land because these two factors are fixed costs which reduce steadily as the scale of production increases.

Thus, the proportion of fixed assets on buildings for small establishments, medium establishments, and medium firms was 20.9 per cent,

21.3 per cent, and 17.2 per cent respectively, all smaller than that of tiny establishments (27.8 per cent). Similarly, the proportion of fixed assets on land for small establishments (28.3 per cent), medium establishments (12.8 per cent), and medium firms (15.9 per cent) was smaller than that of tiny establishments (29.9 per cent).

The proportion of fixed assets on machinery for tiny establishments, small establishments, and medium establishments was 30.7 per cent, 36.2 per cent, and 55.3 per cent respectively. For medium firms, the proportion of fixed assets on machinery was only 50.8 per cent.

The proportion of fixed assets on transport equipment did not increase as firm size increased. It was 10.1 per cent, 11.3 per cent, 6.8 per cent, and 8.5 per cent for tiny establishments, small establishments, medium establishments, and medium firms respectively.

9. Market orientation also differs as firm size varies. For tiny establishments, the export–sales ratio was 19.3 per cent, compared to 26.7 per cent for small establishments and 21.0 per cent for medium establishments. The medium firms had the highest export–sales ratio (34 per cent). Large firms quite surprisingly only catered for the domestic market with the export–sales ratio being only 14.8 per cent.

10. Sources of methods of production also varies as firm size changes. Among the tiny establishments surveyed, 53.6 per cent designed their own products, 17 per cent copied foreign designs without any adaptation, and 16.5 per cent improved on foreign designs. For small establishments, 53.5 per cent had their own product designs, 20.3 per cent improved on foreign designs, and 18 per cent copied foreign designs without any adaptation. About 44.8 per cent of the medium establishments surveyed designed their own products, 20 per cent improved on foreign technology, and 13.8 per cent copied foreign designs without any adaptation. The corresponding figures for medium firms were 43.8 per cent, 20.8 per cent, and 13.5 per cent, and for large firms were 27.1 per cent, 10.4 per cent, and 18.8 per cent respectively.

There is almost a consistent positive relationship between firm size and the adoption of foreign technology. The percentages of firms surveyed which brought in foreign technology for tiny establishments, small establishments, medium establishments, medium firms, and large firms were 2.1 per cent, 4.4 per cent, 9.9 per cent, 8.3 per cent, and 14.6 per cent respectively.

With regard to receiving advice from the government, only 1 per cent of tiny establishments benefited from the government. The corresponding figures for small establishments, medium establishments, medium firms, and large firms were 2.7 per cent, 7.2 per cent, 4.2 per cent, and 10.4 per cent respectively.

11. The form of management differs as firm size varies. There is a negative relationship between firm size and management by owners. The percentage of firms which were run by owners for tiny establishments, small establishments, medium establishments, medium firms, and large firms were 93.1 per cent, 88.8 per cent, 76.6 per cent, 62.2 per cent, and 86.2 per cent respectively.

12. The source of capital also depends on firm size. Using personal funds was an important source of capital for 89.6 per cent of the tiny establishments surveyed. The corresponding figures for small establishments, medium establishments, medium firms and large firms were 65.0 per cent, 70.6 per cent, 71.6 per cent, and 81.3 per cent respectively.

13. The subcontracting system is not well established in Thailand for the following reasons: (i) The tax system, which is based on sales of each firm, encourages vertical integration; (ii) It is difficult to control the quality of products produced by subcontracting firms; and (iii) As labour is cheap in Thailand, labour hoarding is not too costly and thereby causes large firms to rely less on subcontracting as a buffer against fluctuation in business.

Small Firms in Japan

The Japanese success in economic development since World War II needs no introduction. In 1950, Japan accounted for 2 per cent of the GNP of the world market economies, while the US contributed almost 50 per cent and the European countries 21.7 per cent. By the late 1960s, Japan ranked with the US and the Soviet Union as the world's industrial powers, making herself Asia's undisputed industrial leader. Japan's economic development gained such momentum that she contributed 10.6 per cent to the world GNP in 1980, in contrast with 26.3 per cent for the US and 28.7 per cent for the whole of Europe. Hence, Japan has emerged as the second economic power, next to the US.

During the nine-year period 1965–73, Japan's average annual growth rate was 9.9 per cent. Over the same time span from 1974 to 1982, her real economic growth rate slowed down to 4.4 per cent, indicating that the country has shifted from an era of high growth to one of stable growth. The major factor supporting Japan's economic success is her manufacturing sector.

In 1964, there were 487,050 manufacturing establishments. This rose to 744,337 establishments in 1978. The number of workers employed in manufacturing firms increased from 8,169,484 in 1964 to 10,475,000 in 1982. In terms of value-added, in 1964, manufacturing firms had value-added of ¥4,837.1 billion while in 1982, the figure expanded to ¥76,180.4 billion.[5]

Table 8.11 indicates the percentage of the total manufacturing employment in various industries. In 1954, textiles, machinery, and food and drink were the three important employers in the manufacturing sector. By 1980, the machinery industry had become the main employer, accounting for 25.5 per cent of the total manufacturing employment. The percentage of the total manufacturing value-added in various industries is reported in Table 8.13. In 1954, chemicals, machinery, and textiles accounted for 16.5 per cent, 14.5 per cent, and 13.1 per cent respectively of the total manufacturing value-added. In 1980, the machinery industry contributed 24.8 per cent of the total value-added, followed by chemicals with only 12.2 per cent.

Thus, in the past, textiles, ceramics, woodworking, and food and drink dominated the Japanese manufacturing sector. However, the Japanese industrial structure has shifted toward skill-intensive and science-based industries. Machinery-related industries have become the leaders in the manufacturing sector. The remarkable economic restructuring in the manufacturing sector has made an indispensable contribution to Japan's rapid economic growth.

The definition of small firms in Japan is the same as the definition of small firms in Singapore, Taiwan, and Thailand, i.e. establishments with less than 100 workers are classified as small firms. Medium firms in Japan refer to firms with 100–299 workers, while large firms are those with 300 workers or more.

As Table 8.12 shows, Japanese small firms accounted for 97.6 per cent and 84.9 per cent of total industrial establishments in 1970 and 1982 respectively. With respect to employment, small firms contributed 51.6 per cent and 55.5 per cent towards total industrial employment in 1970 and 1982 respectively. The proportion of small firms' output towards total industrial output was 32.0 per cent and 33.9 per cent in 1970 and 1982 respectively. Thus, small firms are still important in a large economy such as Japan, contributing more than half of Japanese industrial employment and one-third of Japanese industrial output.

Medium firms in Japan are also significant employers and producers, contributing 16.4 per cent and 17.6 per cent toward total industrial employment and output respectively in 1982. Needless to say, large firms in Japan contributed almost half the total industrial output in 1982.

Recently, the industrial structure of the small firms in the manufacturing industry is tending towards:

1. an increase in the share of heavy processing industries such as the machine industry; and

2. a decline in the share of light materials industries, such as the pulp, paper and paper products, lumber and wood products, and textiles industries.

The reasons for such developments include the innovations based on electronics technology, found mainly in the processing and assembling industries, the sharp rise in energy prices, and the growth of exports.

The Japanese economy has attained industrial maturity. Interdependence between the various sectors is high and competition is strong. The improved living standards have led to increasingly discerning and diverse demand. Manufacturing firms respond to the growing sophistication of the consumers by either of two means: internal supply within the firm, or external supply by entrusting work to outside organizations. The small and medium firms tend to seek internal supply for reasons of preservation of secrecy and traditional practice. Other reasons include low cost for some operations and unavailability of services to meet special needs from outside organizations. Although large firms more often use the services of subcontractors, an increasing number of small and medium firms are resorting to this method.

Table 8.14 shows the export propensity of small and medium firms in the manufacturing sector in 1981. The proportion of exports to sales ranged from 2.6 per cent in food to 39.5 per cent in transport equipment. The ratio of firms which engaged in exports ranged from 2.8 per cent in publishing and printing to 40.7 per cent in chemicals.

Small and medium firms in Japan have been involved in a relatively large number of overseas ventures. According to *White Paper on Small and Medium Enterprises*, the most important motive for small and medium firms to invest in developing countries is the cheap local labour.[6] The other two important motivations are internationalization of corporate management and securing of overseas markets. With respect to investment in developed countries, the motivations of small and medium firms are, in order of importance: (i) securing of overseas markets; (ii) internationalization of corporate management, and (iii) utilizing local human resources.

Table 8.15 shows the regional distribution of overseas ventures set up by Japanese small and medium firms in manufacturing.[7] They definitely have a strong propensity to invest in Asia, in particular, in South Korea and Taiwan. Unfortunately, due perhaps to rising trade protectionism in the West, Japanese small and medium firms have very apparently shifted their overseas investments from Asia to North America.

With respect to the type of industries Japanese small and medium firms have invested in overseas, Table 8.16 shows that electric machinery and sundries top the list within the manufacturing sector.

The 'Keiei Senryaku Jittai Chosa' or 'Survey on the State of Managerial Strategies', conducted by the Small and Medium Enterprises Agency in December 1983 in Japan highlights some interesting features of small and medium firms in the Japanese manufacturing industry:

1. Small and medium firms emphasized 'low prices through mass production' during the period of high growth (i.e. 1965–73) but have gradually moved into high value-added products by developing quality, function, and design (1974 onwards), developing new products, and diversifying the product field.

2. Physical productivity has increased tremendously. The basic unit of energy consumption has been steadily declining since 1976 because of energy conservation, and the labour input (number of employees × total number of actual labour hours) has been increasing only slowly after 1974.

3. Technology and information, planning, design, and marketing have become increasingly important. After the two oil crises, small and medium manufacturers shifted their focus from hardware-related production factors, such as raw materials, which have a direct impact on the production process, to software-related production factors, represented by technology, information, and design.

4. The growing pattern of consumerism towards individuality and

quality in high fashion goods, etc. and towards value and utility in everyday goods has prompted greater mechanization and rationalization in the production process. About 57 per cent of the small and medium manufacturing firms made no plans for on-line system application, compared with 8.7 per cent of the large firms. On the other hand, 30.2 per cent of the small and medium firms were considering on-line system applications, compared to 22.5 per cent of the large firms. Those actually using on-line systems constituted just 12.5 per cent of the small and medium firms and 68.8 per cent of the large firms.

5. The greater complexity of the businesses has made access to information very important to the success of business enterprise. Small and medium firms have therefore intensified efforts to collect, select, process, and utilize information. The source of their information included business and professional magazines, newspapers, television, and business interactions with clients and parent corporations. However, only 6 per cent feel that the information was appropriately selected. About 42 per cent found their efforts in organizing information insufficient. Those using the filing and documentation system and computers were increasing in numbers, although they still lagged behind large firms.

6. The accumulation of technology of small and medium firms, measured by the growth of research expenses and number of researchers, had increased by 4.3-fold and 1.8-fold respectively between 1971 and 1982. However, the percentages were considerably smaller than those of the large firms.

7. In terms of production techniques, 93 per cent of the small and medium firms practised production management in terms of basic quality control. About 76 per cent implemented process control while 78 per cent had cost controls.

8. Venture business, which has been increasingly important in the past few years, largely comprised small and medium firms (84 per cent). Most were found in processing and assembly industries like the electrical machinery, general machinery, and information-related industries.

In a separate survey by the Small and Medium Enterprises Agency, namely, the 'Kogyo Jittai Kihon Chosa' or 'Basic Survey on the Current Situation of Industries', small and medium manufacturers accounted for 26.7 per cent of the total export volume in 1970. This fell to 15.2 per cent in 1983. The share of light industries (such as textiles) has declined while that of heavy industries (such as general machinery) has increased. Half of the small and medium firms have exported their products through trading companies, while the remaining half have used the sales network or borrowed brand names of their parent or related companies. Only 5.5 per cent have directly exported their own goods.

A Comparative Analysis of Small Firms in Singapore, Taiwan, Thailand, and Japan

Our study of small firms in Singapore, Taiwan, Thailand, and Japan shows that the economic contributions and structure of small firms in each country are distinct. What are the essential differences (or similarities) of small firms in these countries?

Before we attempt a comparative analysis of small firms in the four countries, it may be helpful if we recapitulate the slightly different classifications of small firms in each country. The relative differences are provided below:

| | Number of Workers | | | |
Country	Small Firms	Tiny Establishments	Small Establishments	Medium Establishments
Singapore	5–99	5–9	10–49	50–99
Taiwan	1–99	1–9	10–49	50–99
Thailand	5–99	5–9	10–49	50–99
Japan	1–99	n.a.	n.a.	n.a.

Taiwan has a much higher percentage of tiny establishments than Singapore. In 1981, 70 per cent of Taiwan's manufacturing sector comprised tiny establishments while Singapore's tiny establishments accounted for 37 per cent of the total number of manufacturing establishments in 1983. The same is true of Thailand, whose tiny establishments accounted for 51 per cent of the total number of establishments in 1978.

On the other hand, small establishments are more numerous in relative terms in Singapore than in Taiwan and Thailand. In 1983, 46 per cent of the total number of establishments were small establishments in Singapore while the corresponding figure for Taiwan was 22 per cent in 1981 and that for Thailand was 39 per cent in 1978.

The medium establishments are more dominant in Singapore's manufacturing sector than in Thailand's or Taiwan's. The respective figures are 8 per cent (1983), 5 per cent (1978) and 4 per cent (1981) of the total number of manufacturing establishments.

Thus small firms accounted for 96 per cent of the total number of establishments in Taiwan (1981), 95 per cent in Thailand (1978), 91 per cent in Singapore (1983), and 85 per cent in Japan (1982) (see Table 8.17). Small firms are therefore slightly more dominant in Taiwan and Thailand than in Singapore and Japan.

However, small firms are more important contributors of industrial employment and output in Japan than in the other three countries. Small firms in Japan accounted for 55.5 per cent of total industrial employment while the corresponding figures for Thailand, Taiwan, and Singapore were 45 per cent, 42 per cent, and 35 per cent respectively. Japanese small firms contributed 33.9 per cent towards total industrial output while small firms in Thailand, Taiwan and Singapore contributed 25 per cent, 27 per cent, and 26 per cent towards their respective industrial output. In terms of contribution to total industrial value-added, Taiwanese small firms topped the list with 26 per cent, followed by Thailand (25 per cent) and Singapore (22 per cent). (Data on value-added by Japanese small firms are not available.)

A comparison of the production characteristics of small firms between Singapore and Taiwan is attempted below. (The comparison does not include Thailand and Japan due to the lack of data.)

From our discussion in Chapter 4, we know that the relative contributions of tiny establishments in Singapore's manufacturing sector in the number of establishments, employment, output, and value-added diminished from 1963 to 1978 and then increased from 1978 to 1983 (see also Figure 4.1). Taiwan's tiny establishments are quite different. Rather, their relative contributions in the number of establishments and employment increased from 1971 to 1981, while the relative contribution in value-added initially increased between 1971 and 1976 but declined in 1981. The relative contribution in output declined continuously in the period 1971–81. Clearly, the tiny establishments sector has increased in importance in Taiwan in terms of the number of establishments and employment.

Small establishments in Singapore exhibit a similar trend to tiny establishments except that the declining trend was arrested in 1973. Thereafter, the relative importance increased slightly and then stabilized around that level in 1975–6 (see Figure 4.2). Small establishments in Taiwan, unlike tiny establishments, were losing relative importance in the number of establishments in the period 1971–81 but maintained relative importance in output in the same period.

Medium establishments in Singapore followed the same path as small establishments, i.e. the relative contributions fell from 1963 to 1973–4, rose slightly and then stabilized in the early 1980s (see Figure 4.3). In the case of Taiwan, medium establishments exhibit a similar pattern to small establishments, except that the relative contributions in output increased steadily from 1971–81 and value-added stabilized over the period 1976–81. Therefore, medium establishments in Taiwan, like small establishments, are still increasingly important in employment and output.

It can be seen, therefore, that the small firms sector in Singapore declined in relative importance from 1963 to 1973–4, then rose slightly and stabilized in the early 1980s. On the other hand, the relative importance of the small firms sector in Taiwan in the number of establishments and employment was still on the rise in the early 1980s, but showed a downward trend from 1976 to 1981 in output and value-added.

Next, we will look at the labour intensity of small firms in Singapore and Taiwan. In Chapter 4, we found that tiny and small establishments in Singapore were more labour intensive than the average establishment while medium establishments were less labour intensive than the average establishment from 1963 to 1968 but more so from 1968 to 1983. In the case of Taiwan, tiny, small, and medium establishments were all more labour intensive than the average establishment (their contribution in employment being greater than their contribution in output). Further-more, small firms in Singapore and Taiwan were more value-added oriented in 1975–6; i.e. their respective contributions in value-added exceeded their respective contributions in output.

In Taiwan, we find that sole proprietorships still dominated the manufacturing firms in 1984 (59 per cent) while registered companies were the next most common form of legal organization (39.6 per cent). Partnerships were the least favoured, constituting only 1.3 per cent of manufacturing firms in 1984. On the other hand, sole proprietorships and partnerships became the least common form of business organiz-ation in Singapore in 1983, accounting for 12 per cent and 17 per cent of manufacturing firms respectively. Private limited companies dominated the manufacturing sector, constituting 69 per cent of manufacturing firms in Singapore.

With regard to export orientation, the data available limits any comparison between Singapore's small firms and the small and medium firms in Taiwan is their high export orientation, contributing 71.84 industries in Taiwan is their high export orientation, contributing 71.84 per cent of total exports in 1981. However, the share of exports has declined after 1982, accounting for 62.53 per cent of the total exports in 1984. In contrast, small firms in Singapore contributed only 12 per cent of the total exports of the manufacturing sector in 1983. An interesting point to note is that small and medium firms in Taiwan are even more export oriented than those in Japan. The latter accounted for 26.7 per cent of the total exports in 1970 and 15.2 per cent in 1983.

Another unique feature of small and medium firms in Taiwan is that most of their products are exported under borrowed brand names, i.e. they produce for foreign companies. Taiwanese small and medium firms are therefore cost effective but have little control over markets. As for Japanese small and medium firms, half exported their products through trading companies, about half used borrowed brand names, and only 5.5 per cent directly exported their own products.

With respect to the industrial composition of exports of small firms, Japan is quite different from Singapore and Taiwan. The exports of small firms in Singapore and small and medium firms in Taiwan are concentrated in the light industries while the exports of Japanese small and medium firms are found in both the light and heavy industries. In fact, the proportion of heavy industries in the exports of Japanese small and medium firms have increased in recent years.

Generally speaking, small firms in the four countries have shown great potential in steering their respective economies through different phases of industrialization. Their industrial potential, however, can only be maximized with appropriate government policies. In the next chapter we will look at the role of the government in helping small firms in the four countries.

1. NT$ represents the New Taiwanese dollar. The exchange rate between the NT$ and US$ was 40 in the 1970s.

2. See Busaba Kunasirin, *The Role of Small- and Medium-Scale Industries in the Economic Development of Japan and Thailand: A Comparative Analysis*, Tokyo, Institute of Developing Economies, Visiting Research Fellow Series No. 109, March 1984.

3. Unfortunately, data on output and value-added contribution by tiny and medium establishments are not available. The contribution and value-added by firms with 50–199 workers was 34 per cent and 33 per cent respectively (Kunasirin). The estimate of 25 per cent for small firms' contribution towards output and value-added seems reasonable.

4. S. Tambunlertchai and C. Loohawenchit, 'Small Manufacturing Enterprises in Thailand', in Victor Fung-Shuen Sit (ed.,) *Strategies For Small-Scale Industries Promotion In Asia*, Hong Kong, Longman, 1984.

5. The exchange rate of Japanese yen per US$ was 194.5 in 1978.

6. Japan, Small and Medium Business Agency, *Chusho Kigyo Hakusho*, White Paper on Small and Medium Enterprises, 1980, p. 208.

7. Terutomo Ozawa, 'The Transnational Spread of Japan's Small and Medium Enterprises and Technology Transfer', paper submitted to the United Nations Conference on Trade and Development, Geneva, December 1984.

TABLE 8.1
Number, Employment, Output, and Value-added of Tiny Establishments in Manufacturing, Taiwan, 1971–1981

Industrial Characteristics	Year	Tiny Establishments (Below 10 Workers)			Total Number of Establishments	
		Number/ NT$Million	Percentage of Total	Percentage Increase	Number/ NT$Million	Percentage Increase
Number of establishments	1971	19,317	59.1	—	32,688	—
	1976	47,358	68.1	145.2	69,517	112.7
	1981	64,318	70.3	35.8	91,499	31.6
Employment	1971	113,614	9.5	—	1,202,239	—
	1976	192,848	10.1	69.7	1,907,581	58.7
	1981	237,500	10.8	23.2	2,196,691	15.2
Output	1971	19,238	7.9	—	243,135	—
	1976	54,361	6.6	182.6	819,452	237.0
	1981	108,084	5.3	98.8	2,044,254	149.5
Gross value-added	1971	2,497	6.0	—	41,421	—
	1976	10,656	7.7	326.8	138,812	235.1
	1981	34,085	6.4	219.9	536,048	286.2

Source: Taiwan, *Industrial and Commercial Census Report*, various years.

TABLE 8.2

Number, Employment, Output, and Value-added of Small Establishments in Manufacturing, Taiwan, 1971–1981

Industrial Characteristics	Year	Small Establishments (10–49 Workers)			Total Number of Establishments	
		Number/ NT$Million	Percentage of Total	Percentage Increase	Number/ NT$Million	Percentage Increase
Number of establishments	1971	9,822	30.0	—	32,688	—
	1976	15,875	22.8	61.6	69,517	112.7
	1981	19,702	21.5	24.1	91,499	31.6
Employment	1971	203,862	17.0	—	1,202,239	—
	1976	332,827	17.4	63.3	1,907,581	58.7
	1981	416,467	19.0	25.1	2,196,691	15.2
Output	1971	28,870	11.9	—	243,135	—
	1976	97,803	11.9	238.8	819,452	237.0
	1981	243,445	11.9	148.9	2,044,254	149.5
Gross value-added	1971	4,076	9.8	—	41,421	—
	1976	17,400	12.5	326.9	138,812	235.1
	1981	60,446	11.3	247.4	536,048	286.2

Source: See Table 8.1.

TABLE 8.3

Number, Employment, Output, and Value-added of Medium Establishments in Manufacturing, Taiwan, 1971–1981

Industrial Characteristics	Year	Medium Establishments (50–99 Workers)			Total Number of Establishments	
		Number/ NT$Million	Percentage of Total	Percentage Increase	Number/ NT$Million	Percentage Increase
Number of establishments	1971	1,600	4.9	—	32,688	—
	1976	2,988	4.3	86.8	69,517	112.7
	1981	3,758	4.1	25.8	91,499	31.6
Employment	1971	110,785	9.2	—	1,202,239	—
	1976	209,702	11.0	89.3	1,907,581	58.7
	1981	261,075	11.9	24.5	2,196,691	15.2
Output	1971	16,849	6.9	—	243,135	—
	1976	71,685	8.7	325.5	819,452	237.0
	1981	195,349	9.6	172.5	2,044,254	149.5
Gross value-added	1971	2,359	5.7	—	41,421	—
	1976	11,141	8.0	372.3	138,812	235.1
	1981	43,084	8.0	286.7	536,048	286.2

Source: See Table 8.1.

TABLE 8.4

Number of Establishments, Employment, Output, and Value-added of Small Firms in Manufacturing, Taiwan, 1971–1981

Industrial Characteristics	Year	Small Firms (Below 100 Workers)			Total Number of Establishments	
		Number/ NT$Million	Percentage of Total	Percentage Increase	Number/ NT$Million	Percentage Increase
Number of establishments	1971	30,739	94.0	—	32,688	—
	1976	66,221	95.3	115.4	69,517	112.7
	1981	87,778	95.9	32.6	91,499	31.6
Employment	1971	428,261	35.6	—	1,202,239	—
	1976	735,377	38.6	71.7	1,907,581	58.7
	1981	915,042	41.7	24.4	2,196,691	15.2
Output	1971	64,957	26.7	—	243,135	—
	1976	223,850	27.3	244.6	819,452	237.0
	1981	546,878	26.8	144.3	2,044,254	149.5
Gross value-added	1971	8,932	21.6	—	41,421	—
	1976	39,197	28.2	338.8	138,812	235.1
	1981	137,615	25.7	251.1	536,048	286.2

Source: See Table 8.1.

TABLE 8.5

Number of Establishments, Employment, Output, and Value-added of Medium Firms in Manufacturing, Taiwan, 1971–1981

Industrial Characteristics	Year	Medium Firms (100–449 Workers)			Total Number of Establishments	
		Number/ NT$Million	Percentage of Total	Percentage Increase	Number/ NT$Million	Percentage Increase
Number of establishments	1971	1,628	5.0	—	32,688	—
	1976	2,851	4.1	75.1	69,517	112.7
	1981	3,235	3.5	13.5	91,517	31.6
Employment	1971	339,389	28.2	—	1,202,239	—
	1976	576,084	30.2	69.7	1,907,581	58.7
	1981	632,700	28.8	9.8	2,196,691	15.2
Output	1971	63,121	26.0	—	243,135	—
	1976	239,107	29.2	278.8	819,452	237.0
	1981	537,169	26.3	124.7	2,044,254	149.5
Gross value-added	1971	8,483	20.5	—	41,421	—
	1976	38,665	27.9	355.8	138,812	235.1
	1981	126,942	23.7	228.3	536,048	286.2

Source: See Table 8.1.

TABLE 8.6

Number of Establishments in the Manufacturing Sector by
Total Amount of Assets, Taiwan, 1976
(Percentage)

Number of Workers	Assets (NT$Million)					
	Below 1	1–10	10–50	50–500	Above 500	Total
Below 10	72.2	27.4	0.3	0.03	0.002	100.0
10–49	18.8	71.0	9.4	0.8	0.03	100.0
50–99	1.9	49.0	41.2	7.8	0.1	100.0
100–499	0.7	19.9	43.4	33.6	2.4	100.0
500 & above	0.0	3.1	7.0	49.2	40.7	100.0
Total	53.6	37.8	6.0	2.2	0.4	100.0

Source: Taiwan, *Industrial and Commerical Census Report*, 1976.

TABLE 8.7

Number of Establishments in the Manufacturing Sector
by Total Amount of Assets, Taiwan, 1981
(Percentage)

Number of Workers	Assets (NT$Million)					
	Below 1	1–10	10–50	50–500	Above 500	Total
Below 10	34.7	63.6	1.6	0.07	0.0	100.0
10–49	5.0	69.4	22.9	2.7	0.0	100.0
50–99	0.6	28.4	50.1	20.9	0.03	100.0
100–499	0.09	11.7	34.3	53.9	0.03	100.0
500 & above	0.6	1.0	4.3	87.0	7.0	100.0
Total	25.5	61.2	9.4	3.9	0.04	100.0

Source: Taiwan, *Industrial and Commercial Census Report*, 1981.

TABLE 8.8

Exports of Small and Medium Firms (SMFs) in the Manufacturing Sector,
Taiwan, 1981–1984

Year	Total Exports (NT$ Billion)	Exports by SMFs (NT$ Billion)	Share of Exports (Per Cent)
1981	1.47	1.06	71.84
1982	1.44	1.06	73.53
1983	1.63	1.09	66.90
1984	1.98	1.24	62.53

Source: Taiwan, Ministry of Economics, Institute of Small and Medium Industries, *Report on Small and Medium Industries*, various years.

Note: Firms which have assets less than NT$10 million are considered to be small and medium firms. This definition of small and medium firms may not be the same as those classified by number of employees.

TABLE 8.9
Percentage of Small and Medium Firms by Legal Organization,
Taiwan, 1984

Legal Organization	Percentage of All SMFs
Sole proprietorship	59.7
Partnership	1.3
Registered company	38.9
Others	0.1
Total	100.0

Source: See Table 8.8.

TABLE 8.10
Distribution of Industrial Establishments and Employment, Thailand, 1978

Establishment Size	Number of Establishments	% of Total	Employment (% of Total Labour Force)
5–9	18,618	51	10
10–49	14,200	39	24
50–99	1,908	5	11
100–499	1,364	4	24
Over 500	243	1	31
Total	36,333	100	100

Source: Busaba Kunasirin, *The Role of Small- and Medium-Scale Industries in the Economic Development of Japan and Thailand: A Comparative Analysis*, Tokyo, Institute of Developing Economies, Visiting Research Fellow Series No. 109, March 1984.

TABLE 8.11

Percentage of Total Manufacturing Employment in Various Industries,
Japan, 1954–1980

Industry	1954	1960	1972	1977	1980
Food & drink	12.7	11.0	9.3	10.6	10.6
Textiles	18.5	15.1	9.8	8.2	6.3
Apparel	3.1	3.4	4.2	4.9	4.2
Woodworking	7.0	5.6	4.2	3.9	3.5
Furniture	2.3	2.4	2.7	2.8	2.5
Paper & pulp	3.1	3.2	2.7	2.8	2.7
Publishing & printing	4.6	4.0	4.4	4.4	4.6
Chemicals (including petroleum & rubber)	8.3	8.1	6.7	5.8	5.9
Leather goods	0.8	0.7	0.8	0.8	0.8
Ceramics	5.2	5.0	5.1	4.8	4.9
Metals	6.3	6.2	5.8	6.3	6.0
Fabricated metal goods	4.8	5.9	8.5	7.5	7.2
Machinery (including electrical equipment & precision instruments)	13.6	18.1	22.5	23.0	25.5
Transport equipment	6.2	6.3	7.9	8.5	8.6
Others	3.5	4.9	5.4	5.6	6.6

Source: See Table 8.10.

TABLE 8.12

Percentage of Establishments, Employment, and Output
of Industrial Firms, Japan, 1970–1982

Firms Size by Employment	Percentage of Establishment		Percentage of Employment		Percentage of Output	
	1970	1982	1970	1982	1970	1982
Small firms (less than 100 workers)	97.6	84.9	51.6	55.5	32.0	33.9
Medium firms (100–299 workers)	1.7	11.3	15.9	16.4	16.9	17.6
Large firms (more than 300 workers)	0.7	3.8	32.5	28.1	51.1	48.6

Source: Japan Statistical Year Book, Statistical Bureau, Japan Government, Tokyo, 1984.

TABLE 8.13
Percentage of Total Manufacturing Value-added in Various Industries, Japan, 1954–1980

Industry	1954	1960	1972	1977	1980
Food & drink	11.4	8.5	9.1	10.3	9.3
Textiles	13.1	9.4	6.2	4.8	4.0
Apparel	1.2	1.0	1.8	2.1	1.9
Woodworking	3.7	2.9	2.9	2.5	2.3
Furniture	1.0	1.1	1.8	1.8	1.6
Paper & pulp	4.0	3.6	2.9	3.0	2.7
Publishing and printing	5.6	4.1	4.7	5.1	5.1
Chemicals (including petroleum & rubber)	16.5	14.1	11.5	11.2	12.2
Leather goods	0.4	0.4	0.5	0.6	0.5
Ceramics	5.7	4.7	5.0	5.0	5.1
Metals	10.6	11.6	9.0	8.0	10.3
Fabricated metal goods	3.7	4.7	6.7	6.5	6.2
Machinery (including electrical equipment & precision instruments)	14.5	22.2	23.8	23.2	24.8
Transport equipment	6.8	9.2	9.8	11.0	9.6
Others	1.7	2.5	4.3	4.7	4.4

Source: See Table 8.10.

TABLE 8.14
Export Orientation of Small and Medium Firms, Japan, 1981

Industry Group	Exports Sales (Per Cent)	Ratio of Firms Which Engaged in Exports (Per Cent)
Food	2.6	6.2
Textiles	10.3	21.2
Lumber & wood products	—	3.6
Furniture & furnishings	4.4	5.8
Pulp, paper & paper products	11.6	11.9
Stone, clay & glass products	7.5	15.3
Publishing & printing	8.8	2.8
Ferrous metal	—	21.2
Non-ferrous metals	33.5	24.6
Chemicals	19.2	40.7
Metal products	12.9	15.7
Non-electric machinery	27.9	34.5
Electric machinery	29.9	23.0
Transport equipment	39.5	14.2
Precision machinery	36.7	36.2
Sundries	11.3	24.1

Source: Tokyo, Small and Medium Business Agency, *Chusho Kigyo Hakusho*, White Paper on Small and Medium Enterprises, 1983, pp. 15 and 71.

TABLE 8.15

Regional Distribution of Overseas Ventures in Manufacturing Set Up
by Small and Medium Firms, Japan, 1951–1982

Region	Number of Establishments			
	1951–1971[a]	1972–1975[b]	1976–1979	1980–1982
Asia	387	741	274	158
South Korea	70	403	46	23
Hong Kong	27	38	44	20
Taiwan	170	132	76	56
Others	120	168	108	59
North America	13	94	84	107
Central & South America	16	70	19	7
Europe	2	15	23	17
Middle East	2	0	1	1
Africa	13	4	0	0
Oceania	6	7	4	3
Total	439	931	405	293

Source: Tokyo, Small and Medium Business Agency, *Chusho Kigyo Hakusho*, White Paper
on Small and Medium Enterprises, various years.
[a]Up to the end of September 1971.
[b]For 1974 and 1975, statistics cover only the 1 April–31December period.

TABLE 8.16

Sectoral Distribution of Overseas Ventures in Manufacturing Set Up
by Small and Medium Firms, Japan, 1951–1982

Industry Group	Number of Firms				1951–1982[c]	
	1951–1971[a]	1973–1977[b]	1976–1979	1980–1982	Number of Firms	Percentage of Total
Food	28	42	48	38	156	9.3
Textiles	72	53	25	22	172	10.3
Lumber, pulp & paper	19	31	15	9	74	4.4
Chemicals	28	37	36	28	129	7.7
Metals	26	56	28	18	128	7.6
Non-electric machinery	50 ⎫					
Electric machinery	55 ⎬	177	148	100	535	31.9
Transport equipment	5 ⎭					
Sundries	156	143	105	78	482	28.8
Manufacturing (total)	439	539	405	293	1,676	100.0

Source: See Table 8.15.

[a]The fourth quarter statistics are not available for 1971. Statistics for 1972 are not available.

[b]The first quarter statistics are not available for these years.

[c]The above statistical deficiences apply.

TABLE 8.17

Number of Establishments, Employment, Output, and Value-added of
Small Firms in Singapore, Taiwan, Thailand, and Japan

Industrial Characteristics	Singapore (1983)	Taiwan (1981)	Thailand (1978)	Japan (1982)
Contribution to total number of industrial establishments (%)	91	96	95	85
Contribution to total industrial employment (%)	35	42	45	56
Contribution to total industrial production (%)	26	27	25	34
Contribution to total industrial value-added (%)	22	26	25	n.a.

Sources: For Singapore, see Tables 4.2–4.5, 4.7–4.10, 4.12–4.15.
        For Taiwan, see Table 8.4.
        For Thailand, see Table 8.10.
        For Japan, see Table 8.12.
Note: n.a. refers to not available.

9

THE ROLE OF THE GOVERNMENT:
A COMPARATIVE ANALYSIS

In Chapter 2 we analysed the industrialization process in Singapore. We pointed out that much of the success of Singapore can be attributed to the PAP government. The government has been able to provide an excellent industrial infrastructure, good industrial relations climate, and a trainable and disciplined work-force. With the inflow of substantial foreign investment, Singapore achieved an impressive economic performance during the period 1966–83.

In the twenty-five years since Singapore obtained self-government, the government undoubtedly relied on foreign investment for economic growth. This policy has produced desirable results. However, during this period of rapid industrialization, the government did not pay sufficient attention to the problems faced by local firms, and consequently local firms, especially small local firms, did not develop to the fullest extent.

To counter the effects of the 1985–6 recession, the government is very determined to help small local firms develop and compete in both domestic and foreign markets. The emphasis on small local firms has been brought about by the following factors:

Firstly, many workers were retrenched by MNCs in 1985. A typical MNC has a number of plants in various countries. In the event of a world-wide recession, the management will decide on where to cut production. Since plants in Singapore are less cost effective due to high wages than those in Hong Kong, Taiwan, and Korea—the consequence of a full employment economy—most MNCs decided to trim costs in Singapore. MNCs are therefore not committed to Singapore and their management philosophy is pro-cyclical, which destabilizes the economy. The same cannot be said of small local firms. They are committed to Singapore and their profits also stay within the country. In other words, small local firms act as stabilizers in the economy.

Secondly, local employers are now more outspoken and more organized in presenting their views to the government for action. Consequently, the government is well aware of various problems facing small local firms.

The purpose of this chapter is to assess the role of the government in helping small firms in Singapore as well as in Taiwan, Thailand, and Japan. The comparison of these four countries with respect to policies on small firms is useful as Singapore is economically as developed as Taiwan, economically more developed than Thailand, and economically less developed than Japan. The Taiwanese experience shows that government policies have been largely ineffective in helping small firms; the Thai experience shows that small firms receive far less government attention than is commensurate with their contribution to national development; the Japanese experience demonstrates the vital role that government policies can play in the development of small firms. The Singapore experience shows that, after the recession in 1985, the government is very determined to help small firms.

The Case of Taiwan

The Taiwanese government has been instrumental in steering the country from a labour-intensive agricultural economy to a capital-intensive and technology-intensive industrial economy.[1] Several bodies under the Executive Yuan[2] have been set up to help small firms.

The Ministry of Economic Affairs (MOEA)

The MOEA administers the nation's economic affairs and promotes and supervises agricultural, mining, industrial, commercial, trade, and water conservancy programmes. In May 1974, the MOEA established the Centre of United Services which assists small and medium firms in seven areas: fund procurement, technological improvement, production management and quality control, management efficiency and export promotion, resolution of financial and/or accounting problems, establishment of satellite factories, and special assistance for small and medium firms participating in the production of military goods. At the local level, the provincial governments supervised the Centre of United Services in raising NT$100 million in March 1982 to help solve financial problems encountered by strategic industries and promising small and medium firms. A special division, the Small and Medium Firm Division, was also set up by the MOEA in January 1981 to provide guidance and assistance to small and medium firms.

The Ministry of Finance

The function of the Ministry of Finance is to administer government finance, customs, taxation, public debts, monetary matters, revenue, and government monopolies. The Ministry of Finance provides direct assistance to small and medium firms. We will cite below, in chronological order, the industrial policies of the Ministry of Finance pertaining to small and medium firms in the 1980s:

1. Assist Export-Oriented Small and Medium Firms Programme (December 1981). The aim of the programme is to ease the stringent conditions for working capital around the end of the year.
2. Financial Assistance for Small and Medium Firms Programme

(March 1983). Under the programme, a ceiling is imposed on the credit that banks can extend to large firms.

3. The stipulation that the relevant authorities organize professional seminars for clerks from financial intermediaries to equip them with a better understanding of the tasks and duties involved in providing assistance and funds to small and medium firms (December 1983).

4. The stipulation that loan officers will no longer be held personally liable for bad loans unless misdemeanours or fraud are involved (September 1984). It is hoped that loan officers will be encouraged to extend more loans to small and medium firms who are supposedly poorer credit risks.[3]

The Central Bank of China

The Central Bank of China regulates money and credit, issues notes, manages foreign exchange, operates the overseas banking system, and acts as the fiscal agent for the government.

The main kind of assistance provided by the Central Bank of China to small and medium firms is in the form of loans. In November 1972, the Central Bank of China earmarked NT$1 billion to help small and medium firms to finance their medium-term and long-term investments. A further NT$1.5 billion was set aside in 1974 to promote the interests of export-oriented small and medium firms. This was undertaken well in advance of the Assist Export-Oriented Small and Medium Firms Programme introduced in December 1981 which required the Central Bank of China and financial intermediaries to extend loans to small and medium firms in export-oriented industries.

In order to help small and medium firms obtain short-term credit, the Central Bank of China allocated NT$5 billion in July 1979 for extending credit or discounting bills for small and medium firms. In addition, small and medium firms in the machinery industry are able to procure medium-term and long-term loans at preferential interest rates under a bill approved by the Executive Yuan in 1981.

In July 1976, the Small and Medium Business Bank (SMBB) was established with the view of extending loans mainly to small and medium firms. A minimum of 70 per cent of total loans must be extended to small and medium firms. In April 1977, the SMBB, together with the Bank of Taiwan, Chung-Shing Securities Ltd., and the Small and Medium Business Guarantee Fund (set up jointly by the Ministry of Finance, the Central Bank of China, and the Ministry of Economic Affairs in 1974 to solve the problems of small and medium firms that stem from inadequate collateral) agreed to cooperate in assisting small and medium firms issue short-term commercial notes.

In 1981, the Central Bank of China, through the SMBB and commercial banks, extended NT$3 billion of loans to private enterprises. An additional NT$1 billion was allocated to the SMBB to provide small and medium firms with working capital.

In April 1983, the Central Bank of China, through the SMBB, extended NT$8 billion in loans at preferential rates to small and medium firms. Since August 1983, the SMBB has been providing loans to small and medium firms at preferential rates of interest to help them to purchase computerized facilities and to develop new products.

The Economic Council of Cooperation

The Economic Council of Cooperation assists small and medium firms in five major areas, i.e. technology, management, marketing, financial assistance, and promotion of cooperation among firms.

The National Economic Council

In December 1981, the National Economic Council approved a programme which called for the upgrading of the technology of small and medium firms. For this purpose, NT$2.8 billion worth of loans were extended to small and medium firms through financial intermediaries to upgrade technologically.

Yen Gi-li provides empirical evidence on the inadequacy of government policies in relation to small and medium businesses. According to Yen, the success of the industrial policies should mean an increase in the share of loans extended by financial intermediaries to small and medium firms over time. However, the number of small and medium firms has been increasing rapidly over the years. Their share of the total exports has also been rising. Moreover, financial intermediaries represent only one of the various sources of funds. Consequently, a study of the shifts in the overall financial structure over time is in order. Yen finds that the ratio of borrowings of small and medium firms from financial institutions to the total liabilities of small and medium firms has not increased over time. In fact, in the period 1977–81, the ratio declined slightly from 24.3 to 21.4. Together with several other observations, Yen concludes that government policies related to small and medium businesses have been ineffective and have fallen below expectations.

Yen gives several reasons for the ineffective government policies which he has grouped under two main factors. The first relates to the intrinsic weaknesses of the small and medium firms, such as the failure to maintain reliable accounting records and to distinguish between private and business-related transactions, the lack of collateral and financial instruments, the lack of internal finances dictating the allocation of scarce working capital to medium-term or long-term investments, and the weak organizational structure which prohibits efficiency gains through specialization. The second factor involves the practices of financial institutions and government policies. For example, interest rates in Taiwan are fixed by the Central Bank of China. This naturally gives rise to credit rationing, often in favour of large firms, for both economic and political reasons. Another reason is the reluctance on the part of loan officers to extend loans to small and medium firms for fear of bad loans.[4] A third reason is the tax system which taxes small and medium firms on transactions between different firms but leaves similar transactions carried out within the same firm untaxed.

Subsequently, Yen recommends six steps which the government should take to amend the industrial policies:

1. Establish a coherent and integrated industrial policy.

2. Introduce measures to help small and medium firms improve their accounting practices.

3. Deregulate the banking system gradually.

4. Revise the taxation system. In particular, the sales tax should be replaced by a value-added tax because, under the former, small firms, which are often organized as sole proprietorships or partnerships, bear a greater burden than larger entities.

5. Encourage loan officers and other employees of financial institutions to extend loans to small firms. For example, they should not be held personally liable for uncollectable loans so long as no criminal intent is involved.

6. Enlarge and strengthen the Small and Medium Business Guarantee Fund.

The Case of Thailand

The Thai government has been eager to promote small and medium firms in Thailand. In both the Fourth Economic and Social Development Plan (1977–81) and the Fifth National Five-Year Plan (1982–6), special attention was given to the development of small and medium firms. The Department of Industrial Promotion (DIP), under the Ministry of Industry, is the main body looking after the development of small and medium firms. The DIP has a staff of 1,000 persons, nearly half of whom are professionals.[5] Under the DIP, there are five divisions dealing with specific aspects of small and medium firms. We will briefly introduce them:

1. The Division of Industrial Services (DIS). The DIS provides advisory services in the field of production techniques, management, marketing, and product design. The DIS functions have not been fully utilized. According to Sanguanruang et al.,[6] only 30 per cent of the establishments had heard of the existence of the DIS. The main problem facing the DIS is that it has not been able to maintain well-qualified personnel due to its tight budget.[7]

2. The Thailand Management Development and Productivity Centre (TMDPC). The main objective of the TMDPC is to promote management development through training and seminars. The consultancy services of the TMDPC have been effective and have fulfilled the needs of the majority of recipients.[8]

3. The Small Industrial Finance Office (SIFO). The SIFO was established in 1964. The objective of the SIFO is to extend loans to small entrepreneurs to establish factories or for expansion. Firms with fixed assets not exceeding 5 million bahts are eligible to apply. Each given loan, however, is less than 1 million bahts. The SIFO operates through

a joint fund of the government and the Krang Thai Bank, which is a commercial bank with substantial government shares. The SIFO analyses and appraises loan applications but the Krang Thai Bank is responsible for collateral appraisal, the disbursement of loan proceeds and the collection of loan obligations. The SIFO has not been very useful to small and medium firms for two reasons.[9] Firstly, many applications from small and medium entrepreneurs for loans have been turned down due to inadequate collateral. Secondly, many entrepreneurs would like to use loans for working capital, which is not the objective of the SIFO.

4. The Industrial Finance Corporation of Thailand (IFCT). The IFCT is an additional government-affiliated financial institute providing financial assistance to small and medium entrepreneurs. During the 1975–81 period, 78 per cent of the total number of loans were given to small and medium firms.

5. The Textile Division (TD). The TD conducts training courses and provides consultancy services to local textile producers. It has modern laboratories to conduct research and development activities and also a testing laboratory capable of carrying out physical, chemical, microscopic, and colour tests for all sorts of textile materials.[10]

The DIP has also set up many plans to promote small and medium firms. Specifically, the DIP has planned eleven projects to achieve its objectives, namely the Entrepreneurial Development Project, Feasibility Studies, the Loan Facility Expansion Project, the Regional Industrial Service Centre Project, the Establishment of Regional Industrial Areas, the Industrial Technology Transfer Project, the Agro-Industrial Development Project, the Ceramic Industry Project, the Furniture Industry Project, the Engineering Industry Project, and the Thai Silk Industry Project.

The Industrial Estate Authority of Thailand (IEAT) under the Ministry of Industry also plays an important role in promoting small and medium firms. The main objective of the IEAT is to set up industrial estates outside Bangkok. The IEAT will thus help to decentralize the manufacturing activities, moving them away from Bangkok to selected growth poles, increase employment opportunities in areas outside Bangkok, and develop small and medium firms by establishing small-scale industrial estates.

The One-Stop Service Centre under the Ministry of Industry also assists industrialists by providing simplified and speedier procedures in getting factory operation permits.

Apart from the Ministry of Industry, the Department of Labour also provides occupational and skills training in the fields of welding, mechanical and electrical skills, radio and television repair, draftsmanship, and surveying, through the National Skill Labour Development Institute (NSLDI). The NSLDI has two training centres in Bangkok and four regional offices, which are located in Ratburi, Chonburi, Lampang, and Khon Kaen. The activities of the NSLDI have increased the supply of skilled workers and have therefore played an important role in solving the problem of skilled labour shortages in small and medium firms.

In 1984, the Thailand Institute of Scientific and Technological Research (TISTR) under the Ministry of Science, Technology and Energy (MOSTE) obtained government approval to set up joint ventures with industries in the private sector in four high-technology areas—microwave isolators and circulators, solar cells, bio-technology, and computer software. Since August 1985, two joint ventures, one in microwave isolators and circulators (Microtek) and the other in solar cells (Thai Solar Corp.) have been established. As yet, strong government support is not forthcoming as the Board of Investment is far from granting high-technology industries top priority.[11]

Kunasirin finds that government assistance extended to small and medium firms has been rather poor and insignificant in Thailand.[12] However, with the strong intention of the government to help small and medium firms as demonstrated by the implementation of the eleven DIP projects and others, it is believed that small and medium firms will increase their importance in the Thai national economy provided that entrepreneurs themselves are willing to cooperate and, more importantly, to adopt changes.

The Case of Japan

The manifestly important economic role of small and medium firms has led the Japanese government to give priority to their development and support. The Japanese economic strategy in the post-war period has been first to carefully select industries, next to prevent them from excessive competition at the infancy stage, then to nurse them to competitive stature, and finally to expose them to outside competition.[13] In this way, government-selected target industries are given a chance to grow and develop into a strong base from which they can compete with foreign companies in world markets.

In order to promote small and medium firms in Japan, the Japanese government enacted the 1963 Basic Law for Small and Medium Enterprises.

The Law stipulated that the government must enforce necessary measures in a comprehensive manner in all areas of government policy to help small and medium firms in the following aspects:[14]

1. Modernizing equipment and other facilities;
2. Improving technology;
3. Rationalizing of management;
4. Upgrading the structure of small and medium firms;
5. Rectifying disadvantages in business activities;
6. Increasing demand;
7. Securing fair opportunities for business activities;
8. Establishing proper relations between management and labour.

There are in total four main measures adopted by the Japanese government in helping small and medium firms:

1. The first encompasses those activities which help firms to modernize facilities, rationalize management, improve technology, develop personnel, and strengthen the overall entrepreneurial capacity.

2. The second is meant to rectify the disadvantages faced by small and medium firms in external business activities. Small and medium firms are handicapped by two factors: (i) they are not strong enough to face fierce competition, and (ii) they do not have established markets for their products. The small and medium entrepreneurs are therefore encouraged to set up cooperative associations in order to avoid excessive competition and to increase competitive power. More importantly, such measures will increase the opportunities of small and medium firms to receive procurement orders from the government and other public agencies in order to increase demand in small and medium firms.

3. The third is aimed at the small firms which operate under the handicap of sole proprietorship. It aims to ensure that such small firms can effectively utilize the policies meant for small and medium firms in general.

4. The fourth aims to strengthen the financial situation through the facilitation of procurement of funds and improvement of equity position. Small and medium firms can procure funds from three government affiliated institutions: the Small Business Finance Corporation, the People's Finance Corporation, and the Central Cooperative Bank for Commerce and Industry.

Besides the above measures, tax incentives are also extended to small and medium firms. Bankruptcy prevention and disaster assistance are also extended to small and medium firms. The bankruptcy prevention and mutual relief system was set up in 1978 to prevent domino-effect bankruptcies. Disaster assistance in the form of financial aid is provided through government affiliated financial institutions and special credit guarantees.

Other fiscal measures are the Small and Medium Enterprise New Technology Investment Promotion Tax System, which aims to promote higher productivity and modernization of management through mechanization and computerization, the Investment Promotion System for Efficient Utilization of Energy, the Special Allowance for Irrecoverable Loans of Small and Medium Enterprises, and the Reserve Fund System for the Structural Improvement of Smaller Enterprises.[15]

In addition, the Japanese government encourages subcontracting by means of a law which prevents delayed payments of subcontracting fees and a system which introduces business to subcontractors.

Development of human resources is also within the purview of the government in the form of the Small and Medium Enterprise University. Technological development is promoted through technology transfer and exchange activities. Information is made readily available by the Small and Medium Enterprise Information Centre of the Japan Small Business Corporation.

At the regional level, small and medium firm development is enhanced through the Regional Industry Promotion Centre. At the international level, small and medium firm development is promoted by means of facilitating overseas investment and mutual international exchange among small and medium firms.

There is also good rapport between the government and small and medium firms. The government collects and analyses opinions and requests of small and medium firms on various economic issues and also informs small and medium firms about policy changes.

Needless to say, Japanese small and medium firms receive much more substantial assistance from the government than their Taiwanese and Thai counterparts, especially in terms of procurement orders from the public sector and financial incentives. It should, however, be noted that the Japanese small and medium firms were developed during a period when foreign investment was limited and suppressed. In the case of Taiwan, Thailand, and Singapore, foreign investment is indispensable for rapid industrial development and consequently the governments find it difficult to openly adopt policies to protect their small and medium firms in the respective countries.

The Singapore Experience

In our theoretical discussion in Chapter 3, we hypothesized that there are three types of small firms, i.e. firms with a capital constraint, firms with an output constraint, and firms with an entrepreneurial constraint.[16] The government can therefore help capital-constrained companies to obtain loans at low interest rates, output-constrained companies to secure markets overseas, and entrepreneurial-constrained companies to speed up the process of economic restructuring by producing high value-added products through upgrading and by retraining workers. As will be discussed below, the Singapore government has been actively helping small firms in these three areas of operation.

During the past two decades of economic development, the small firms sector in Singapore has never enjoyed official promotion and recognition on a scale as large as that for the giant MNCs. Nevertheless, the Singapore government is aware of the importance of small firms in its economy. Generally, the official support for small firms comes from five main organizations: the Economic Development Board, the Skills Development Fund, the Singapore Institute of Standard and Industrial Research, the National Productivity Board, and the Trade Development Board.

The Economic Development Board (EDB)

The EDB was formed in August 1961. The primary function of the EDB is to promote the establishment of new industries in Singapore and the growth of existing ones. With this objective of promoting rapid industrialization in Singapore, the EDB was organized into four main areas of administration: the Promotion Division, the Financial Division, the Projects and Technical Consultant Service Division, and the Industrial Facilities Division.[17] But no special attention was given to small firms until the Light Industries Services (LIS) Unit was set up in 1962 within the Technical Consultant Service Division which had been separated from the Projects Division.

The LIS Unit assisted small industrialists with their financial, organizational, and technical problems. In particular, the EDB made an initial grant of $3 million for the loans service to aid small firms. The loans service included hire purchase schemes for equipment as well as short-term loans for working capital, which small firms found difficult to obtain. The loans service was operated through local commercial banks. The applications for loans were assessed on the basis of the integrity and experience of the small entrepreneur, and the prospects of improvement of the enterprise.

The LIS Unit was active in assisting small firms. In 1964, it received 522 requests for assistance from small firms. These included 241 requests for assistance in site location, 140 requests for loans for equipment and working capital, 109 requests for technological advice on machinery, process and plant layout, and 32 requests for marketing, accounting and management services.

Among the 140 loan requests for equipment and working capital, 41 cases involving $292,700 for working capital and $233,295 for the purchase of machinery and equipment were approved. Of the 41 cases, the LIS Unit assumed risks only in 6 cases. The private banks assumed all risks solely on the basis of the evaluations submitted by the LIS Unit, reflecting the close working relation between the banks and the LIS Unit in industrial financing.

It was estimated that through the financial assistance extended, the LIS Unit was responsible for the creation of 1,000 jobs and of an additional output of over $10 million in 1968.[18] The LIS Unit, however, ceased operations in 1973 when its functions were taken over by other units of the EDB.

The Local Operation Section within the Investment Services Division was set up in 1973 with the objective of promoting the expansion, upgrading and diversification of local firms through various means, including the encouragement of joint ventures with foreign or local partners which can provide higher levels of skills and technology or new markets, either in existing or new product lines. Moreover, the Bureau for Joint Ventures was established in 1975 under the Local Operation Section to promote industrial joint ventures and to provide any necessary assistance in monitoring and expediting the implementation of joint venture projects.

The Capital Assistance Scheme under the Project Division was established in 1974 to provide equity capital and loan financing at attractive terms to assist local investors to set up high technology industries in Singapore. The local investors are given the option to buy up the EDB's share within a period of five years under terms mutually agreed upon at the outset of the venture. The Capital Assistance Scheme has been used rather sparingly. For example, in March 1985, only $34 million in loans were extended under the Capital Assistance Scheme, leaving a balance of $258 million.[19]

The Investment Allowance Scheme was established to enable firms with at least 31 per cent local ownership to make tax deductions ranging from 10–50 per cent of approved new fixed investments. Firms that qualify for the scheme are those in manufacturing, engineering and technical services, research and development, computer-related services, and construction. In 1986, the scheme was extended to encompass new service areas such as management and consultancy services, educational services, exhibition services, financial services, laboratory and testing services, mechanized warehousing, medical services, publishing, and tourism-related projects. In addition, a standard rate for investment allowances of 30 per cent across-the-board has been used. Processing of applications has also been speeded up with the EDB handling investment allowances of less than $1 million and the Ministry of Trade and Industry handling projects of more than $1 million.

Another investment scheme administered by the EDB is the Product Development Assistance Scheme (PDAS) which provides grants of up to 50 per cent of the direct development costs of a project. Local firms or joint ventures developing high-technology products are eligible for the grants. In 1986, the PDAS was extended to include up to 50 per cent of the costs of market feasibility and technical feasibility studies. A ceiling of $5,000 was imposed. The scheme was redefined to include any firms which produce a commercially marketable product, have a satisfactory track record and have adequate resources to market the product.[20]

The EDB in collaboration with the Development Bank of Singapore (DBS) also set up and operated the Small Industries Finance Scheme (SIFS) in 1976. The SIFS aims at encouraging the further development and technical upgrading of the operations of small firms. An applicant to the SIFS should not have, inclusive of the loan applied for, more than $1 million in fixed productive assets, defined as factory buildings, machinery, equipment, and tools.

The SIFS has since grown rapidly. Now the EDB operates the SIFS with sixteen financial institutions, including, of course, the DBS. The SIFS has also been extended to include firms which have assets not exceeding $3 million and firms which have assets between $3 million and $8 million. Moreover, to qualify for the SIFS, the applicant has to be locally owned or jointly owned by local and foreign entrepreneurs with a minimum 30 per cent local share.

Since 1985, the SIFS has offered factory loans, machinery loans, and working capital loans at a fixed interest rate of 7.75 per cent per annum. The maximum loan allowed to the local entrepreneur is $2 million and the loan is granted for varying periods of up to 10 years at fixed and lending rates. If the enterprise grows and its fixed assets grow beyond

$3 million, another loan of up to $3 million may be approved under the Extended Small Industries Finance Scheme at a fixed interest rate of 7.75 per cent per annum.

The SIFS, which had been initially extended only to the manufacturing sector, was expanded in 1985 to encompass the service sector.[21] This is in line with the government's objective to promote the service sector as the other major area of growth.

Export Factoring under the SIFS was launched by the EDB in conjunction with DBS Finance Ltd. in 1985. The aim of Export Factoring is to improve the competitiveness of small local exporters who stand to enjoy the following benefits:[22]

1. A cash advance of up to 90 per cent of the invoice value after the goods are shipped. A discount fee of 6 per cent per annum is charged, much lower than the current market rate of 9.5–10.0 per cent.

2. The ability to sell goods to overseas buyers on an open account basis without the need for letters of credit.

3. Full protection against the non-payment of approved invoices by importers.

4. Political and non-commercial risk protection such as losses arising from wars, disturbances, and political and legal changes in the buyer countries.

5. Collection and sales ledgering services. If the local exporter's trading deals are in various currencies, he can opt for a specialized multi-currency sales ledger service.

In 1986, the SIFS was further augmented by a new scheme to help small local firms in the manufacturing and service sectors upgrade technologically. It is a soft loan scheme which comes with an interest grant and a packaged deal ranging from advice on buying, installation, implementation, and software programming to provision of management expertise. The effective interest rate is 3.5–4.0 per cent, much lower than the market rate which was about 9–10 per cent in 1986. Firms must have not more than $8 million in fixed assets in order to qualify for the scheme. In addition, firms in the service sector should not have more than 50 workers.

The growth of the SIFS has been remarkable. SIFS loans increased from $1.2 million in 1976 to $64 million in 1985, and reached $250.1 million in 1986, bringing the total amount approved since the inception of the scheme to $752 million. By March 1986, 1,131 firms had benefited from the scheme.[23]

A $100 million Venture Capital Fund was also set up by the EDB in 1985 to help local firms through low interest loans and co-partnerships. Singapore firms that go into venture capital investment may get loans from the EDB at concessionary interest rates.[24] The EDB is prepared to co-invest with Singapore partners in new technology firms, both in Singapore and overseas, and consequently share with Singapore firms the business risk involved in such ventures. If the project is successful, Singapore investors have the option to buy out the EDB's share within a specified period at a fair market price.

The main purpose of the Venture Capital Fund is to encourage the eventual transfer of technology and investments back to Singapore. Indeed, a number of local firms have already ventured into new technology investments in the US with the intention of transferring some projects back to Singapore.[25] Small firms are expected to benefit from the Venture Capital Fund too.

According to a founding partner of Abacus Venture Pte. Ltd., the $100 million Venture Capital Fund can create 20–30 new high-technology firms.[26] However, businessmen in general feel that the incentives given so far are inadequate to stimulate the growth of venture capital in the long run. Since Singapore should not rely solely on MNCs to acquire know-how, they feel that a comprehensive strategy is needed to integrate indigenous capital and entrepreneurial talent with external know-how.[27]

In January 1986, the EDB's Small Enterprise Bureau (SEB) was set up to act as a one-stop consultancy centre for local businesses. The SEB comprises three departments: the General Assistance Department, the Loans and Grants Department, and the Planning and Co-ordination Department. The General Assistance Department, as its name indicates, provides general assistance to small firms. Visits are made to the business premises by the department's extension officers. The Loans and Grants Department gives advice on the types of loans that local businessmen can arrange with banks, and on the types of grants available from the EDB. The department also manages the SIFS. In the Planning and Co-ordination Department, officers coordinate the work of sister agencies like the Singapore Institute of Standards and Industrial Research, the Trade Development Board, the National Productivity Board and the Skills Development Fund. Local businessmen can get advice on upgrading their management skills and on technical matters. They can also get help in selling to new markets and in securing loans.[28] The SEB is under the supervision of the Committee on Small Enterprise Policy which was formed in 1985. The Committee, which comprises representatives from the various Ministries and statutory boards, coordinates government efforts to help small businesses.[29]

In the initial period, the Bureau, which has a multi-million dollar budget, is to concentrate on helping the following groups of firms:

1. Firms which directly or indirectly export their products and services, and those with the potential to do so;

2. Support industries for export-oriented firms, and

3. Traditional businesses which can be upgraded and modernized.

The response to the SEB has been encouraging. Eighty cases were received within the first two months of operation, most of which were requests for financial assistance.[30]

In order to further help local firms to upgrade technologically, the SEB has introduced the Local Industries Upgrading Programme (LIUP). MNCs are given a grant if they train local supplier firms in areas such as management, quality control, production process, technology, and equipment. The SEB is prepared to reimburse up to 90 per cent of the MNC's training costs, which include costs incurred in workshops, training, consultancy services, and factory visits. The balance falls on the local supplier firms. The SEB budgeted $500,000 for the LIUP for the year 1986. Local supplier firms must have not more than $8 million in fixed assets and must have at least 30 per cent local equity. In addition, non-manufacturing supplier companies should also have not more than 50 workers.[31]

Both MNCs and local firms stand to benefit from the scheme: the MNCs will have higher quality products from better-trained and more knowledgeable local suppliers, while the local firms will gain easy access to the latest technological developments. However, a potential obstacle to the success of the scheme is the element of distrust between local suppliers and MNCs. Official indications are that there have been antagonistic relations between some MNCs and their suppliers. To overcome this problem, greater interaction and more effective communication are essential to promote trust and openness and to reduce the chances of conflict. Nevertheless, by early 1986 at least ten MNCs had expressed a desire to work with local supporting firms under the scheme,[32] two of which took the grants under the LIUP in July 1986.[33]

The SEB has also expressed its eagerness to promote educational and training programmes for small firms, such as 'clinics' or 'teaching' sessions in financial management and marketing techniques.[34] Three international consultant firms have also been appointed to identify the strengths and weaknesses of small firms to enable the SEB to provide the best form of assistance possible.[35]

In addition, the EDB has combined forces with the National University of Singapore (NUS), the National Computer Board (NCB), and Telecoms in joint schemes to help small firms. A Small Business Consultancy Unit has been set up by the NUS under the auspices of the EDB. Management audit services from the School of Accountancy and Business Administration are available to small firms at a highly subsidized fee.[36]

In early 1987, the EDB allocated $847 million for the period 1988–91 to finance an umbrella scheme called the Economic Development Assistance Scheme (EDAS) with the primary objective of helping small local firms in Singapore.[37] The umbrella scheme, which started on 1 February 1987, brings together the following eight schemes:

1. Small Industries Finance Scheme. Soft loans for small local firms to purchase machinery and factories.[38]

2. Capital Assistance Scheme. Fixed or floating rate term loans from 5–15 years for investors. Technology transfer is a must for qualification.

3. Product Development Assistance Scheme. Grants for developing products, production processes, acquiring new technology and licences. Grants at 50 per cent of the total cost of $1 million, whichever is lower, are repayable under certain conditions. Applicants must have at least 30 per cent local equity.

4. Small Industries Technical Assistance Scheme. Grants given to small local firms to seek external expertise to upgrade their operations.[39]

5. Venture Capital Scheme. A grant of $100 million to invest in venture fund and high technology projects. The aim is to encourage transfer of technology and foster the local venture capital industry.

6. Initiatives in New Technology.[40] Grants to both manufacturing and service sectors for developing new capabilities and for selected training programmes. The maximum grant for a single project is $5 million or 70 per cent of the total cost, whichever is lower.

7. Robot Leasing Scheme.[41] Soft loans to acquire robots and other industrial automation equipment.

8. Business Development Scheme. The newest scheme in which grants are given to small local firms with a minimum of 30 per cent local equity to explore overseas marketing and technology tie-up opportunities.

Three of the eight schemes—the Small Industries Technical Assistance Scheme (SITAS), Initiatives in New Technology (IINT), and the Robot Leasing Scheme (RLS) have been taken over from the Skills Development Fund (SDF). Four are existing EDB schemes which have been discussed earlier. The Business Development Scheme was officially implemented on 10 February 1987.

Furthermore, the EDB is planning to launch a Convertible Loans Scheme in connection with the Stock Exchange of Singapore Dealing and Automated Quotation System (SESDAQ) which was launched on 18 February 1987. Firms which cannot obtain financing from banks can get convertible loans at low interest under the SIFS. When these firms show profits, the loans can be converted into equity, which can then be traded on the SESDAQ.

In May 1987, the National Computer Board launched a scheme, called the Small Enterprise Computerized Accounting Programme (SECAP), to enable small firms to computerize their accounting systems quickly and at low cost. By June 1987, twenty small firms had taken advantage of the scheme.[42] They each had to pay a fee of $1,775, which entitled them to training and the services of consultants to advise them on the most suitable computer equipment to use. The Small Industries Technical Assistance Scheme pays for 70 per cent of the fees for each of the twenty small firms.

Another important organization which also provides assistance to local firms is the Singapore Institute of Standards and Industrial Research (SISIR). The SISIR is an autonomous technical and consultant agency of the EDB. It was established in 1969, taking over the activities of the EDB's Industrial Research Unit. In the past, the Industrial Research Unit mainly provided testing facilities for local firms. But the activities of the SISIR have been extended to provide quality control, standardization, improvement in the design of products and processes, and development of new products. The purpose of the SISIR is to provide these additional facilities to local firms and also to develop a permanent standards and industrial research organization.

In 1986, the SISIR embarked on a new role of providing industrial research technology to small firms. A $30 million budget has been allocated to the SISIR for the period 1981–91 to help small firms in three areas:

1. Assistance in the transfer of technology relevant to the needs of small firms;
2. Technical assistance in their export drive;
3. Assistance in improving production and quality-control systems.

In order to promote technology transfer, the SISIR has set up the Food Technology Centre, the Materials Technology Centre, the Design and Development Centre, the Industrial Research Centre, and the Technical Information Centre, and is the process of setting up a Hardware Demonstration Centre. With the resources of these centres, the SISIR has been able to provide information on the latest developments in technology relevant to small firms and to help firms to innovate by offering technical services, research services, and development support.

To help small firms improve their export performance, the SISIR provides information on overseas technical requirements and helps local firms meet these criteria by inspecting and testing their products. Since 1986, sixteen foreign authorities have been appointed to inspect or test Singapore-made products. In turn, the SISIR will test purchases made by international purchasing offices of MNCs.

As testing is an important economic activity, the SISIR has introduced the Singapore Laboratory Accreditation Scheme (SINGLAS), among other things, to maintain and improve the standard of testing and related activities in Singapore. Since August 1987, four laboratories have been accredited with SINGLAS. The laboratories provide services in the fields of chemical and biological testing, mechanical testing, and calibration.

In the area of production and quality control, the SISIR has set up a Quality Systems Department to implement, among other things, Total Quality Control Programmes. Officials from the SISIR have visited many firms in 1986 and 1987 to identify their problem areas.

The National Productivity Board (NPB),[43] which was established in 1972 to undertake the EDB's responsibility of formulating and organizing programmes to improve work attitudes, productivity, and labour-management relations, set up the Management Guidance Centre in early 1986 to help boost the performance and efficiency of small firms. An advisory panel comprising eighteen members from top-level positions in local and multinational firms was appointed to provide expert advice on the manner in which the NPB can help small firms. The advisory panel will eventually have thirty chief executives with experience covering the whole spectrum of Singapore industries. A pool of part-time consultants has also been engaged to take on consultancy projects with firms on an individual or sectorial basis. In addition, a group of foreign consultants and professional consultancy agencies has been enlisted to assist the NPB. Small and medium firms receive advisory, diagnostic, and consultancy services in four ways:

1. Diagnosis and review of management problems;

2. Analysis of training requirements and training programmes to solve efficiency problems;

3. Schemes or mechanisms to help solve specific productivity problems, and

4. Help to make full use of the assistance from various government agencies and private consultants.

The priority groups the NPB is focusing on are the manufacturing and commerce sectors. The various programmes organized by the Management Guidance Centre have proceeded well.[44]

In mid-1986, the NPB launched five training programmes to provide managers of small firms with management know-how and skills. The courses cover topics in management assistance, financial management and accounting, corporate planning and control, and corporate strategy in the manufacturing and retail sectors. The courses focus on the problems and issues commonly faced by small firms. The Skills Development Fund offers grants to firms which have staff taking the courses.[45]

Other plans on the agenda of the NPB include networking—through informal, after-office-hour gatherings of small entrepreneurs in similar industries to establish contacts, exchange views and gather information—and the production of a bulletin on value-added statistics by the NPB's research and development centre.[46]

The Skills Development Fund (SDF)

The SDF was established in 1979 to provide financial assistance to employers for the training of skills relevant to Singapore's economic restructuring effort. The SDF Secretariat was staffed by officers seconded from the EDB until August 1986, when the SDF was taken over by the NPB. It is financed through a levy on firms, originally amounting to 4 per cent of the salaries of all employees earning less than $750 a month. In 1985, the rate of contribution was reduced from 4 to 2 per cent.

Until 1 February 1987, the SDF offered the following schemes of financial incentives.

THE TRAINING GRANT SCHEME

The scheme provides grants to employers for structured training programmes undertaken to upgrade the skills of their workers. The amount of a grant varies with the individual merits of the application. Generally, it covers either 30 per cent, 50 per cent, 70 per cent, or 90 per cent of allowable training costs.

THE INTEREST GRANT FOR MECHANIZATION SCHEME

The scheme, which was introduced in December 1980, encourages firms to invest in new machinery and equipment to replace inefficient labour-intensive methods of operation. Firms which require term loans or hire purchase financing for the purchase of such machinery and equipment are eligible to apply for an interest grant to help reduce the interest cost.

The interest grant is equal to half the actual interest incurred in financing the equipment or machinery purchase, subject to a maximum of 9 per cent per annum, calculated on a six-monthly equal-instalment basis.

THE SMALL INDUSTRIES TECHNICAL ASSISTANCE SCHEME

The scheme, which was launched in 1982, helps small firms upgrade their technical operations and management techniques. Firms which satisfy the above criteria for loans may obtain grants of 30–90 per cent of fees incurred when they hire consultants to help them decide on software requirements.[47]

ROBOT LEASING SCHEME (RLS)

The scheme, which was introduced in 1984, helps firms to computerize and automate. No distinction was made between the MNCs and the small firms. With the shift of government focus to small firms in 1985, RLS relaxed its policies to enable small firms to obtain easier access to loans. RLS has two arms—the Automation Applications Centre, which is a low-cost consultancy unit, and the head office, which offers financial services. The RLS publishes a regular newsletter called 'Automation News' and has a library of information on the latest developments in automation. By November 1985, RLS had invested $30 million in about 40 robotic/automation systems, 12 of which have been completed.[48]

THE DEVELOPMENT CONSULTANCY SCHEME

Introduced in August 1981, this is the only scheme packaged specially for local firms, with the needs of smaller employers in mind. It provides financial assistance to local firms in need of external expertise for short-term assignments in the areas of business operations, technical know-how, management and manpower training. Grants provided under the scheme are based on either 30 per cent, 50 per cent, or 70 per cent of the cost of engaging experts.

THE INITIATIVES IN NEW TECHNOLOGIES SCHEME (INTECH)

Launched in August 1984, INTECH aims to provide financial assistance to projects in the knowledge-intensive field that will fit into Singapore's present stage of industrial development. The objective is to develop a core group of highly trained scientists and professionals to catalyse knowledge-intensive activities in new technology. The duration and extent of the support varies depending on the nature of each project and the risks involved.

CORE SKILLS FOR EFFECTIVENESS AND CHANGE (COSEC)

The SDF embarked on an important training scheme in February 1986, namely the COSEC scheme, which addresses the training needs of workers earning less than $800 a month. Assistance is provided for firms to recruit experts and train supervisors to help the workers gain a set of five core skills: communications, personal effectiveness, problem solving, work economics, and computer literacy. These skills enable workers to overcome three common areas of inadequacy: commitment to work, job competence, and capacity for change. With the COSEC programme, the SDF provides nine-tenths of the development cost and the trainer's salary and half of the trainees' absentee payroll. A pilot project involving 6,000 sales and clerical workers in ten retail and banking companies commenced in June 1986 and lasted for about a year. The SDF hopes to extend the scheme eventually to the 300,000 sales, service and clerical workers, and to another 100,000 workers in the manufacturing and other sectors, earning less than $800 a month. In 1986, 60 per cent of the work-force in Singapore earned less than $800 a month but received only 30 per cent of the employers' training budget. So far, COSEC has met with favourable response from workers and employers. The civil service, with 22,000 clerical workers, has also expressed a desire to join the scheme.[49]

Since the SDF was taken over by the NPB from the EDB, all the above schemes, except COSEC, have been integrated by the Economic Development Assistance scheme under the EDB. The transfer of the SDF from the EDB to the NPB indicates that the SDF has been given the sole responsibility of providing incentives to promote worker's training by only focusing on the COSEC scheme, leaving the EDB to work on the technical aspects of upgrading firms.

The SDF has been making greater efforts to reach out to small firms. It has looked into their limitations in undertaking upgrading programmes and has accordingly worked out various means to assist them. In the case of the Training Grant Scheme, between January 1980 and December 1984, 5,080 firms were awarded grants. Of these firms, 62 per cent were tiny and small establishments (with 5–49 workers). However, in terms of the number of employees who received the training, large firms were the main users of the SDF. Of those trained under SDF-approved programmes, 52 per cent worked for firms employing 500 workers or more.[50]

This shows that small firms generally do not put much emphasis on training. At the same time, it is sometimes difficult for small firms to design a training programme that is acceptable to the SDF. Nevertheless, the SDF is fully aware of the circumstances faced by small firms. While a seemingly weak training effort offered by a large firm is likely to be rejected, the SDF may approve it for a smaller applicant, on the grounds that it is a small but good first effort in the direction of training.[51]

Table 9.1 gives a profile of the users of SDF grants for the period January 1980–March 1984. Only 1.5 per cent of firms with fewer than 10 workers benefited from SDF grants. The percentage of firms which benefited from SDF grants increased with the size of the firm. It is worth noting that there were 217 firms with 500 or more workers in the early 1980s and all of them benefited from the SDF.

In terms of the number of employees trained under SDF grants, large firms again benefited more than small firms. Only 1.5 per cent of the employees of firms with fewer than 10 workers received training through SDF grants, while 28.5 per cent of the employees of firms having 500 or more workers benefited from such grants.

Thus, the SDF has to work harder to come up with various schemes to attract small firms to utilize SDF grants. On the other hand, small firms must also play their role in taking the training and retraining of workers seriously. With the transfer of the SDF to the NPB, it would appear that the SDF will have more funds to allocate to training. This is because the SDF's resources, since the streamlining, are devoted only to workers' training schemes.

The Trade Development Board (TDB)

Against a backdrop of international economic recovery and rising trade protectionism, the TDB was established in January 1983 in response to strong requests from the business community. The private sector also felt that mechanization was not likely to be successful unless Singapore was able to secure new markets overseas.

Among other things, the TDB quickly established a one-stop trade information service to provide personalized advisory service to exporters and traders. An average of 1,000 firms are serviced each month. Table 9.2 shows the main users of the TDB's services. Although the TDB did not design a special scheme to help small local firms, it is thought that the main users of the TDB's resources are usually small local firms, which do not have the same degree of overseas market connections as large and foreign firms.

In September 1985, the TDB introduced a Market Development Assistance Scheme (MDAS) to help small local firms. The MDAS offers dollar-for-dollar cash grants for export promotion activities, such as setting up overseas offices, improving product and package designs, marketing new products and services, and developing new markets.[52] Under the MDAS, firms pay only half the cost incurred in export promotion activities. The TDB pays the other half with the range set at $2,000–$250,000. The MDAS has a budget of $25 million. The main purpose of the MDAS is to help firms meet the initial costs of export promotion. Thus, cast grants are given for a one-to-two-year period only. But since grants are made on a project-by-project basis, firms which come up with activities aimed at promoting new products can send in fresh applications.

The following firms are eligible to apply to the MDAS for grants:

1. Firms which have less than $3 million in fixed assets excluding land and buildings. They should also be employing fewer than 100 workers.

2. Both service and manufacturing firms, provided that their goods and services have at least 25 per cent Singapore content. Furthermore, they must export to independent customers and not to their parent or affiliated firms overseas.

Small firms are expected to benefit from the MDAS because many do not have the necessary funds to increase their marketing efforts overseas. They are likely to use the MDAS to help pay for overseas marketing trips to promote exports, to pay for trade fairs and missions, and to provide promotional publications and package designs.

The TDB has recently embarked on an aggressive broad-base trade programme to help local exporters sell their new products. In the financial year 1986–7, the TDB has pursued a four-pronged plan to:[53]

1. Break into new markets, including North and West Africa, Eastern Europe, Canada, India, and China;

2. Export new products to existing markets, such as jewellery to Japan, industrial machinery to the Middle East and South-East Asia, and electronics to Australia;

3. Export technical know-how and professional services to developing nations, such as services in industrial engineering and building construction, plant design and engineering, and plant and building maintenance, and professional services like accounting, training and legal services; and

4. Export more high-end products to developed countries, such as industrial electronics, high-fashion apparel, quality furniture, speciality furniture, speciality food, and jewellery.

Since 1986, the TDB has organized many trade missions to various countries. Local exporters have also been assisted in countertrade[54] by means of the Countertrade Services Unit—a matchmaker of sorts that helps bring trading parties together. International countertrade houses can be considered for pioneer status in Singapore for five years if they satisfy the following criteria:[55]

1. The firm engages only in countertrade activities.

2. The firm has established international trading links and employs an agreed number of specialist countertraders.

3. At least one leg of each countertrade transaction, whether a financial or physical movement of goods, must be made through Singapore.

Other Measures

The Stock Exchange of Singapore Dealing and Automated Quotation System (SESDAQ) may offer another form of assistance to small firms.[56] The SESDAQ can help small firms with growth potential to raise their capital through share issues. Young and growing firms which do not yet qualify for a listing on the main board of the Stock

Exchange of Singapore due to their limited track record will find the SESDAQ useful as it provides an alternative source of long-term funds for them. The EDB is confident that the SESDAQ will be a success, given the right sort of direction, adding that similar markets in the US and Britain have been very successful.

Small firms are generally pleased with the setting up of the SESDAQ. The chairman of the Singapore Manufacturers' Association described the move as timely and enlightened as it will help small firms, particularly high-risk venture companies, to raise funds more easily and cheaply.[57] He added that the SESDAQ will be a success if there is public confidence and people have the money to invest. Firms listed should also comply with appropriate requirements and standards of disclosure.

In accord with the Economic Committee,[58] the government formed the Business Enterprise Committee (BEC) in January 1986 to remove unnecessary or over-restrictive regulations which smother private initiative and hinder the growth of firms. The BEC consists mainly of civil servants, with representatives from the private sector. The committee reviews government regulations and seeks to eliminate those rules that give rise to unnecessary red tape and procedural delays so as to develop an 'innovative, creative and enterprising society'.[59]

Concerned with the spate of dissolutions that have hit a total of 350 firms in 1985,[60] the concept of judicial management was introduced in the Companies (Amendment) Bill 1986.[61] The Bill allows for a moratorium period during which the rights of all creditors are suspended so as to allow the judicial manager time to reorganize the operations of an insolvent but still viable company. If these provisions are enacted, firms, including small firms, can have an alternative to receivership and liquidation.

Conclusion

In this chapter we have studied the role of the government in helping small firms in Taiwan, Thailand, Japan, and Singapore. The governments in these countries have been taking explicit measures to help local and small firms. However, the effects of government policies on small firms have not been the same for all.

The Taiwanese government has provided assistance to small firms through various ministries and agencies, namely, the Ministry of Economic Affairs, the Ministry of Finance, the Central Bank of China, the Economic Council of Co-operation, and the National Economic Council. Most of its industrial policies are aimed at eliminating or alleviating the financial burdens of small firms. A study by Yen, however, shows that government policies have been largely ineffective. Several reforms in the industrial policies are called for, and these have been discussed in the first section of this chapter.

In the case of Thailand, the government has helped small firms through various organizations, such as the Division of Industrial

Services, the Management Development and Productivity Centre, and the Small Industrial Finance Office. The budgets and manpower resources of these organizations, however, are not really adequate for the needs of local firms in Thailand. Consequently, the government policies for helping small firms have not been too effective.

Japan is one of the few countries which practises an industrial strategy. The Japanese industrial strategy has been to select and protect industries with great potential to excel not only in the domestic market but also in foreign markets. The Japanese government has been able and willing to protect them from foreign competition. Moreover, small firms in Japan have also benefited from government assistance by receiving procurement orders from the public sector. Many Japanese giant corporations, such as National, were once small firms which have benefited from government policies.

The government in Singapore has also taken many measures to help small firms. As early as 1962 the EDB set up the LIS Unit to help local and small firms. It is a common belief that the presence of many foreign companies discouraged local entrepreneurs from forming enterprises. This is not exactly true. Few small firms compete with large and foreign firms in Singapore. As a matter of fact, the relationship between small, and large and foreign firms is more complementary than substitutional. Nevertheless, small firms have to compete with large and foreign firms for semi-skilled and skilled workers and the former always lose. Fortunately, the government has been able to alleviate this problem by increasing the supply of such workers through effective manpower planning.

The entrepreneurs of small firms in Singapore often complain that there is unfair competition between them and government-owned firms in a number of fields. In response to requests from the business community, the government has taken various measures to privatize some government-owned firms.

In 1985, the government introduced numerous policies to help small firms in Singapore. It is hoped that small firms can quickly capitalize on these facilities and thereby improve their business competitiveness.

It should be highlighted here that the entrepreneurs of small firms must also help the government by helping themselves. They should take training of workers seriously and always be prepared to upgrade technology and management know-how. The Japanese have been successful in economic development because there is good rapport between the government and the private sector. Japanese entrepreneurs are also capable of adapting Western technology and management know-how to their unique cultural environment. It is imperative that entrepreneurs in Singapore learn from the experiences of their Japanese counterparts.

1. The material of this section is obtained from two main sources, namely, Yen Gi-li, 'Industrial Policies as They Relate to SMBs—A Financial Perspective', paper presented at the *1984 Joint Conference on the Industrial Policies of the Republic of China and the Republic of Korea*, held in Taiwan, 27–28 December 1984; and T. K. Djang, *Industry and Labour in Taiwan*, Institute of Economics, Academia Sinica, Monograph Series No. 10, Republic of China, 1977.

2. The Executive Yuan is the highest administrative organ of the State and has under it a president, a vice president, several ministers without portfolio, and a number of ministries, commissions, and agencies. For more information on the organization of the Taiwanese government, see Executive Yuan, Research, Development and Evaluation Commission, *Annual Review of Government Administration, Republic of China*.

3. Yen gives a number of reasons why small and medium businesses are deemed poor credit risks. See Yen, op. cit., p. 10.

4. It is hoped that this reservation on the part of the loan officers will be removed with the 1984 ruling of the Ministry of Finance that acquits loan officers from being personally liable for bad loans except in the case of misdemeanours or fraud.

5. Thailand, Ministry of International Trade and Industry, 'Country paper (Thailand) on small and medium enterprise policies', delivered at the International Conference on Small Enterprise Policy, held in Osaka, 18–20 January 1983.

6. Saeng Sanguanruang, Nisa Xuto, Preeyanuch Saengpassorn, and Chuchup Piputsitee, *Development of Small and Medium Manufacturing Enterprises in Thailand*, Bangkok, December 1970.

7. Jacques Amyot, *Small Industries Enterprise Supportive Institutions: A Preliminary Assessment*, Report for Rural Off-Farm Employment Assessment Project (ROFEAP), Kasetsart University, Bangkok, 1981.

8. Busaba Kunasirin, *The Role of Small- and Medium-Scale Industries in the Economic Development of Japan and Thailand: A Comparative Analysis*, Institute of Developing Economies, Visiting Research Fellow, Series No. 109, March 1984.

9. Ibid.

10. Ibid.

11. *Asian Business*, August 1985.

12. Kunasirin, op. cit.

13. Okita Saburo, *The Developing Economies and Japan*, Tokyo, University of Tokyo Press, 1980, p. 97.

14. Japan, Small and Medium Enterprise Agency, Ministry of International Trade and Industry, *Outline of Small- and Medium-Scale Enterprise Policies of the Japanese Government*, January 1983, p. 3.

15. Japan, The Japan Institute of International Affairs, *White Papers of Japan 1983–84*, annual abstract of official reports and statistics of the Japanese government, p. 127.

16. We have not, however, ruled out the possibility that small firms in Singapore might face a labour constraint. Indeed, it is unfortunate that some small firms in Singapore face both capital and labour constraints. See Chapter 7 for a discussion on the problem of shortage of workers faced by small firms.

17. In June 1986, the EDB was re-organized into three departments—the Markets Department, the Support Department and the Product Department. The latter includes the Small Enterprise Bureau. The change is in tandem with the goal of selling Singapore as an investment centre. See *The Business Times*, 23 June 1986.

18. Economic Development Board, *Annual Report*, 1968, p. 30.

19. Economic Development Board *Annual Report*, 1985.

20. *The Straits Times*, 5 June 1986 and 20 June 1986.

21. *The Straits Times*, 13 November 1985.

22. *The Business Times*, 24 January 1986.

23. *Singapore Statistical News*, Vol. 70, No. 1, 1984; *The Straits Times*, 27 March 1986; *The Business Times*, 28 May 1986.

24. *The Straits Times*, 29 July 1985.

25. Ibid.

26. *The Straits Times*, 24 August 1985.

27. *The Business Times*, 5 November 1985.

28. *The Straits Times*, 25 January 1986.

29. *The Straits Times*, 13 November 1985.

30. *The Straits Times*, 24 February 1986.

31. *The Business Times*, 1 July 1986 and 10 July 1986.

32. *The Straits Times*, 23 January 1986; *The Business Times*, 10 April 1986.

33. *The Business Times*, 1 July 1986. The two MNCs are Philips and Hewlett Packard.

34. *The Business Times*, 24 February 1986.

35. *The Business Times*, 18 April 1986.

36. *The Straits Times*, 16 April 1986.

37. *The Straits Times*, 11 February 1987.

38. The SIFS incorporates a former Skills Development Fund (SDF) scheme, the Interest Grant for Mechanization. The SDF is discussed later.

39. The SITAS incorporates another SDF scheme, the Development Grant for Consultancy.

40. Initiatives in New Technology was formerly administrated by the Skills Development Fund.

41. The Robot Leasing Scheme was formerly administrated by the Skills Development Fund.

42. *The Straits Times*, 28 May 1987.

43. With effect from 1 August 1986, the NPB came under the Ministry of Trade and Industry. At the same time, the SDF was moved to the NPB from the Economic Development Board. It is expected that skills training and productivity will be better coordinated with this move.

44. *The Straits Times*, 21 February 1986.

45. *The Business Times*, 8 July 1986. The SDF is discussed below.

46. *The Business Times*, 7 June 1986.

47. *The Business Times*, 2 June 1986.

48. *The Business Times*, 18 June 1987.

49. *The Business Times*, 6 February 1986.

50. *The Business Times*, 18 March 1985.

51. Ibid.

52. *The Straits Times*, 22 September 1985.

53. *The Straits Times*, 10 January 1986.

54. Countertrade is a complex form of barter trade involving several parties which now accounts for 8–10 per cent of world trade.

55. *The Straits Times*, 17 July 1986.

56. *The Straits Times*, 17 September 1985.

57. Ibid.

58. The Economic Committee was formed in March 1985 to review the progress of the economy and to identify new directions for its future growth.

59. *The Straits Times*, 27 January 1986.

60. *The Straits Times*, 12 March 1986.

61. *The Straits Times*, 6 May 1986.

TABLE 9.1

Users of the Skills Development Fund Grants, January 1980–March 1984

Employment Size	Firms in Singapore		Employees in Singapore	
	Number	Per Cent Reached*	Number	Per Cent Reached*
Less than 10	50,405	1.5	153,476	1.5
10–50	9,862	17.5	195,210	9.5
51–99	1,183	53.3	82,098	12.4
100–199	603	79.8	83,044	12.5
200–499	367	86.7	113,373	29.6
500 & above	217	100.0	304,432	28.5

Source: The Business Times, 18 March 1985.
* Supported by SDF grants.

TABLE 9.2

Users of the Trade Development Board, 1983 and 1984

Service	Industrial Products[a]		Consumer Products[b]		Commodities[c]		Services[d]		Total	
	1983	1984	1983	1984	1983	1984	1983	1984	1983	1984
Singapore manufacturers visited[e]	80	121	150	201	46	13	10	54	286	329
Incoming buyers serviced[f]	65	104	85	167	23	23	5	10	178	304
Serious trade enquiries services[g]	323	229	471	386	162	39	75	39	1,031	693

Source: Singapore, Trade Development Board, *Annual Report*, 1983 and 1984.

[a] Refers to electronic components, industrial electronics, chemical and pharmaceuticals, and packaging.

[b] Refers to apparel, jewellery, furniture and houseware, food and beverages, consumer electronics, printing and publishing, and general merchandise.

[c] Refers to timber, coffee, and others.

[d] Refers to infrastructure consultancy, marine and ocean engineering, industrial plant, and machinery.

[e] Refers to the number of Singapore manufacturers who made use of the Board's facilities.

[f] Refers to the number of foreign buyers in Singapore who received help from the Board.

[g] Refers to the number of serious trade enquiries from abroad via telephone and telex.

10

DOMESTIC ENTREPRENEURSHIP IN SINGAPORE

A Definition of Entrepreneurship

THE important role of entrepreneurship in economic development is well recognized.[1] According to Schumpeter, the driving force in economic development under capitalism is the entrepreneur.[2] An entrepreneur has three unique roles to play.[3] He is (i) an innovator who has the ability to seize business opportunities for introducing a new product, a new method of production, a new market, and a new factor of production; (ii) a business organizer who has the ability to plan, control, and coordinate the various factors of production to obtain revenue-generating products, and (iii) a risk taker who is willing and able to bear the calculated risk of the business.

There has been extensive discussion in the literature on whether the unique characteristics of the entrepreneur are determined by nature or nurture. According to J. P. Roscoe, entrepreneurship is a state of mind or a certain quality in an individual and therefore cannot be taught.[4] But C. J. Grayson argues that it can be taught.[5] The truth probably lies somewhere in between.

This chapter looks at domestic entrepreneurship in Singapore. In actual fact, there is no lack of entrepreneurship in Singapore: there are a few outstanding hotel and bank entrepreneurs; construction entrepreneurs are numerous; Singapore trading and merchant entrepreneurs are well known, and an abundance of Singapore entrepreneurship is found in the hawker food industry. There is, however, a lack of industrial entrepreneurship in Singapore. As is implied in the discussion on the manufacturing sector in Chapter 2, local entrepreneurs could have played a more important role in the industrial development of Singapore.

Factors Affecting Industrial Entrepreneurship

Singapore was an immigrant society. She was a society trading in primary commodities. As Singaporeans had no experience in dealing with industrialization until the early 1960s, this may explain why Singapore does not lack trading entrepreneurs but lacks industrial entrepreneurs.

The purpose of this chapter is to present an economic analysis of the factors influencing domestic industrial entrepreneurs in Singapore. It is argued that the higher the opportunity cost of becoming an entrepreneur and the lower the rate of return on investment, the smaller the pool of entrepreneurs. The opportunity cost of being an entrepreneur is measured by the alternative choice in employment, i.e. the wages as an employee. The rate of return on investment is assessed in terms of operating cost and market share.

Most people are reluctant to become entrepreneurs if they can have a stable career with high earnings. This is especially true for graduates in Singapore. We shall now examine the factors affecting domestic industrial entrepreneurship in Singapore.

High Wages

The wages of Singapore graduates are high even by international standards. As Table 10.1 shows, the starting wage of a production engineer in Singapore is the highest compared to Malaysia, Taiwan, South Korea, and even Japan. After three years in employment, the production engineer in Singapore still draws the highest salary. Similarly, the Singapore accountant is also the best paid among those in the same group of countries. Thus, graduates in Singapore draw very attractive salaries. It is only natural that most people in Singapore, especially if they have good paper qualifications, are more inclined to be employees. This is consistent with our survey findings that most entrepreneurs are not highly educated (see Chapter 7).

It has also been reported that most entrepreneurs in Singapore are Chinese educated.[6] Since English is the medium of administration in both the private and public sectors, the Chinese educated, especially graduates, whose jobs demand a good command of English are naturally at a disadvantage compared to the English educated. As Table 10.2 shows, English-educated graduates earned 85 per cent more than Chinese-educated graduates in 1966. The margin was reduced to 38 per cent in 1978. This shows that the opportunity cost of being an entrepreneur (measured in terms of wages) plays an important role in the decision on whether to be one.

High Growth Rate of Earnings

Singaporeans, especially graduates, also enjoy a high growth rate of nominal earnings. Table 10.3 presents nominal earnings growth by education for the period 1973–84. Clearly, the nominal earnings of all workers increased rapidly between 1973 and 1984, irrespective of education. This is particularly true since 1979, when the Wage Correction Policy was launched to correct the anomalous situation of the low-wage phenomenon coexisting with a tight labour market during the latter half of the 1970s.

Although the Wage Correction Policy was intended to last for only three years, nominal earnings continued to rise rapidly across the board.

In particular, the growth of nominal earnings of graduates has been most spectacular, rising from 4.4 per cent in 1973–8 to 8.7 per cent in 1979–81 and to 21.1 per cent in 1982–4. In fact, nominal earnings of graduates grew at the fastest pace for the period 1982–4, compared to those of workers with other levels of educational attainment.

The prospect of increasing earnings, with the rate being highest among graduates, increases the opportunity cost for workers striking out on their own to become entrepreneurs. In the words of Dr Wong Kwei Chong, the then Minister of State for Trade and Industry,

We are, in a sense, victims of our own success. In successfully eradicating unemployment, we have created more jobs than there are takers. This has led to an environment in which good jobs are easy to find. Unfortunately, this environment has also reduced the motivation on the part of individuals to strike out on their own.[7]

The Public Sector as the Leading Wage Sector

The Singapore government has stressed time and again that the brightest and the best citizens should be working in the public sector.[8] In order to retain the best people in the public sector, the wages in the public sector have to be very attractive compared to those in the private sector. Table 10.4 illustrates the pay differentials between the public and private sectors for graduates for 1978–84. The percentage of graduates employed in the public sector increased from 49.7 per cent in 1978 to 55.9 per cent in 1984. It is reasonable to conclude that most of the top graduates are with the public sector.

The public sector comprises government departments and statutory boards. The pay differential of graduates in the private and public sectors has been shifting slightly in favour of the public sector. For example, the pay differential of graduates in the private sector over the overall average of the public sector was 1.02 in 1978 but dropped to 0.96 in 1984. If we look at government departments alone, the public sector stands out clearly as the better paymaster as the pay-differential ratio was 0.95 in 1983 and 0.88 in 1984. In 1984, for example, graduates in government departments earned about 12 per cent more than their counterparts in the private sector.

Indeed, a government committee set up in 1985 to study the wage structure in the public sector found that 'on the average, starting salaries for civil service appointments were much higher than those for equivalent occupations in the private sector'.[9]

Moreover, the public sector offers the additional attraction of stable employment. Following the government committee's report, the government decided to lower the starting salaries of all workers in the public sector by $30–$200 on 1 November 1985—excluding officers in five key services, namely the Administrative Service, the Administrative Service (Foreign Service Branch), the Singapore Armed Forces (Senior Grade), the Police Service (Senior Grade) and the Intelligence

Service (Senior Grade)—to bring public sector wages more in line with wages in the private sector. This helped correct the bias of wages in favour of employees in the public sector.

The Central Provident Fund (CPF) Scheme

Under the CPF scheme in Singapore, employers and employees have to contribute a proportion of the employees' salaries to the employees' CPF accounts. When the scheme was first introduced in 1955, the rate of contribution was 5 per cent of the gross monthly wages each by the employers and employees, subject to a maximum monthly contribution of $50. The rate of contribution and the ceiling have been increasing steadily over the years. In 1984, the CPF rate of contribution was 25 per cent each payable by the employers and the employees, with the maximum monthly contribution fixed at $2,500. The CPF scheme thus makes it even more attractive to remain as employees.

Lim Chong Yah et al. simulate the CPF savings of a hypothetical worker.[10] They make the following assumptions: (i) Inflation is 4 per cent and real wages increase at 3 per cent annually throughout the period of projection; and (ii) Interest rate on the CPF balances is 6.5 per cent, making the real rate of interest earned by the CPF balances 2.5 per cent. They consider a worker starting work at the age of 25, earning an initial monthly wage of $800. The worker's CPF balances, in real value terms are given in Table 10.5.

Given the above conditions, which are reasonable in the light of our discussion earlier in this chapter, the worker will have a total of $335,035 CPF money in real terms at the age of 55. This represents part of the opportunity cost if the worker becomes self-employed.

For a graduate whose starting salary is about $1,944 (see Table 10.1) with the growth rate of earnings around 21.1 per cent (see Table 10.3), the CPF balance will be much larger than that of the hypothetical worker in Table 10.5. Therefore, the CPF scheme increases the opportunity cost of being an entrepreneur.

The employer's CPF contribution was reduced to 10 per cent in April 1986. This change in policy has significantly reduced the CPF balances of employees and hence the opportunity cost of being an entrepreneur. Moreover, in view of the recession in 1985–6, the growth rate of earnings is expected to increase at only 3–5 per cent per annum in the late 1980s.[11] This will certainly encourage entrepreneurship in Singapore.

The above discussion shows that a favourable employment climate in terms of attractive wages and stable employment is not conducive to the development of domestic entrepreneurship. But the favourable employment climate in Singapore is brought about by full employment and not by decree. This implies that if Singapore wants to encourage local industrial entrepreneurship, a concerted effort must be made to cultivate it.

The Domestic Market

The rate of return on capital is largely determined by the market share of the product. We will first examine the size of the domestic market in Singapore. This can be measured either by the size of the population or the GDP (GNP).

Using either yardstick, Singapore's domestic market is small in contrast with Taiwan's, Hong Kong's, South Korea's, Malaysia's, Thailand's, and Japan's (see Table 10.6). Taiwan's GNP is more than three times that of Singapore's, and Thailand's GNP is twice that of Singapore's. In terms of population, Singapore's population is less than half of Hong Kong's and about 17 per cent of Malaysia's and 13 per cent of Taiwan's.

The importance of a sizeable domestic market to industrial firms should not be underestimated. The domestic market provides the first contact point for the local (and often) small firms. It is easier to penetrate the domestic market than the foreign market as the former is less competitive. The theory of the firm suggests that firms can practise price discrimination, where the price of the product is higher in the less competitive domestic market and lower in the more competitive foreign market. Thus, having a sizeable domestic market will enable the firm to make full use of the price discrimination strategy and ultimately enjoy economies of scale if its penetration into the foreign market is sustained and extensive.

Since the domestic market in Singapore is very small, small firms in Singapore will not have the advantage of being sheltered by the domestic market and subsequently have to compete in the world markets before economies of scale occur.

The Public Enterprises

The market share of a product is also affected by the extent of involvement of public enterprises. In Singapore, there are numerous government wholly-owned companies and subsidiaries.[12] Some of the public enterprises are regulated monopolies and some are natural monopolies. Others are export oriented in nature. But many public enterprises compete in the local market.[13]

The Local Business Committee[14] has made three observations concerning public enterprises: (i) There are more than 450 government-owned companies, subsidiaries, and associated companies in Singapore; (ii) These government enterprises have become increasingly involved in activities formerly the exclusive domain of the private sector; and (iii) They usually have high financial and market leverage over firms in the private sector. The government's policy of privatization introduced in 1986 is thus consistent with the objective of promoting entrepreneurship in Singapore.

The High Statutory Cost of Operation

We have already examined the size of the domestic market and the participation of public enterprises in Singapore which affect the market share of the product and ultimately the rate of return on capital. We will now look at the various factors which affect the cost of production, one of them being the statutory cost of operation in Singapore.

One reason for the paucity of domestic entrepreneurship in Singapore is the high statutory cost of operation in Singapore. This has affected the profitability of local businesses and subsequently weakened their international competitiveness.

A government survey in 1984 showed that Singapore was losing her competitiveness in imported goods, compared to London, Paris, New York, and Hong Kong.[15] The survey compared a list of popular tourist items belonging to thirteen categories, namely various brands of ladies' wear, shoes and handbags, men's wear, shoes, belts and wallets, perfumes, ladies' and men's watches, cameras, radio-cassette recorders and video-cassette recorders, sold in Singapore and six other cities. Most of the goods sold in Hong Kong were found to be the least expensive.

Table 10.7 shows that compared to Hong Kong, Singapore was losing her competitiveness in the majority of the items. In fact, some of the goods sold in Singapore were found to be twice as expensive as similar items sold in Hong Kong. Retailers in Singapore cited, *inter alia*, higher rentals and the stronger Singapore dollar for the higher cost of the products sold in Singapore. Moreover, Singapore had a higher corporate tax rate than Hong Kong and she had taxes on utilities charges which were absent in Hong Kong (see Table 10.8).

Since July 1985, however, the Singapore government has taken steps to reduce the cost of operating a business in Singapore. These steps are summarized below:[16]

PROPERTY TAX

From 1 July 1985 to 31 December 1988, industrial and commercial properties enjoy a 50 per cent property tax rebate. In addition, from 1 July 1986 all properties that are being developed privately are exempt from property tax from the time construction commences to the issue of Temporary Occupation Licences.

CORPORATE TAX

For the year of assessment 1987, the corporate tax rate has been reduced from 40 per cent to 33 per cent. Companies may also pay an effective tax rate of a minimum of 5 per cent after the expiration of their pioneer status. In addition, approved companies that set aside 20 per cent of their taxable income for research and development (to be spent within three years) are exempt from tax on that amount. And to promote venture capital, firms or investors which incur losses arising from the sale of shares in an approved company may write-off an amount up to the full value of their investments. They may also carry forward losses for write-offs against future profits.

PERSONAL INCOME TAX

To bring the personal income tax rate in line with the reduction in corporate tax rate, a 25 per cent personal income tax rebate was provided across the board for the year of assessment 1986.

RENTS

From 1 August 1985, the Jurong Town Corporation (JTC) has provided a 10–15 per cent rebate on warehouse and land rentals. The Housing and Development Board (HDB) commercial/industrial tenants and lessees enjoy a rent-free fitting-up period. Payment of advance rent has also been scaled downwards. In addition, Urban Renewal Authority (URA) tenants can enjoy a 15 per cent rent rebate up to the end of 1987.

TELEPHONE CHARGES

From 1 October 1985, international telephone and telex services, telephone extensions, and pager charges have been reduced by 10–50 per cent.

PORT CHARGES

The Port of Singapore Authority (PSA) has also provided a 10–33 per cent rebate on warehouse and handling rates from 1 August 1985. This is over and above the 10–15 per cent discounts on the use of JTC port facilities.

AIRPORT CHARGES

There has been a 15 per cent reduction in airport rentals and in concessions on fees of airport shops, ground handling, and aviation fuel from 1 August 1985.

UTILITIES CHARGES

The Public Utilities Board (PUB) has imposed lower electricity and gas charges. It also suspended the 10 per cent tax on electricity and gas charges for a period of two years on 1 November 1985. Owners of factories and large commercial buildings will suffer lower penalties if they are unable to reach their estimated power needs under the five-year agreements with the PUB from 1 April 1986.

LAND CHARGES

The URA has offered six concessions which essentially aim to give property developers more time to complete their projects on URA sites and to enable them to have more time to pay for land bought from the URA. Concessions have also been given to encourage entrepreneurs to renew their land leases and to expand investments.

EXPORT DUTY

The export duty on timber and wood products was lifted on 1 April 1986.

DIESEL TAX

The diesel tax for taxis was reduced from $6,600 to $1,100 on 1 October 1985. The fuel-oil duty was eliminated and the pump price of petrol was reduced on 1 September 1985 with price adjustments to be made every three months to reflect the prevailing exchange rate.

The effects of the above measures on the statutory cost of operation in Singapore have been encouraging. Indeed, according to a survey conducted by the Singapore Tourist Promotion Board in 1986 on the prices of fifty-two items sold in duty-free, speciality, and fixed-price stores in Singapore and Hong Kong, the prices of goods sold in Singapore were on average 2.5 per cent to 5.5 per cent cheaper than similar items sold in Hong Kong.[17]

High Labour Cost

Wages in Singapore are high and labour costs are even higher. Table 10.9 shows the hourly compensation costs for production workers in the manufacturing sector of a number of selected countries. For Singapore, the average hourly earnings was $3.32 in 1984. The labour cost per hour, however, was not equal to $3.32. It was 56 per cent more than the average hourly earnings. This ratio of additional compensation to hourly earnings was the highest in Singapore, compared to the US (37.1 per cent), Hong Kong (11.0 per cent), Japan (16.8 per cent), Korea (20 per cent), Taiwan (5.0 per cent), and the United Kingdom (33.1 per cent).

Table 10.10 lists the breakdown of the ratio of additional compensation to hourly earnings for Singapore. It may be observed that the ratio of 56 per cent in 1984 comprised 33.6 per cent of statutory contributions, namely the Central Provident Fund (28.8 per cent), and the Skills Development Fund.[18] Bonus and annual wage supplements account for 12.6 per cent. Thus, by international standards, the employment of production workers in Singapore is very costly. This certainly increases the cost of manufacturing products in Singapore.

Workers' Health, Safety Regulations, Environmental Control, and Labour Legislation[19]

In Singapore, there are numerous laws to protect workers' health and safety at the place of work. For example, the Factory Act 1973 protects a worker from accidents and diseases arising from his working environment. Other examples are the Employment Act Chapter 22 (1970), which includes (i) control of hours of work, (ii) prohibitions of employment of children and young persons, (iii) protection of women during their maternity period, and (iv) health, accommodation and medical care; the Workmen's Compensation Act 1975; the Factories Safety Committee Regulations 1975; and the Factories (Registration and Duties of Safety Officers) Regulations 1975. In addition, environmental protection is enforced by the Clean Air (Standards) Regulations 1972 and the Trade Effluent Regulations dealing with the Water Pollution Control and Drainage Act 1975 (Article 29).

Needless to say, all these regulations and controls have increased the cost of production. Large and foreign firms are least affected because they generally can comply with the requirements. However, small firms are the worst hit as their working conditions are generally inferior.

Similarly, regulations exist in Taiwan, such as the Labour Safety and Health Act 1974, the Lead Poisoning Prevention Ordinance 1974, and the Tetra-Alkyl Lead Poisoning Prevention Ordinance 1974.[20] However, enforcement of such regulations in Taiwan is not as stringent as in Singapore. It may be said that to some extent the Taiwanese small firms are able to flourish because of the greater laxity in the control of working conditions. But the Taiwanese government has been taking safety and environment problems more seriously since the mid-1980s.[21]

There have also been major changes in labour legislation in Singapore. Since the 1960s, the government has instituted a series of legislative measures aimed at controlling labour costs. The Industrial Relations Ordinance 1960 has legislated collective bargaining procedures through compulsory conciliation and arbitration. Under this legislation, strikes and lockouts are prohibited once an industrial dispute has been referred to the Industrial Arbitration Court by either party or the government. The Industrial Relations (Amendment) Act 1968 has given greater discretion to employers in the deployment of their work-force, and has removed decisions on promotions, internal transfer of employees, hiring, and dismissals from being subject to negotiation with unions. Furthermore, the Employment Act 1968 has reduced labour costs by limiting the sums payable on bonuses, annual paid leave, retrenchment benefits, and overtime.

All these legislative measures have, to a large extent, benefited large firms which have to deal with trade unions. Small firms in Singapore, however, do not gain from these legislative measures as most of them are not unionized (see Chapter 5 for a discussion on unionization).

Conclusion

It is always difficult to pin-point the main determinants of development in general and entrepreneurship in particular. According to his EGOIN Theory of Development, Lim Chong Yah concludes that it is the quality of people that determines development.[22] His definition of quality of people includes good government, good economic and political leadership, and good entrepreneurship in both the private and public sectors.

Specifically, on the quality of entrepreneurship, he writes:

... not all people in the world have been given or have developed the enterprising spirit. The levels of enterprise are likely to vary from people to people and from time to time even with the 'same' people. If an enterprising people whose enterpreneurial activities have been restricted by Government intervention, the removal of Government intervention logically would stimulate the growth or revitalization of enterprise. . . . However, if the people concerned have no enterprise or have lost their enterprise, the removal of Government restrictions per se can do very little to stimulate the enterprising spirit, particularly in the short run.[23]

Singaporeans are an enterprising people but many opt to work in the private and public sectors. Therefore, appropriate policies by the government can stimulate the enterprising spirit of Singaporeans.

In the past two decades or so, all Singaporeans have been given the opportunity to educate themselves. Few leave school out of economic hardship. Many regard academic achievement as an important goal in life. It may therefore be safely concluded that the quality of people is positively related to the level of education.[24] In the above section, we have seen that the economic opportunity cost of graduates setting up their own businesses is enormous. Thus, the manufacturing sector has not been getting its fair share of talented people as entrepreneurs. It can be concluded that, if it were not for the lack of talented entrepreneurship, the contribution of small firms towards industrial output, value-added, and exports would have been greater.

However, we can say with confidence that small firms in Singapore will continue to play an important role in the manufacturing sector on the following three counts:

1. Statistically and economically the importance of small firms in the national economy will not decline as the economy matures (Chapters 4 and 8).

2. The government is very determined to promote small local firms through economic incentives (Chapter 9 and the second section of this chapter).

3. The recession in 1985–6 has made Singaporeans realize that the days of double-digit growth in earnings are over. This, coupled with the 15 percentage point reduction in the employer's CPF contribution rate, has greatly reduced the opportunity cost of graduates becoming entrepreneurs. According to the *1985 Report on the Labour Force Survey of Singapore*, the unemployment rate for graduates in mid-1984 was 3.1 per cent, 0.4 per cent above the 2.7 per cent rate for the work-force as a whole. This was higher than the 2.9 per cent unemployment rate for graduates in mid-1983, which was 0.3 per cent below the then prevailing national unemployment rate. Thus, graduates are finding jobs increasingly difficult to come by.[25] The less favourable employment climate for graduates will help promote entrepreneurship.

1. See, for example, P. Kilby (ed.), *Entrepreneurship and Economic Development*, New York, The Free Press, 1971, and B. Higgins, *Economic Development*, New York, W. W. Norton and Co. Inc., 1968.

2. J. Schumpeter, *The Theory of Economic Development*, New York, Oxford University Press, 1961.

3. For a detailed discussion on the functions of the entrepreneur, see H. Schollhammer, 'Internal Corporate Entrepreneurship' in C. Kent, O. Sexton and K. Vesper (eds.), *Encyclopaedia of Entrepreneurship*, New Jersey, Prentice-Hall Inc., 1982, and H. Schrage, 'The R & D Entrepreneur: Profile of Success', *Harvard Economic Review*, Vol. 43, November–December 1965.

4. J. P. Roscoe, 'Can Entrepreneurship be Taught?', *MBA Magazine*, Vol. 51, June–July 1973, p. 12.

5. C. J. Grayson, 'Let's Get Back to the Competitive Market System', *Harvard Business Review*, Vol. 51, November–December 1973, p. 11.

6. Lim Boon Heng, Assistant Secretary-General of the National Trades Union Congress and Member of Parliament for Kebun Bahru, at a scholarship award ceremony of the National Transport Workers Union on 19 October 1985, as reported in *The Sunday Times*, 20 October 1985.

7. Wong Kwei Chong, the then Minister of State (Ministry of Trade and Industry) and Chairman of the National Productivity Board, at the opening ceremony of the Fourth Singapore National Academy of Science Congress on 28 May 1984, *Singapore Government Press Release*, May 1984.

8. See, for example, the ministerial statements on the administrative and professional services in the Singapore civil service by Tony Tan Keng Yam, Minister for Trade and Industry, on 3 March 1982, *Singapore Government Press Release*, March 1982, and by the Prime Minister, Lee Kuan Yew, during a parliamentary debate on ministers' salaries on 22 March 1985, as reported in *The Straits Times*, 23 March 1985.

9. *The Straits Times*, 23 October 1985.

10. Lim Chong Yah *et al.*, 'Report of the Central Provident Fund Study Group', *Singapore Economic Review*, Special Issue, Vol. XXXI, No. 1, April 1986.

11. In his 1986 National Day Message, Lee Kuan Yew stated that the future GDP growth rate for Singapore would not be 8–10 per cent but only 3–5 per cent. Certainly, the rate of wage increase is not expected to be greater than the rate of GDP growth. See *The Straits Times*, 9 August 1986.

12. For a detailed discussion, see Tan Chwee Huat, *State Enterprise System and Economic Development in Singapore*, London, University Microfilms International, 1975.

13. See Linda Low, 'Privatisation Policies and Issues in Singapore', Staff Seminar Paper No. 7, Department of Economics and Statistics, National University of Singapore, 1985.

14. Singapore, Federation of Chambers of Commerce and Industry, Report of the Subcommittee and Local Businesses, August 1985.

15. *The Straits Times*, 31 January 1984.

16. The sources are:
(a) Budget for financial year 1986/7.
(b) Budget for financial year 1986/7 and First Deputy Prime Minister's response to the Economic Committee's Report.
(c) First Deputy Prime Minister's response to the Economic Committee's Report.
(d) *The Straits Times*, 27 July 1985, and *Business Times*, 1 April 1986.
(d) *The Straits Times*, 27 July 1985, and *Business Times*, 1 April 1986.
(e) *The Straits Times*, 27 July 1985.
(f) *The Straits Times*, 27 July 1985.
(g) *The Straits Times*, 27 July 1985.
(h) *The Straits Times*, 25 October 1985 and 15 March 1986.
(i) *The Straits Times*, 12 March 1986 and 31 March 1986.
(j) *The Straits Times*, 15 March 1986.
(k) *The Straits Times*, 1 September 1985.

17. *The Straits Times*, 26 August 1986.

18. For a discussion on the SDF, see Lim Chong Yah, *Economic Restructuring in Singapore*, Singapore, Federal Publications, 1984.

19. See J. Wong and K. Kalirajan, 'Industrial Regulations and Licensing in Singapore', Department of Economics and Statistics, National University of Singapore (unpublished), 1983.

20. For a further discussion on the safety and health regulations on factories in Taiwan, see T. K. Djang, *Industry and Labour in Taiwan*, The Institute of Economics, Academia Sinica, Monograph Series, No. 10, Republic of China, 1977.

21. One should never compromise workers' safety to promote industrialization. Singapore's policies on safety requirements are commendable.

22. Lim Chong Yah, 'The Causes of Development', *Singapore Economic Review*, Vol. XXIX, No. 2, October 1984.

23. Ibid., p. 74.

24. Tertiary refers only to the first degree from university education and does not include post-graduate studies. Many Singaporeans consider university education as a basic requirement in a career. Normally, only those who are interested in research would pursue post-graduate studies.

25. According to Lim Boon Heng, university degrees are no longer as prized as they used to be because of the increasing number of graduates in the labour market. The difference in earnings between graduates and other workers would also narrow (see *The Straits Times*, 20 October 1985). Indeed, graduates are now facing increasing difficulties in getting jobs (see, for example, *The Straits Times*, 23 October 1985).

TABLE 10.1

Comparative Wage Cost of Non-bargainable Employees for
Selected Occupations in Selected Countries, 1984

Country	Production Engineer		Accountant	
	Start	After 3 Years	Start	After 3 Years
Singapore	2,244	3,156	1,944	2,938
Malaysia	1,748	2,203	1,748	2,203
Taiwan	733	989	746	1,006
South Korea	940	1,107	856	1,021
Japan	1,449	1,715	1,478	1,750

Source: NWC Secretariat.

Note: The wage data include provident fund contributions, fringe benefits, and other allowances.

TABLE 10.2

Median Monthly Income of Men by Broad Education Level and
Stream of Education, 1966 and 1978
(in S$)

	1966			1978		
Level of Education	Chinese Stream	English Stream	English/ Chinese	Chinese Stream	English Stream	English/ Chinese
No schooling/ some primary	146	144	1.01	251	251	1.00
Completed primary/ some secondary	164	187	1.14	275	299	1.08
Completed secondary	200*	352*	1.76	325	386	1.19
Tertiary	358	663	1.85	1,004	1,388	1.38

Source: Pang Eng Fong, 'Returns to Schooling and Training: Postscript', in Education, Manpower and Development in Singapore, Singapore, Singapore University Press, 1982, Chapter 8.
*Includes some workers with post-secondary and A-level qualifications.

TABLE 10.3

Nominal Earnings Growth by Education, 1973–1984
(Percentage)

Group	1973–1978	1979–1981	1982–1984
Total	8.0	12.8	17.6
No education	11.4	8.7	12.2
Below PSLE	9.8	9.9	11.4
PSLE	10.8	10.1	11.8
Post-primary	0.8	12.5	17.2
Secondary	8.1	11.6	12.0
Post-secondary	12.4	13.3	12.0
Tertiary	4.4	8.7	21.1

Source: Computed from Ministry of Labour, Singapore, Labour Force Survey of Singapore, various years.

TABLE 10.4

Public Sector–Private Sector Pay Differentials for Graduates, 1978–1984

Year	Per Cent Employed in Private Sector	Per Cent Employed in Public Sector	Pay Ratios		
			Private/ Overall Mean	Private/ Govern- ment	Private/ Statutory Board
1978	50.3	49.7	1.02	—	—
1979	49.3	50.7	1.01	—	—
1980	52.5	47.5	0.99	—	—
1981	57.2	42.8	1.01	—	—
1982	50.9	49.1	0.99	—	—
1983	43.1	56.9	1.03	0.95	1.06
1984	44.1	55.9	0.96	0.88	1.01

Source: Computed from Survey of Graduates, National University of Singapore, various years.
Note: Estimates before 1982 are based on median monthly pay.

TABLE 10.5

Wages, Contributions, and Balances of a Hypothetical Worker
(Monetary Values in Real Terms)

Age	Monthly Wages	Annual Contributions	Maximum Attainable Balance
25	800	5,200	0
26	824	5,356	5,133
27	849	5,517	10,553
28	874	5,682	16,256
29	900	5,853	22,261
	Housing Withdrawal = $19,463		
30	927	6,028	28,990
35	1,075	6,988	65,777
40	1,246	8,101	112,480
45	1,445	9,392	171,190
50	1,675	10,888	244,395
55	1,942	12,622	335,053
60	2,251	14,632	446,676
65	2,610	16,963	583,423

Assumptions:

Annual wages	13 months
Real wage increase	3 per cent per annum
Inflation rate	4 per cent per annum
CPF interest	6.5 per cent per annum

Housing Loans:

Year taken	Age 30, after 5 years of working
Housing withdrawal	$19,463 real
Loan from HDB	$41,189 real
Total sum for flat	$60,652 real
Monthly repayment	$312 real
Interest on loan	6.5 per cent per annum
Term of repayment	20 years

Source: Lim Chong Yah *et al.*, 'Report of the Central Provident Fund Study Group', *Singapore Economic Review*, Special Issue, Vol. XXXI, No. 1, April 1986.

Note: The schedule was first generated on the basis of nominal values, using 7.12 per cent as the wage increase rate. The resulting figures were then deflated at 4 per cent throughout to obtain the real or present dollar values.

TABLE 10.6

GNP and Population of Singapore, Taiwan, Hong Kong, South Korea, Malaysia, Thailand, and Japan, 1984

Country	GNP (US$ Million)	Population (Million)
Singapore	17,710	2.5
Taiwan	57,510	18.9
Hong Kong	67,948[a]	5.4
South Korea	80,200	42.0
Malaysia	65,334	15.3
Thailand	41,550	51.7
Japan	2,665,544[b]	119.9

Source: *Asian Business*, May–December 1985.

[a]GDP figure.

[b]For the fiscal year.

TABLE 10.7
Comparison of Prices of Selected Items Sold in Singapore and Hong Kong, 1984

Item	Singapore	Hong Kong
Ladies' 100 per cent cotton dress		
Celine	570	287
Men's cotton shirt		
Van Heusen	50–55	45
Manhattan	44–55	27
Men's T-shirt		
Fred Perry	25–38	19
Ladies' leather shoes		
Bally	265–335	243
Charles Jourdan	215–275	260–273
Men's leather shoes		
Lanvin	269–295	206–232
Ladies' leather handbag		
Christian Dior	150–209	232
Charles Jourdan	150–295	328
Men's belt		
Pierre Balmain	69–89	27–30
Ladies' perfume		
Estee Lauder (White Linen) 50 ml	88	194
Ladies' watch		
Rolex	2,100–3,000	2,636
Seiko	148–300	68–123
Men's watch		
Rolex	2,900–3,805	3,434
Camera		
Canon Auto-focus AF-35	250	216
Yashica Auto-Focus AF-35	215–230	163
Nikkon Auto-focus L-35-AF	285–299	260
Kodak Disc 8000 with lens	125	145
Polaroid No. 660	230	139
Radio-cassette recorder		
Sony Walkman	215	189
Philips Đ8343	187	150
(made in S'pore)		
Video-cassette recorder		
National NV 777	950–1,200	1,025
National NV 788	1,350	1,503
Akai VS-3	950	1,011
Philips OVR 901	1,280	1,175

Source: The Straits Times, 5 September 1984.
Note: All prices are converted to S$ based on the exchange rate as at 31 January 1984.

TABLE 10.8
Comparison of Selected Costs of Operation in Singapore and Hong Kong, 1984

Cost of Operation	Singapore	Hong Kong
Office rents* (US$)[a]	327	301
Currency per unit of Singapore dollar (S$)[b]	1	0.2729
Corporate tax (%)[c]	40	18.5
Tax on electricity and gas charges (%)[d]	10	Nil

Sources: (a) *The Straits Times*, 15 November 1985; (b) Singapore, Department of Statistics, *Yearbook of Statistics, 1984/85*; (c) Singapore, Ministry of Trade and Industry, Report of the Economic Committee, *The Singapore Economy: New Directions*, February 1986; (d) The Public Utilities Board.
*Total occupancy cost (net rent plus service charges and property tax) for a suite of 1000 m² of air-conditioned offices in a central location.

TABLE 10.9
Hourly Compensation Costs for Production Workers in Manufacturing, 1984

Country	National Currency Unit	Exchange Rate National Currency Units per US Dollar	Average Hourly Earnings in National Currency	Ratio of Additional Compensation to Hourly Earnings	Hourly Compensation National Currency	US Dollars	Index US=100
United States	Dollar	–	9.18	37.1	12.59	12.59	100
Hong Kong*	Dollar	7.819	11.25	11.0	12.49	1.60	13
Japan	Yen	237.400	1290.00	16.8	1507.00	6.35	50
Korea	Won	806.000	912.00	20.0	1094.00	1.36	11
Singapore	Dollar	2.133	3.32	56.0	5.18	2.43	19
Taiwan	Dollar	39.600	64.13	5.0	67.34	1.70	14
United Kingdom	Pound	0.748	3.29	33.1	4.38	5.85	46

Source: US Department of Labour, Bureau of Labour Statistics, August 1985.
*Average of selected manufacturing industries.

TABLE 10.10

Ratio of Additional Compensation to Hourly Earnings of
Production Workers in Manufacturing, Singapore, 1975–1984

Compensation Item	1975	1976	1977	1978	1979	1980	1981	1982	1983	1984
Average hourly earnings*	100.0	100.0	100.0	100.0	100.0	100.0	100.0	100.0	100.0	100.0
Pay for leave time										
Holidays	4.0	4.0	4.0	4.0	4.0	4.0	4.0	4.0	4.0	4.0
Vacation	2.8	3.2	3.2	3.2	3.2	3.2	3.2	3.2	3.2	3.2
Bonus and annual wage supplement										
Bonus	4.5	6.2	6.2	6.2	6.2	1.8	5.4	5.4	5.4	5.4
Annual wage supplement	5.3	5.4	5.4	5.4	5.4	8.9	7.2	7.2	7.2	7.2
Total cash pay	116.5	118.8	118.8	118.8	118.8	117.9	119.8	119.8	119.8	119.8
Pay in kind										
Meals	0.2	0.2	0.2	0.2	0.2	0.3	0.2	0.3	0.3	0.3
Housing	0.6	0.6	0.5	0.4	0.7	0.7	1.0	1.1	1.1	1.1
Transportation	0.4	0.4	0.5	0.5	0.6	0.6	0.7	0.7	0.8	0.8
Employer contributions to funds										
CPF	17.5	17.8	18.2	19.0	22.0	24.2	24.6	25.5	27.0	28.8
SDF						1.2	4.7	4.8	4.8	4.8	4.8
Total compensation costs	135.2	137.8	138.2	138.9	143.4	148.4	151.1	152.2	153.7	155.5

Source: See Table 10.9.

*Average hourly earnings include basic time and piece-rates, overtime and other work-related premiums, and cost-of-living and social allowances paid regularly each pay period, and are computed per hour worked. Payroll tax is included with the SDF. The CPF contribution rate in this table is not a nominal rate but the effective rate.

BIBLIOGRAPHY

Amyot, Jacques, *Small Industries Enterprise Supportive Institutions: A Preliminary Assessment*, Report for Rural Off-Farm Employment Assessment Project (ROFEAP), Kasetsart University, Bangkok, 1981.

Asian Business, August 1985.

Asian Computer Yearbook, 1981–82, Hong Kong, Computer Publications, 1982.

Bain, G. S., and Elias, P., 'Trade Union Membership in Great Britain: An Individual-Level Analysis', *British Journal of Industrial Relations*, Vol. 1, March 1985.

Benson, Anthony, 'Transfer of Software Technology from the Developed Countries', in *Developing Singapore into a Software Centre*, Proceedings of a Data Processing Managers' Association Seminar, Singapore, 19 January 1982.

The Business Times, various issues.

Chng Hak Kee, 'A Study of the Characteristics of Local Small Industries and Entrepreneurs', Case Studies No. 3, Department of Industrial and Business Management, Nanyang University, July 1978.

Djang, T. K., *Industry and Labour in Taiwan*, Institute of Economics, Academia Sinica, Monograph Series No. 10, Republic of China, 1977.

Grayson, C. J., 'Let's Get Back to the Competitive Market System', *Harvard Business Review*, Vol. 51, November–December 1973.

Herzog, Helge, 'Small and Medium-sized Firms in Sweden and Government Policy', *American Journal of Small Business*, Vol. VII, No. 2, December 1982.

Higgins, B., *Economic Development*, New York, W. W. Norton and Co. Inc., 1968.

Hsuan Owijang, 'Definition and Role of Small Industries in Singapore', paper presented at a Symposium on Small Industries in Singapore, Singapore, March 1977.

Hughes, H., and You Poh Seng, *Foreign Investment and Industrialization in Singapore*, Canberra, Australian National University Press, 1969.

International Bank for Reconstruction and Development, *Current Economic Position and Prospects of Singapore*, International Development Association, 1973.

Japan, The Japan Institute of International Affairs, *White Papers of Japan 1983–84*, annual abstract of official reports and statistics of the Japanese government.

Japan, Ministry of International Trade and Industry, 'Small and Medium Enterprises', *White Papers of Japan 1979–80*, Tokyo, Institute of National Affairs, 1979.

Japan, Small and Medium Business Agency, *Chusho Kigyo Hakusho*, White Paper on Small and Medium Enterprises, 1980.

Japan, Small and Medium Enterprise Agency, Ministry of International Trade and Industry, *Outline of Small- and Medium-Scale Enterprise Policies of the Japanese Government*, January 1983.

Kilby, P. (ed.), *Entrepreneurship and Economic Development*, New York, The Free Press, 1971.

Kunasirin, Busaba, *The Role of Small- and Medium-Scale Industries in the Economic Development of Japan and Thailand: A Comparative Analysis*, Tokyo, Institute of Developing Economies, Visiting Research Fellow Monograph Series No. 109, March 1984.

Lau Puay Choo, 'The Role of Small Industries in Singapore's Economic Restructuring', Honours thesis, Department of Economics and Statistics, National University of Singapore, 1983/4.

Lee Kuan Yew, *Extrapolating from the Singapore Experience*, Singapore, Ministry of Culture, 1978.

Lee Soo Ann, 'Export-Led Growth with Particular Reference to Small Industry Experiences of Singapore', Paper presented at Asian Productivity Organization Symposium on Export-Oriented Small Industries, Lahore, Pakistan, 10–14 November 1984.

———, *Industrialization in Singapore*, Camberwell, Victoria, Longman, 1973.

Lim Chong Yah, 'The Causes of Development', *Singapore Economic Review*, Vol. XXIX, No. 2, October 1984.

———, 'Economic Development of Singapore since Self-Government in 1959', in Boulding, K. E. (ed.), *The Economics of Human Betterment*, London, The Macmillan Press, 1984.

———, *Economic Restructuring in Singapore*, Singapore, Federal Publications, 1984.

——— *et al.*, 'Report of the Central Provident Fund Study Group', *Singapore Economic Review*, Special Issue, Vol. XXXI, No. 1, April 1986.

——— and You Poh Seng, *The Singapore Economy*, Singapore, Eastern Universities Press, 1971.

Low, Linda, 'Privatisation Policies and Issues in Singapore', Staff Seminar Paper No. 7, Department of Economics and Statistics, National University of Singapore, 1985.

Minato, Tetsuo, 'The Japanese System of Subcontracting', *Sumitomo Corporation News*, Vol. 48, January 1985.

Oi, Walter Y., 'Labour as a Quasi-Fixed Factor', *Journal of Policy Economy*, Vol. 70, December 1962.

Ozawa, Terutomo, 'The Transnational Spread of Japan's Small and Medium Enterprises and Technology Transfer', paper submitted to the United Nations Conference on Trade and Development, Geneva, December 1984.

Pang Eng Fong, 'Return to Schooling and Training: Postscript', in *Education, Manpower and Development in Singapore*, Singapore, Singapore University Press, 1982.

Pang Eng Fong and Tan, Augustine, 'Employment and Export-led Industrialization: The Experience of Singapore', in Amjad, Rashid (ed.), *The Development of Labour-Intensive Industry in ASEAN Countries*, Bangkok, Asian Regional Team for Employment Promotion, 1981.

Republic of China, Executive Yuan, Research, Development and Evaluation Commission, *Annual Review of Government Administration, Republic of China*.

Roscoe, J. P., 'Can Entreprenuership be Taught?', *MBA Magazine*, Vol. 51, June–July 1973.

Rothwell, R., and Zegveld, W., *Innovation and the Small and Medium-Sized Firm*, Hingham, Massachusetts, Kluwer Nijhoff Publishing, 1981.

Saburo, Okita, *The Developing Economies and Japan*, Tokyo, University of Tokyo Press, 1980.

Sanguanruang, Saeng; Xuto, Nisa; Saengpassorn, Preeyanuch; and Piputsitee, Chuchup, *Development of Small and Medium Manufacturing Enterprises in Thailand*, Bangkok, December 1970.

Schollhammer, H., 'Internal Corporate Entrepreneurship', in Kent, C.; Sexton, O.; and Vesper, K. (eds.), *Encyclopaedia of Entrepreneurship*, New Jersey, Prentice-Hall Inc., 1982.

Schrage, H., 'The R & D Entrepreneur: Profile of Success', *Harvard Economic Review*, Vol. 43, November–December 1965.

Schumpeter, J., *The Theory of Economic Development*, New York, Oxford University Press, 1961.

Singapore, Budget for financial year 1986/7.

Singapore, Department of Statistics, *Monthly Digest of Statistics*, various issues.

Singapore, Department of Statistics, *Report on the Census of Industrial Production*, various years.

Singapore, Department of Statistics, *Yearbook of Statistics*, various years.

Singapore, Economic Development Board, *Annual Report*, various years.

Singapore, Economic Development Board, 'Singapore Investment News', October 1982.

Singapore, Federation of Chambers of Commerce and Industry, Report of the Subcommittee and Local Businesses, August 1985.

Singapore, First Deputy Prime Minister's response to the Economic Committee's Report.

Singapore, Ministry of Finance, *Economic Survey of Singapore*, various years.

Singapore, Ministry of Labour, *Report on the Labour Survey of Singapore*, various years.

Singapore, Ministry of Trade and Industry, Report of the Economic Committee, *The Singapore Economy: New Directions*, February 1986.

Singapore, NWC Secretariat.

Singapore Government Press Release, various issues.

Singapore Statistical News, Vol. 70, No. 1, 1984.

Sit, Victor Fung-Shuen, *Small Scale Industries in a Laissez-Faire Economy*, Hong Kong, University of Hong Kong Press, 1980.

Star, A. D., 'Estimates of the Number of Quasi and Small Businesses 1948 to 1972', *American Journal of Small Business*, Vol. IV, No. 2, October 1979.

Staley, E., and Morse, R., *Modern Small Industry for Developing Countries*, New York, McGraw-Hill Book Company, 1965.

The Straits Times, various issues.

Tambunlertchai, S., and Loohawenchit, C., 'Small Manufacturing Enterprises in Thailand', in Sit, Victor Fung-Shuen (ed.), *Strategies for Small-Scale Industries Promotion in Asia*, Hong Kong, Longman, 1984.

Tan Chwee Huat, *State Enterprise System and Economic Development in Singapore*, London, University Microfilms International, 1975.

Tan Thiam Soon, 'Management Guidance for Small and Medium Enterprises—Japan, Taiwan and Singapore', unpublished Asian Productivity Organization Report, 1983.

Tanaka, Hiroshi, 'Position and Role of Small and Medium-Sized Enterprises in the Japanese Economy and their Overseas Investment', paper presented at a conference on the Role of Small Industries in the ASEAN National Economies, Singapore, November 1978.

Thailand, Ministry of International Trade and Industry, 'Country paper

(Thailand) on small and medium enterprise policies', delivered at the International Conference on Small Enterprise Policy, held in Osaka, 18–20 January 1983.

United Nations Industrial Development Organization, *Subcontracting for Modernizing Economies*, New York, United Nations, 1974 as quoted in Germidis, Dimitir (ed.), *International Subcontracting: A New Form of Investment*, Paris, OECD, 1980.

Wong, Amy, *A Study of Selected Small-Scale Manufacturing Industries in Singapore*, Singapore Economic Research Centre, University of Singapore, 1975.

Wong, J., and Kalirajan, K., 'Industrial Regulations and Licensing in Singapore', Department of Economics and Statistics, National University of Singapore (unpublished), 1983.

World Bank, *Employment and Development of Small Enterprises*, Sector Policy Paper, Washington DC, World Bank, 1978.

Yen Gi-li, 'Industrial Policies as They Relate to SMBs—A Financial Perspective', paper presented at the *1984 Joint Conference on the Industrial Policies of the Republic of China and The Republic of Korea*, held in Taiwan, 27–28 December 1984.

Yoon-Bae Ouh, *International Research Project on Korean Small Industry Development*, Seoul, Soong Jun University, 1978.

Yoshihara, Kunio, *Foreign Investment and Domestic Response: A Study of Singapore's Industrialization*, Singapore, Eastern Universities Press, 1976.

Youngson, Al, *Hong Kong: Economic Growth and Policy*, Hong Kong, Oxford University Press, 1982.

INDEX